The Apostle John

STUDIES IN
HIS LIFE AND WRITINGS

BY

Dr. W. H. GRIFFITH THOMAS
Late Principal, Wycliffe College, Toronto

PICKERING & INGLIS
14 PATERNOSTER ROW, LONDON, E.C.4
229 BOTHWELL STREET, GLASGOW, C.2
29 GEORGE IV BRIDGE, EDINBURGH

CONTENTS

INTRODUCTION

This volume is intended to help those who are called upon to preach and teach, and on this account the material is set out largely in outline form. It is a great satisfaction to know that a former book, "The Apostle Peter," covering his life and writings, has been found of service to fellow-workers. I hope the present work will be similarly useful, and will also provide an introduction to the larger books included in the Bibliography, all of which, though often varying greatly in their attitude to Scripture and in their spiritual teaching, have been consulted or otherwise used in the preparation of "The Apostle John"

W. H. GRIFFITH THOMAS

I

THE LIFE OF THE APOSTLE

The Apostle John

I

FIRST DAYS

There are few things more interesting than the study of biography. To trace a career from start to finish, to note the various features, circumstances, and crises, to discover the springs of character and the secret of power, to follow the course of a life from its opening to its close—all this is at once fascinating and profitable. It is probable that the vital interest of the New Testament is largely due to the fact that it is so definitely concerned with life, with human problems, needs, sins, weaknesses, conquests, blessings.

Of the lives recorded in Scripture there are none more truly valuable than those of the Apostles of our Lord, because their association with Christ gave them exceptional opportunities of development and progress. Of these apostolic lives it is probable that not one is more important than that of the Apostle John, because of his very intimate fellowship with his Master. In these studies an attempt will be made to look at the various circumstances and stages of his career with special reference to the development of his spiritual life.

In John 1:37–41, we are given certain hints of the way in which he commenced his discipleship to Christ, but it will be well to try to discover something of his antecedents in order that we may become more fully acquainted with the man and his subsequent life as a follower of Christ.

1. His name, John, corresponds to the Old Testament Jonah, which means "a dove," and although it would be going too far to say that the name had anything to do with his character, it is hardly possible to avoid noticing the dove-like elements in this apostle of love.

2. His age when first we see him is unknown, but there are certain circumstances which seem to suggest that he was quite young, and certainly the youngest of the twelve apostles. Thus, on running to the tomb of Christ (John 20:4), John outran Peter, as though he were able to do so by his youth. Then, too, his youth would readily explain the special relation that he bore to Jesus Christ, which was apparently accepted by the other disciples without any feelings of jealousy. It has also been suggested that his youthfulness will probably account for the difference between his Gospel and the other three, since his impressionableness would enable him to receive and assimilate the teaching of Christ in a way impossible to older men, whose intellectual habits had become firmly fixed.

3. His relatives are mentioned. His father was Zebedee; his mother Salome, who may have been a sister of the mother of our Lord (Mark 15:40; John 19:25). His brother was James, and from the fact that the two are always described as James and John, James would seem to have been the elder of the two.

4. His work was that of a fisherman, and his usual sphere of labor was on the Lake of Galilee, near his home.

5. His position was probably one somewhat better than that of an ordinary fisherman, because we read of the servants of Zebedee, his father.

6. His character may perhaps be indicated by the name given to him and his brother by our Lord: they were called "Sons of Thunder," a term which is usually considered to express their earnestness, zeal, and enthusiasm.

7. His religion. He was a follower, and, indeed, a close disciple, of John the Baptist, from which we may infer that he was an earnest, thoughtful, pious Jew, who had been impressed by the preaching of the great forerunner of Christ, and had thrown in his lot with those who were thus being prepared for the advent of the Messiah.

We may now look at the circumstances of his conversion. It is always interesting to see something of the way in which a man finds Christ. While there are many ways, there is but one goal, and the story of John's conversion is not without its practical value for us today.

1. As a disciple of the Baptist, he heard his master's testimony to Jesus Christ as "the Lamb of God." How far this led his mind back to Old Testament times and truths it is impossible to say, but it is clear that some special thought must have arisen in John's mind as he heard the reference to Jesus Christ as "the Lamb of God." This was not the first time that the forerunner had proclaimed Jesus Christ in this way, for the day previous he had said, "Behold the Lamb of God that taketh away the sin of the world" (John 1:29). In this there may have been an allusion to the Passover Lamb, and also to the prophetic word concerning the Messiah (Isa. 53:7). If so, it would speak of sin and of sacrifice provided by God to remove the sin. This message is the very heart of the Christian Gospel, and the theme of the preacher should always, in one way or

another, be that of "the Lamb of God." We can see the importance of this as we contemplate other parts of the Bible in which the two truths of sin and sacrifice are emphasized (Acts 8:32; 1 Pet. 1:19; Rev. 5:6).

2. This testimony of the Baptist influenced John to leave his old teacher and to follow Jesus. It is significant that such a proclamation should have this effect, and it is a reminder of what has often since happened through the attractive power of Christ: "I, if I be lifted up from the earth, will draw all men unto Me" (John 12:32). Happy the preacher and happy the hearer who find their theme and their attraction in the atoning death of our Lord and Saviour.

3. He inquired about Jesus as the result of the act of following. When our Lord turned and beheld him and the other disciple following, he asked them what they were seeking, and they replied, "Teacher, where dwellest thou?" This spirit of inquiry marked their interest in Christ, and when our thoughts have been turned to him, especially as the Lamb of God, it is natural and inevitable that we shall want to know something more of our Lord's presence and work.

4. The outcome of this inquiry was an invitation, which was accepted. "He saith unto them, Come and see." They came, therefore, and saw where he dwelt, and they abode with him that day. The personal invitation of Christ to the soul is noteworthy here, as always, and the response of the soul is equally important. Our Lord's "Come and see" is met by an acceptance and a stay with Christ that day. The result was that by his contact with Jesus Christ John became convinced that he was indeed "the Lamb of God."

5. The next day John set out to find his brother. This seems to be clearly implied by the references to Andrew. "He findeth first his own brother Simon." This is understood to imply that John in like manner found his own brother, his elder brother, James, and brought him to Jesus. It was a beautiful and yet very simple testimony. "We have found the Messiah." This was all, but it was sufficient. There was no argument, no elaborate reasoning, but a simple witness based on personal experience: "We have found." And then, with equal simplicity, we read, "he brought him unto Jesus." Mark how personal it is: "*he* brought *him.*"

From all this we are enabled to see the characteristics of every true conversion. Whatever may be the precise method, there are certain essential facts which are true in every case.

1. Conversion is a personal relation to Jesus Christ. As the late Earl Cairns was so fond of saying, "Conversion is a personal transaction between the soul and God." The testimony of John the Baptist led to John the son of Zebedee seeking Jesus Christ and coming into association with him. Thus his conversion was due to contact with Christ, the touch of soul with soul.

2. This personal relation to Christ necessitated a definite step—that of inquiry, trust, and obedience. When Jesus Christ invited John to "come and see," the invitation was accepted, and in this act of intelligent confidence we see the initial stage of every genuine conversion. The soul must be willing to venture in response to the invitation of Christ, and when this definite step is taken the result is always sure.

3. The immediate outcome was a new attitude expressed in new activities. The personal experience of Jesus Christ immediately led John to endeavor to make known to his brother what he had received, so that the latter might share in the new-found interest and joy. This is a sure mark of definite conversion, the desire to let others know, the longing that others may share in that which has become so precious to us.

II

FIRST EXPERIENCES

The early days of the Christian life are vital and important. Much depends on them, because with proper teaching it is possible to prevent error and backsliding. From the moment of the conversion of John the son of Zebedee, there came into his life certain experiences of his new position which enabled him to see and enter upon the sphere of a follower of Jesus Christ with strength and confidence.

When our Lord saves an individual and unites that one to himself, a new relationship is thereby constituted between the individuals thus separately joined to Christ. And so the immediate outcome of the two men leaving their old master, John the Baptist, and following the new one, Jesus Christ, was that a relationship immediately and inevitably sprang up between them. This community is given several titles in the New Testament, that of "the Church" being perhaps the most important, as it is the most familiar. Thus the disciple soon found himself in connection with a new social life. The community of Christians is intended for fellowship, for the individual relation to our Lord must necessarily have a corporate and social outcome. Christianity is social as well as personal, and the very nature of Christ's salvation is to create a community. Paganism may show the beauty of the old humanity, but Christianity creates a new one. We are told that "Christ Jesus came into the world to save sinners," and when he has united each separate sinner to himself, his followers may be said to become a "society of saved sinners."

Thus the Church began on that day when these two men followed Christ, and the simple beginnings are worthy of special notice, because they provide the germ of all else that appears later in an elaborated form in the New Testament. Christianity has room for "all sorts and conditions of men," and when they are spiritually united to Christ they are enabled to express through their own individual temperaments and circumstances the glory of the grace of God.

The New Testament doctrine of the Church is one of great importance, and it is essential that it be kept in mind and emphasized in every proper way. There is something unutterably sad in the description of the non-Christians as "they that are without," for in reality it means a great deal to be "inside" the fold and to enjoy the fellowship provided by Christ. It is hardly possible to exaggerate the importance of the Church to the individual. The Church, in the New Testament inclusive sense, is "the blessed company of all faithful people," or, as Paul calls it, "the Church which is his body." It has often been pointed out how significant is the reference in the Creed to "the Communion of Saints," coming, as it does, after the words, "Holy Catholic Church." It is known that the reference to the Saints is decidedly later than that to the Church, and was originally intended as an explanation of the real meaning of the latter word. When the Church is thus realized as the fellowship of all those who belong to Christ, something like the New Testament teaching is seen. Individualistic Christianity is at once a contradiction and an impossibility. We are justified solitarily and alone in association with Christ direct, but we are sanctified in connection with others. Christian character needs the Church for development, and while, as the familiar phrase has it, talent may be developed in solitude, character needs the stream of life (Eph. 3:18; 6:18). It is not too much to say that there is no real future for Christianity along New Testament lines, except through a Church or a community. Mysticism in general is too vague and individualistic. Christianity is mysticism, but it is far more. Individualism is equally impossible, for unattached Christians are not found in the New Testament, and even what may be wrongly described as ultra-spirituality must not be opposed to corporate Christianity, for as Dr. Forsyth has well said, "Free lances are futilities."

This was the earliest experience of the son of Zebedee, and, although it doubtless did not make a distinct impression at the time, there is hardly any question that the power of fellowship with others in Christ was felt from the very first, especially as very soon three or four other men were similarly united in the same blessed bonds. Bishop Moule has well pointed out that our view of the Church in its widest sense as "the body of Christ" should dominate all our thinking and affect all other interpretations of the idea of the Christian community. When we look at this subject in what is, perhaps, the most important place, the Epistle to the Ephesians, we find a fourfold reference to the Church—as a Body, a Building, a Bride, and a Brotherhood. Be it ours to emphasize the necessity and importance of this fellowship, and to derive from it all possible inspiration for life and service.

It was not long after John's conversion and fellowship with other believers that he was led into fuller light by a deeper experience of his Master. This took place on the occasion of the marriage in Cana of Galilee, where John, with the other disciples, was present (John 2:1–11). One of the essentials of a disciple's earliest life is a fuller knowledge of his master. At the outset the joy of forgiveness is so great that it may seem to be everything, but new difficulties, new temptations, new trials, new problems, arise, and to meet these it is vital to enter into a fuller, deeper, richer knowledge of Jesus Christ.

Perhaps the first knowledge of the Master was that of his power on the occasion of this miracle. When the wine failed Jesus Christ worked the miracle of providing what was needed, and we are told of the significant result: "This beginning of his signs did Jesus in Cana of Galilee, and manifested his glory, and his disciples believed him." The miracle was thus a "sign" of his glory, and we may try to put ourselves in the place of the disciple John and ask what rays of glory were likely to appear.

It is hardly possible to doubt that the first ray was the *fact* of our Lord's divine commission as the Messiah. At the beginning of his public work it was necessary to prove that he came from God. Remembering his lowly birth, obscure parentage, and village education, we can readily understand the difficulty he would have in proving the truth of his claims, and this would necessarily lead to the working of something which would first excite wonder, then suggest the thought of some unseen power at work, and so would lead naturally to the inquiry as to the real meaning. Such were our Lord's miracles, "signs" of his divine mission, calling attention to him as the Messiah and Saviour, and thereby manifesting his glory.

Then, too, the *object* of his divine commission was pretty certainly manifested in this miracle. Not only the fact that he came from God, but the reason why he came, to change the lives of men from sin to holiness, the change from water to wine being an emblem of his whole life and work. This is not to say that the disciples understood this meaning at the time, but it is certainly easy and natural to pass from such a miracle of beneficence to the spiritual purpose of our Lord's coming into the world. Everything in the world up to that time had attested the fact that men wanted something which they themselves could not provide. Both individuals and nations had attempted this, but had failed, and then, when this failure was complete, our Lord appeared, and in him men found what they had vainly sought elsewhere (Luke 4:18, 19).

Perhaps, too, we may include as a ray of his glory on this occasion the thought of the *sympathy of man with men*. He entered into all natural relationships, for he "adorned and beautified marriage with his presence and first miracle." He was no hermit or ascetic—a fact all the more remarkable when we contrast him with his forerunner the Baptist. Christ had intense sympathy with the social side of life, with those feelings and affections which play so great a part in human affairs. Then, too, he sympathized with all natural enjoyment. Not only did he attend a marriage, but a marriage feast. Not only was he there, but he supplied the means of their satisfaction. He is not an enemy, but a friend of all true joy, and his sympathy is not only for times of sadness, but also for times of gladness. Many seem to imagine that Christianity is almost joyless, but the presence of Christ on this occasion shows that he does not take away joy, but adds to it, purifies it, and heightens it. The life of austerity and singularity is never the ideal life; that is the true life which is everywhere "in," but not "of," the world.

It is particularly significant that we read, "His disciples believed on him," namely, the five referred to in the earlier chapter, and who had been invited with him to the marriage. Not a word is said as to any such effect upon his mother or his brethren, or any of the other assembled guests. Indeed, we should gather from the subsequent conduct of Mary and his brethren that they were not affected by it. Apparently, only those who were already his disciples were impressed and convinced. From this we derive the truth that our Lord's miracles were wrought almost exclusively for the purpose of strengthening the faith of his disciples, and not for the purpose of winning over the outside world. These men were already his disciples, and the story of their acceptance of Christ is entirely natural, for, having heard of him as the Messiah, they simply believed and followed. It was only afterwards that they had miracles to confirm their faith. This truth is seen all through our Lord's life, for he kept his miracles as secret as possible. When he healed the leper, raised the dead, descended from the Mount of Transfiguration, he said, "See thou tell no man."

There is a very real and important application of this to us today. Those who are already believers have daily, hourly instances of his special guidance, strength, and blessing which are little short of miraculous, and which help to strengthen the faith that already exists. Yet every avowal of such inward experiences to those who are outside would probably be laughed to scorn or disbelieved. Such avowals are not appreciated, though there are few more convincing proofs to the believer himself than the constant experience of God's grace in his soul.

But some one may ask whether there is no sign for those outside, no proof to convince them. There is, and a careful consideration of John 2:18 will show what this is. When our Lord began clearing and cleansing the Temple, the Jews came asking a "sign" why he did such things. Instead of working a miracle, he said, "Destroy this temple, and in three days I will raise it up," speaking of the temple of his body. That was the sign for them, his death and resurrection. So, also, when the Pharisees came seeking a sign, he told them that none should be given but the sign of Jonah, again referring to his own death and resurrection. This was the sign for the unconverted Jews of that day, and it is also the one for the unconverted people of the present age.

After this miracle of Cana of Galilee we are not told anything of the effect of association with Christ on the disciples, and it is, of course, possible—some think, absolutely certain—that these five men returned at once after the miracle to their own homes. If, however, they accompanied our Lord to Jerusalem, we can well understand the constant and deepening influence of his words and works, as the variety of circumstances of his stay at the capital occurred (John 2:13 to 3:36). But greater than all the influences of his teaching and actions would be the impress of his personality, and we know that this is the one essential for the early life of disciples—a personal and growing experience of Jesus Christ. Nothing can compare with this for deepening the life of a believer and enabling him to realize more of his Master's spirit and learn more of his Master's will. Long years afterwards the Apostle John described the growing Christian life under the three figures, of children, young men, and fathers, and in each case the life was only made possible by a personal experience of the Lord himself (1 John 2:12–14).

III

LIFE WORK

One of the most important points in the Christian life is the necessity of showing the young convert the duty of doing some work for him who has done so much for us. "That we being delivered … might serve" (Luke 1:74). This was the next lesson to be learned by John. Although a disciple of Jesus Christ, it would seem clear that he returned home some time after the first interview with, and acceptance of, his new Master (John 1:36–39). But the time was at hand when he was to be called to definite work, and the occasion is recorded in three Gospels (Matt. 4:18–22; Mark 1:16–20; Luke 5:1–11). John and the others were now to be called from discipleship in general to specific ministry, and it is this ministry which we have to consider with special reference not only to John, but also to all disciples.

The work was that of soul winning, expressed by the figure "fishers of men." This has been rightly called "the greatest work of the world," for whether we think of non-Christian multitudes at home or unevangelized millions abroad, we cannot fail to see that the work of every individual Christian is first and foremost that of soul winning. Our Lord spoke of catching men alive (Luke 5:10, Greek), and it is significant that the only other phrase where the word is used refers to the power of Satan to take men alive (2 Tim. 2:26). There seems no real doubt that the proper rendering of this last passage refers to Satan, and not to the Christian worker.

It is important to give special attention to this turning point in the life of John, the son of Zebedee, by means of which he was led from the outer circle of discipleship to the inner circle of what may be termed "ministry." Along the lines of this subject emerge some great principles of Christian life and duty, which deserve earnest and constant consideration.

I. The Divine Purpose

Our Lord intended John to become a "fisher of men," to win men alive, and lead them into the sphere of fellowship with his Master. This is still the purpose of the Lord with every one of us, and as we consider what it meant for John, we shall be enabled to see what it means for us.

It is a definite service. We are called upon to deal with human beings, and are expected to "catch" them. Nothing short of this will suffice for our Master's work. We can see this among other things in the various titles given to the children of God in the New Testament. They are called "witnesses" (Acts 1:8). They are described as "ambassadors" (2 Cor. 5:20). They are designated "heralds" (1 Tim. 2:7, Greek). These titles clearly imply a distinct and pointed purpose, and we must not rest with anything short of definite results of service. Not merely are we to put the message before men, but we must use means to lead them to accept the message, and to become disciples of Christ. The fisherman is never content with merely throwing out the line or the net. If he does not land some fish, he is not in any real sense a fisherman. It is recorded of a French doctor that, full of enthusiasm, he said he had operated upon eight people in connection with some very serious and complicated disorder. When asked how many lives he had saved, he replied, "Not one; but then, you see, the operations were so brilliant." This would never satisfy an ordinary medical man, and certainly in relation to things spiritual Christian men must never be satisfied with mere brilliance of testimony. It is for us "by any means to save some." This is our definite work.

It is a difficult service. Men are not easily "caught." The power of sin is so great, and the character of sin is so varied; the self-will of man is so strong, the heart of man is often so far from God that the Christian fisherman finds it exceedingly difficult to catch the one for whom he is praying and striving. There is no work in its way so arduous and trying as that of endeavoring to save men from their sins and snatch them out of the hands of the Wicked One. Satan does not easily let go his prey, and whenever there are earnest endeavors on the part of Christian people to evangelize and win souls, there, it is perfectly certain, will be found the most intense opposition of the Devil. Soul winning is, indeed, a difficult work.

Yet it is a delightful service. Is there any joy in this world comparable with the bliss of leading an anxious soul to Christ? To hear the question, "What must I do?" to observe the evident interest and anxiety, to mark the genuine repentance, to see the eager acceptance of the Word of truth, and then to notice the soul surrendering to Christ and commencing to rejoice in his great salvation—all this is "joy unspeakable, and full of glory." It is the supreme felicity of life to be permitted to lead a soul into the presence-chamber of the King of kings.

II. The Divine Reminder

Our Lord spoke of his disciples "becoming fishers of men," and this clearly teaches the important lesson that such are not born, but made. The word "become" is in many respects one of the most interesting and suggestive in the New Testament, because it always implies a process and a progress. Thus the Apostle Paul urged the Christians at Corinth to "become" imitators of himself (1 Cor. 4:16; 11:1). He also urged them not to "become" children in their minds, but to "become" mature (1 Cor. 14:20). Many other passages in the New Testament similarly emphasize this idea of "becoming," always suggesting that the disciples were not then what they ought to be, but were to "become" so. Christians "become" fishers of men, and this implies that they are not originally qualified in this respect. What, then, does it mean to "become" a fisher of men, in what does the training consist? Perhaps if we consider some of the more important qualifications of ordinary fishermen, we may learn from them a little of what is needed in order that we may become fishers of men.

A fisherman needs watchfulness. Mark the alertness of the true fisherman; always on the lookout for fish, and for the best ways of catching it. So must it be with the true disciple of Christ, who wishes to win men for his Master. "They watch for your souls" (Heb. 13:17). "I have made thee a watchman" (Ezek. 3:17; 33:2–7; Acts 20:26, 28). The fisher of men must be eager and on the lookout for men. A clergyman once wrote to a friend, asking him whether he could recommend a curate, and said that he wanted a man "whose heart was aglow with the love of souls."

A fisherman needs patience. How wonderfully patient is the fisherman who remains hour after hour on the river bank, waiting for a bite. How utterly impossible it would be for him to fish with success unless he had this element of patience. Much more is this true of the servant of God who wishes to win men to Christ. "The servant of the Lord must be … patient" (2 Tim. 2:24, 26). Men are not always won at the first attempt, and any spirit of impatience will not only hinder the sinner from accepting Christ, but will hurt the worker's own soul. It will only be by prayerful patience that many a captive of the Evil One is rescued and brought to the feet of the Saviour. This patience will demand real strength and energy. The fisherman must be "instant in season, out of season" (2 Tim. 4:2), and persistently, prayerfully wait for every opportunity to lay hold of the one whom he desires to win for Christ.

A fisherman needs courage. Sea fishing in particular needs very great bravery and fearlessness. A fisherman often takes his life in his hands, and we know from our own fishing industry how many lives are lost in the prosecution of this daily task. So also fishing for men is by no means easy, and, as is well known, those who attempt it are often lacking in courage, and they do not find it any easier even after a long life of individual work. Dr. H. Clay Trumbull, one of the ablest and most earnest workers among individuals, has told us in his little work on the subject that he was as much afraid on the last occasion as on the first. Courage is, therefore, a pre-eminent requirement if we would persist in the work of soul winning.

A fisherman needs tactfulness. In the course of a day's fishing a man may often have to change his method, and also to use different kinds of bait. We also know that there are very great differences in fishing for various sorts of fish, and there are other diversities, according to locality and circumstance. All this suggests the need of tactfulness. When we think of spiritual fishing, tactfulness is one of the prime essentials. "The servant of the Lord must not strive, but be gentle unto all men, apt to teach, patient, in meekness instructing those that oppose themselves" (2 Tim. 2:24, 25). Men around us differ so widely in circumstance, character, temperament, and attitude to God that unless the Christian worker is characterized by tactfulness, he will often do more harm than good in his endeavors to win men for Christ. It is as true today as ever that "he that winneth souls is wise," and "he that is wise winneth souls" (Prov. 11:30). We need to know something of the devious ways of sinners, the different snares set by the enemy, and the precise aspects of Gospel truth best fitted to meet particular cases. All this requires and will demand tactfulness, wisdom, and discretion.

A fisherman needs self-forgetfulness. An old fisherman has said that one of the prime requirements of a true fisherman is that he should keep himself out of sight. This quality is pre-eminently necessary in the soul winner. His own individuality must be kept as far as possible in the background, in order that his Master may be first and foremost. There is always danger lest we attach men to ourselves instead of linking them on to

Christ. At the King's levee there comes a point at which, after the introduction of the newcomer, the one who introduces him stands aside, his work being over. In like manner, in bringing a soul to Christ we carry the work to a certain point, and then stand back for the soul to have its own private and personal interview with the Master. "I labored … yet not I, but the grace of God which was with me" (1 Cor. 15:10).

III. THE DIVINE PROMISE

In case we should for a moment imagine that to "become" fishers of men is out of our power, the Lord gives to us, as he did to John, his own blessed assurance, "I will make you" (Mark 1:17). This is at once an indication that "God's biddings are enablings," and that our Lord never requires service without providing equipment.

Thus power for soul winning is possible. "I will make you." The Lord Jesus Christ is able and willing to equip us for the work of spiritual fishing. He himself was the greatest of all soul winners in the days of his earthly ministry, and he is ready now to fit and prepare us for the same blessed work. Let this thought sink deep into our hearts; there is no reason whatever why every Christian should not be a soul winner. Here is the promise of the Lord Jesus Christ offering to prepare us for this blessed work. This should encourage us to believe in the possibility for each of us.

And power for soul winning is certain. "I will make you." This is one of the "I wills" of Christ, those gracious and blessed promises which are intended to encourage and hearten us for life and service. When Jesus Christ our Lord and Saviour says "I will," he means it, and in special connection with soul winning we see the cheer and inspiration of such a promise, giving us a certain guarantee of strength and provision for the difficult task.

And power for soul winning is blessed. To be fitted and equipped for this glorious work is surely a joy, a privilege, and a blessing. Christ our Master takes us into his school, trains us, teaches us, prepares us, and bestows upon us all needed grace and wisdom, and then sends us out into the great ocean of the world, ready to "catch" men. There is surely nothing nobler, nothing more uplifting, nothing more glorious than to be equipped and commissioned by our Master to do "the greatest work in the world."

IV. THE DIVINE SECRET

It is now time for us to consider the precise requirements and conditions laid down for us in the Word of God with reference to the work of soul winning. We are already clearly aware of our duty to "catch" men. We have also seen some of the qualifications required in a spiritual fisherman. We have also been cheered and encouraged by the Master's promise that he will make us to become fishers of men. Now let us consider very carefully our attitude to him and the conditions required by him in order that we may be "thoroughly furnished unto all good works." The answer is found in the words, "Follow Me,"

"Come ye after Me." This is a very familiar message, but one that needs to be analyzed into its constituent parts. What does it mean to follow, to "come after" Christ?

Trust him. To follow Christ means to depend upon him for grace, and the soul winner will never be of any service in the kingdom of God unless he depends constantly and entirely upon the grace of God to equip, guide, strengthen, and bless him in his labors.

Imitate him. Our Lord's life was a life of soul winning, and following him means doing as he did. A study of the Gospels will quickly reveal to us our Lord's wonderful dealing with sinners, as, for example, in the story of the Woman of Samaria, will show some of the methods and secrets of the greatest of all soul winners. "Follow Me" means, among other things, "Imitate My example." As a soul winner, Christ's example is peerless.

Obey him. Following always includes and involves obedience, and, therefore, "Whatsoever he saith unto you, do it." The Lord is calling upon every one of us to do as much as we possibly can in the direction of soul winning. It is not sufficient, blessed though it is, to live a quiet, consistent life. This we must do of course, but, in addition to this, there must be the testimony of the lip, and the endeavor, lovingly, yet aggressively, to win souls to the Master. And if we do not do it, our spiritual life will suffer, and we shall not be following our Master.

Abide in him. Following Christ is not only an act, but an attitude, one that covers a lifetime. Abiding in him means continual and ever-increasing fellowship. It implies living in his presence through faith, prayer, and the Word of God, and in this abiding fellowship with our Master will come that force, freshness, fragrance, and fiber in spiritual life which will be the best possible means of attractiveness in soul winning. As water never rises above its level, so our work for God never rises above the level of our fellowship with him. We must "dwell with the King for his work," and in so doing we shall have his Spirit, his power, and his blessing.

As we continue to study the life of John, we see that at each stage he is being drawn closer to his Master, and enabled to learn more of that Master's will. Little by little it is being revealed to him what he is to be and to do, and whenever, like John, the believer is ready to "leave all and follow" Christ, the outcome is as certain as it is blessed. "Everything may be hoped of men who leave all for Christ. Where there is a noble soul, there is an indefinite capacity for growth" (Bruce, "The Training of the Twelve," p. 14).

IV

SPECIAL SERVICE

The stages of the progress of John the son of Zebedee are decidedly interesting and spiritually valuable. After having been called from the ranks of the disciples of John the Baptist to become a disciple of Jesus Christ, he was led into definite service in what may be called "the ministry" (Luke 5:1–11). Then from this work he was called to still more special service as an Apostle, and it is this that we must now consider.

I. COMMISSION

1. *The Purpose.*—In the original choice of the Twelve by our Lord, we are told that he ordained them that they should be with him and that he might send them forth to preach (Mark 3:14). They were thus to be continually with him in close association, and, at the same time, to go forth on his service proclaiming his message. This is always Christ's purpose for his people, fellowship with him and work for him.

But the appointment of the Twelve was made for much wider reasons. They were definitely selected as one of the three main methods of proclaiming and extending the Kingdom of God. Our Lord was already preaching and teaching, and also working miracles, but the time had come for a fuller development which was to be realized in connection with the work of the Twelve as they went from place to place carrying their Master's message and reproducing their Master's power (Mark 3:15).

Even more than this, the Twelve occupy a unique position in the records of the New Testament (Eph. 2:20), for there can be little doubt that our Lord selected them with a view to the ultimate as well as to the immediate future. It is striking to notice the contrast between the Twelve and the Seventy in two successive chapters (Luke 9:1; 10:1). The Seventy were intended simply for temporary work, and we never hear of them again, while the Twelve were selected both for immediate service, and also for the purpose of being founders of the future Church. The latter point is clear from the words and action of the Apostle Peter, who considered it necessary for some one with proper qualifications to take the place of Judas and to be numbered among the Apostles (Acts 1:21–26). It is evident from this that only those who could fulfill the necessary conditions could be so numbered, and therefore the Apostles, as such, have no successors. They were necessarily unique in position, opportunity, and place.

2. *The Possibility.*—John and his brother James were named by Christ "Boanerges," which means "the sons of thunder" (Mark 3:17). This is usually regarded as a reminder of their past, and is thought to refer to their warm, enthusiastic nature, but it does not appear as though any reproach were intended, but only the reminder that their intensity should be utilized and developed in zeal for their Master's cause. As some one has well said, "When God makes a prophet, he does not unmake the man." It is a profound satisfaction to realize that Christ can utilize all that is good in our past and make it subserve the interests of his kingdom. Whatever may be the nature, and however varied the temperament and circumstances, Christ can use all, for there is room in his Kingdom for every possible variety. The Apostle Peter must have had this in mind when he spoke of the "many-colored grace of God" (1 Pet. 4:10, Greek).

3. *The Plan.*—The great work to be done by these Apostles was that of witnessing to Christ, "Ye shall be my witnesses" (Acts 1:8), and a true witness requires three qualifications—intelligence, candor, and disinterestedness. It is clear that the Apostle John had these features, for nothing could be more impressive than his intelligence, his frankness, and his utter disregard of self in all that he had to say concerning the Gospel. In this respect all Christians are called upon to "witness" for their Master. He has left this work to us, and it can only be done by those who have a personal knowledge and experience of Christ. The Apostle Peter, speaking with John at a later date, said, "We cannot but speak the things we have seen and heard" (Acts 4:20). When the soul is in close and constant touch with Christ the evidence will come out instinctively and inevitably in testimony to him and to his grace.

The one thing essential to this work of witnessing is the training that comes from personal experience. The Twelve, including John himself, were at first very narrow and shortsighted, but the great thing was that they were in the presence of Christ, and, as it were, surrounded by his influence. Devotion to him was the one thing necessary, and when this comes about it is blessedly true that there is an indefinite capacity for growth and expansion. We read of the old workers of David that "they dwelt with the king for his work" (1 Chron. 4:23), and it was the personal influence of the character of Christ that beyond all else made these men, and the Apostle John in particular, what they became. In this respect we may all be "Apostles," that is, those who are sent forth by Christ to do his work, and our power for him will be in exact proportion to our fellowship with him. Just as water never rises above its level, so the strength and character of our work will never be greater than our fellowship with the Lord.

N. B.—Those who desire to study more fully the various elements in the training of the Apostles should give special attention to "The Training of the Twelve," by Bruce, and "Pastor Pastorum," by Latham. There are also several more recent books dealing with the particular characteristics of the Apostles of Christ, of which "The Apostles as Everyday Men," by Dr. R. E. Thompson, and "He Chose Twelve," by Dr. J. Elder Cumming, may be instanced.

II. COMPANIONSHIP

The position of John as one of the Twelve is still more interesting, because out of the Twelve our Lord selected three, of whom John was one, and on several occasions these three were given the privilege of special association with the Master in his work. We do not know exactly why Peter, James, and John were thus selected, but it is more than probable that Christ saw in them such exceptional possibilities that he felt he could and must concentrate upon them the special features of his training for future life and service.

John was one of the three who attended our Lord at the raising of Jairus' daughter (Mark 5:37). Perhaps this was to teach the great lesson that Christ is the Lord of death and life. At any rate, it is an attractive hypothesis that the prominence given in the writings of the Apostle John to "eternal life" may have been due to his close association with the Lord at the death bed of this young girl. It was essential that the disciples should learn, and learn quickly and deeply, the power of their Master over death, and the way in which John thought of death and its contrast, life, is seen in the Fourth Gospel and the First Epistle, and is decidedly striking and impressive. Death is, fundamentally, separation, and is capable of three applications: physical death is the separation of the soul from the body; spiritual death is the separation of the soul from God; everlasting death, in the full sense, is the separation of soul and body for ever from God. Wherever the thought of "death" occurs in John's writings, one or other of these aspects of "separation" will be found. In contrast, there is the thought of life, fundamentally that of union, and again it is threefold: physical life is the union of body and soul; spiritual life is the union of soul with God (John 17:3); everlasting life, in the full sense, is union of soul and body with God for ever. Under one or other of these aspects the complete teaching of the Apostle on "life" can be gathered.

The Transfiguration was another occasion on which John, with Peter and James, was permitted to be in special fellowship with his Master. After the serious and sad conversation a week before about the Cross, it would seem as though a gloom had settled upon the disciples (Mark 8:31–38), and it was therefore necessary that the glory of Christ should be seen by those who were to proclaim him later on. And so, on the Mount of Transfiguration, Christ was transformed before them, and they were permitted to see his glory. He was glorified in person in a way which they had never realized before. In answer to Peter's impulsive suggestion about three tabernacles, the Divine Voice reminded them that Jesus Christ their Master was God's Son in contrast with Moses and Elijah, who were only servants. Then, too, they were permitted to understand something of their Master's glory in connection with the very Cross which had been a stumbling block in that conversation, for the two men, Moses and Elijah, were actually making this death the subject of their conversation (Luke 9:31). In the light of what happened a few months later on the Cross, and in the gift of the Holy Spirit, these three disciples would naturally realize the blessedness and glory of the death from which they had otherwise shrunk as something intolerable (Matt. 16:22).

In these special associations the three Apostles, and John in particular, would find their convictions deepened and strengthened. Truth always becomes confirmed in personal experience and fellowship, for it is only thus that intellectual conceptions can become permanent. Ideas alone may easily degenerate into speculation; they need experience in order to be, as it were, burnt in and made part and parcel of the life. In fellowship with their Master, these men saw light on many mysteries, and long years afterwards John, doubtless referring to the Transfiguration, though perhaps to the life of Christ as a whole, said, "We beheld his glory" (John 1:14).

And yet it is important to remember that there are many experiences too sacred for expression. We know practically nothing of what John felt as the result of this close association with his Master at the bedside of Jairus' daughter and on the Mount of Transfiguration. A true disciple always knows more than he can tell, and, as it has been well pointed out, an author is, or at least ought to be, far greater than his book. We would naturally like to know something of what happened on these special occasions, but, to use familiar words, "something sealed the lips of that Evangelist." Meanwhile, we are sure that, as the outcome of personal experience, Christ always becomes more real and precious to those who are in close fellowship with him. The half of what he is to his people cannot be told (1 Kings 10:7). But although it cannot be "told," it can be lived, and the closer our fellowship with Christ the more precious he will be to our own souls, and the more powerful will be our witness for him.

Thus, whether we think of the commission of John as one of the Twelve, or of his companionship as one of the Three, we are certain it was in close contact with Christ that he derived his knowledge and power, and it will be in the same real fellowship that we shall know and love and serve him today.

V

PERILS

A disciple is always intended to be, as the word indicates, a learner. Lessons are needed all through life. This was especially the case with the Twelve Apostles, and in particular with the Apostle John. Even after the privileges of the Transfiguration there were many things to learn before he could be all that his Master desired him to be. We must now notice some of the dangers to which the Apostles were liable, dangers that were likely to imperil their influence and give a wrong impression of their Master.

I. THE PERIL OF NARROWNESS

In Luke 9:49 we have the record of an experience in the life of the Apostle John which calls for special attention. Our Lord had just spoken (v. 48) of receiving a little child in his "Name," and it would seem as though this reference prompted John to think of an incident which had occurred apparently not long before, for he said, "Master, we saw one casting out demons in thy name." "In the name" always means "by the authority," and based upon the character. The "Name" of God invariably refers to his nature as revealed, and not to any mere title attributed to him. The many passages in the Old Testament referring to "The Name of the Lord" invariably have this meaning of God's nature and character, while in the New Testament the allusions to our Lord's "name" (John 14:14) mean exactly the same thing, his revelation of himself with the authority and power associated with it. The person to whom John referred was some one who had been using Christ's "name" or authority in casting out demons, and this was enough for the Apostle to rebuke and forbid him on the ground that he was not among the recognized followers of Jesus Christ:

"We forbad him because he followeth not us." But Jesus rebuked his disciple, and said: "Forbid him not, for he that is not against you is for you" (v. 50).

In these words the Lord taught his follower the serious danger of narrowness in religion. It is clear that the man was not undervaluing Christ, or he would not have been casting out demons in Christ's name. The trouble seems to have been that he did not recognize the necessity and importance of fellowship with the disciples, and on this ground he had been rebuked by John. This is, perhaps, a hint about the danger of selfishness in religion: "He followeth not *with us*." It is only too possible to become so concerned with our own position and importance in relation to Christ as to regard our cause as identical with his.

But can we get beneath the surface and account for this ebullition of narrowness? What was the explanation? It is often suggested that we have in this an illustration of that want of balance in the Christian life which takes various forms according as particular elements of our nature are affected. Thus, it has been shown that when the conscience is lacking in knowledge the danger of fanaticism arises; when the intellect is wanting in experience the peril of dogmatism is seen; and when the will is short of love the risk of tyranny is evident. So that where narrowness takes the form of fanaticism or dogmatism or tyranny, the result is a want of proper intellectual, moral, and spiritual balance, which cannot but affect character, and then influence for evil whatever we may say and do for Christ. The Apostle John doubtless thought he was vindicating his Master's honor, and the fanatic, or the dogmatician, or the tyrannical person may have the same idea, while in reality the work of the Lord is being hindered. There is scarcely anything more subtle than the way in which the "old Adam" often colors our testimony. We feel compelled to be faithful, and we make our protest accordingly, but all the while our own personal feeling—it may be of severity, or even of anger—enters in and spoils our testimony, and gives people a wrong impression of ourselves and of our Master.

As we ponder this incident, it is important to consider some of the practical truths arising out of it which are continually necessary for our life and service. The first of these is that we may be perfectly certain that work such as here described—that of casting out demons—necessarily has the sympathy of our Lord Jesus Christ. We hear today a great deal about "philanthropy," and this, as Archbishop Benson once characteristically defined it, is "man-lovingness." The love of man as man is essentially true, right, and beautiful, and whenever the effort is made to help our fellows we may be perfectly certain that our Lord approves. There are many "demons" today, as ever, and if they are cast out we ought to rejoice, especially when the work is done in our Master's name.

Another point of great importance, as we read this story, is the reminder that all who work along right lines, casting out demons in the name of Christ, are really one body. The man in doing the work in Christ's name was definitely associated with the Master, whether he knew it or not. It is a useful reminder that our company is not the only one Christ has, and

any idea of rebuking a man "because he followeth not with us" is apt to lead to spiritual pride and self-sufficiency. Just as there are hints in the Old Testament of the true worshipers of God outside the chosen people, so we must never limit the followers of Christ to those who belong to the organized company of his disciples with which we happen to be associated. We may go still further, and observe that the spirit of our Master may be outside our own company, and a very opposite spirit be within it. The tone and temper of the Apostle at this time were obviously much more dangerous to truth, life, and morality than anything the other man had been doing, and it is only too possible today to show a spirit of narrowness, haughtiness, and even bitterness, which will do immense harm to the cause of Christ.

Under these circumstances, we should try to see the good in what other people are doing, and at the same time endeavor to win them to a true Christian unity. It is a constant problem with individual Christians how to combine the extensiveness of sympathy with intensity of conviction. Our principles ought to be part of ourselves, and to go as deep down as possible; but our sympathies should be as wide as they can stretch, extending everywhere, so long as real good is being done. The danger of depth alone is narrowness, and the danger of breadth alone is shallowness. It is for us to seek to blend and harmonize these two principles, so that we may be as narrow as God's truth and as wide as God's love.

Then, too, it is important to remember that outward unity is not adequate as a test of real discipleship. We may have outward and visible unity at the expense of purity and truth. Unity is consistent with the greatest possible variety, and the more we insist upon outward and visible unity, the greater our danger of confusing unity with uniformity. The fact that a man "followeth not with us" is no necessary proof that he does not follow Christ, and the familiar words are as applicable today as ever: "In things essential unity, in things non-essential liberty, in all things charity."

And yet this will not mean that we are to tolerate everything and everybody, for it is clear that the large-heartedness which our Lord urged upon his servant applies only to those who are doing genuinely Christian work. The man was casting out demons in the name of Christ, and it was this that ought to have prevented him from being rebuked by the follower of Christ. An easy-going tolerance of every conceivable opinion and every possible effort is almost as far removed from truth as the narrowness of the Apostle. It *does* matter what a man is attempting, and also why he is making the effort, and if only we bear in mind that the work to be done is in the name of Christ, we shall be kept from an easy-going readiness to accept every one and everything, which is often prejudicial and paralyzing to true life and service.

II. THE PERIL OF VINDICTIVENESS

In Luke 9:54–56 another danger was revealed by John and his brother James. Our Lord was on his way to Jerusalem, and on sending messengers before him to prepare the way a certain community of Samaritans would not receive Christ, because he was going up to the city of their hated foes, the Jews. This was too much for James and John, who at once, in zeal for their Master, said, "Lord, wilt thou that we bid fire to come down from heaven and consume them?" The spirit that prompted this outburst was praiseworthy, for they were jealous for their Master's honor. It is also worth while noticing their faith in the power to call down fire from heaven. They had evidently learned from their Master the secret of miracle-working, and thought they could exercise their authority and power in this way. According to the older text, we are to read, "Even as Elijah did," referring to the well-known incident in that Prophet's career (2 Kings 1:10–12), but whether we include these words or not, it would seem almost certain that an allusion to that story was in the minds of James and John. Yet, notwithstanding the elements of praiseworthiness in this expression of feeling, there was a serious and sad ignorance of themselves and of their Master in what they said, as we can see from the way in which they were at once rebuked. Here, again, some texts read that our Lord added, "Ye know not what manner of spirit ye are of," and then, according to still other authorities, though fewer in number, he is said to have remarked, "For the Son of Man came not to destroy men's lives, but to save them" (Luke 19:10; John 3:17; 12:47). But whether we read these words or not, they express the true attitude of Christ and the spirit of his rebuke. James and John did not know what manner of spirit they possessed, and at least for the moment they had forgotten that their Master had come not to kill men, but to save them. Vindictiveness on the part of a follower of Jesus Christ is utterly abhorrent to the spirit of the Master and the truth of his Gospel. Defense, not defiance, is essentially Christian when the interests of others are at stake, but zeal for our Master, however well-intentioned, must never degenerate into personal feelings such as actuated James and John at this time.

As we contemplate afresh these two dangers of narrowness and vindictiveness, we naturally seek to discover the safeguard against them, as well as the cure for them if they should be expressed. This is found in the simple yet sufficient secret of fellowship with Christ. The closer we draw to him, the more large hearted and the more loving we shall become. In his light we shall see light, and in his love we shall feel and express love. We shall see things from his standpoint, and do only that which is in accord with his spirit. I remember once hearing Bishop Whipple, of Minnesota, so well known as "The Apostle of the Indians," utter these beautiful words: "For thirty years I have tried to see the face of Christ in those with whom I differed." When this spirit actuates us, we shall be preserved at once from a narrow bigotry and an easy-going tolerance, from passionate vindictiveness and everything that would mar or injure our testimony for him who came not to destroy men's lives, but to save them.

VI

A GREAT LESSON

Every incident in the life of the Apostle John is in one way or another a revelation of his character, and, at the same time, of the way in which our Lord dealt with it. The story of the request of the mother of the sons of Zebedee, with her sons, James and John, calls for special attention in this connection as shedding remarkable light on the personal characteristics of John (Matt. 20:20–28; Mark 10:35–45).

I. THE REQUEST

According to Matthew, it was Salome who came with this request, though her sons were with her, and were doubtless personally associated with her in approaching Christ. If, as is generally thought, she was the sister of the Virgin Mary (Matt. 27:56; Mark 15:40), she may have considered that her special position warranted her in making this appeal. The request was definite and, doubtless, honest, even though it was marked by ignorance. Like the rest of the disciples, these two were thinking of an earthly kingdom, and of their own position in it (Luke 19:11). There was not a little faith in proffering such a request at the moment, for if we may press the word "then" (Matt. 20:20), it came immediately after the solemn announcement of the Passion, so that James and John must have believed in spite of these words that Jesus Christ was to be a king. Perhaps, however, they remembered what he had said about his glory and sitting on his throne (Matt. 19:28).

But however honest and confident was the request, there was an element of selfishness in it that reflected seriously on the two brothers, as well as on their mother. They clearly desired some pre-eminence in their Master's Kingdom, which would necessarily affect, and be at the expense of, the rest of the disciples. It is, therefore, impossible to acquit them of an undue consideration of their own interests in their desire to occupy the chief places of honor in Christ's Kingdom.

II. THE REPLY

The Lord met their request in a very striking way by reminding them first of all that they were altogether ignorant of the true meaning of the request, "Ye know not what ye ask." Then he put to them an inquiry, which showed what was in his mind, "Are ye able to drink the cup that I am about to drink?" The "cup" in Scripture sometimes is the symbol of blessing (Psalm 23:5), and at others the symbol of suffering (Mark 14:36). It was, of course, in the latter connection that Christ asked the question, thereby reminding them of an experience altogether different from the place of honor and glory to which they were looking forward. It was a quiet, but forceful reminder that it was necessary to count the cost of such a position as they were anxious to fill. Thus Christ did not set aside their request as impossible or refuse it. Still less did he condemn them as wrong. As on other occasions, he instructed and trained them by pointing out that they possessed an entirely erroneous and false idea of the glory associated with their Master, as well as of the way to the realization of that glory. Christ desired them to understand that there were certain conditions to be fulfilled if their request was to be granted.

III. The Rejoinder

The two brothers at once replied, "We are able." This seems to indicate a superficiality or, at any rate, an ignorance of what was involved in their Master's question. Bishop Chadwick is of the opinion that Salome, with fearlessness, "could see the clear sky beyond the storm. Her sons shall be loyal and win the prize, whatever be the hazard, and however long the struggle. Ignorant and rash she may have been, but it was no base ambition which chose such a moment to declare its unshaken ardor, and claim distinction in the Kingdom for which so much must be endured. And when the stern price was plainly stated, she and her children were not startled; they conceived themselves able for the baptism and the cup" (Mark, p. 288). It is impossible not to admire the frankness and even the courage with which they expressed their ability and readiness to face what Christ had put before them.

IV. The Reminder

Then the Master told them plainly what would happen. "Little as they dreamed of the coldness of the waters and the bitterness of the draught, yet Jesus did not declare them to be deceived, but said, 'Ye shall indeed share this' " (Chadwick). The cup was to be taken, thereby implying submission to suffering. The baptism was promised, thus indicating, like their Master, consecration and designation to the pathway of sorrowful service. The only thing that was impossible in regard to absolute promise was the sitting on Christ's right hand and on his left. This could only be given to those for whom it had been prepared. It was no arbitrary matter, but one involving conditions. Some were to be nearer and others farther away from their beloved Master, but wherever their position was, it was something to be gained, not granted as a gift. "It is for them for whom it hath been prepared of my Father."

V. The Results

It is not surprising that when the rest of the Apostles heard of this request "they were moved with indignation." The action was virtually that of stealing a march on their fellow workers, and their annoyance was so far natural. And yet not long before they themselves had been guilty of a similar offense against the brotherhood, because there had been a dispute as to who was the greatest (Mark 9:34). Their indignation at the two was therefore not quite so surprising as it would have been if they themselves had not been guilty of a similar offense. Then, too, they were as ignorant as James and John, and the annoyance felt was in some respects the measure of their ignorance. Selfishness always tends to divide brethren. There are two Greek words usually rendered "zeal" and "envy." The former implies a definite emulation without any thought of inferiority on the part of others. The latter always involves the desire and determination to get first place, even though it be at the cost of other people. It is right for us to exercise "zeal"; it is altogether wrong to show "envy."

The Lord's instruction was soon given both to the two and to the ten disciples. He showed them first of all the difference between the world's idea of greatness and that which he himself had come to introduce. The Gentiles lorded it over their people, but it was to be the very opposite among the followers of Jesus of Nazareth. The true idea of greatness is that of service—not authority. "Whosoever would become great among you shall be your minister." Not only so, but the very highest place would be filled by the one who rendered the lowliest service (v. 27). The distinction between "minister" and "servant," between "deacon" and "slave," is very striking. Caroline Fry, in her valuable little book, "Christ Our Example," defines humility as "unconscious self-forgetfulness."

Then, as a parting message, Christ showed that he himself was the one and supreme model of greatness in his life of service. "Even as the Son of Man came not to be ministered unto but to minister, and to give his life a ransom for many." Thus the incident was closed, and the two as well as the ten were taught some solemn, searching, practical lessons.

As we review the whole story, we cannot help noticing some of the outstanding truths for our daily life: (1) What a mercy it is that our prayers are not always answered as we desire. There is a world of difference between our "wants" and our "needs." Very often we ask for what we "want," and God, in his mercy, does not answer our prayer, but only gives us what he, in his divine wisdom, sees that we "need." (2) What a solemn thought it is that personal character in the Kingdom of God really determines our position. There is nothing arbitrary in the realm of grace. When we accept the Lord as our Saviour, everything depends upon our faithfulness to what he bestows. Not greatness, but goodness; not ability, but obedience, is the guarantee of true Christian life. Amid the controversy between the followers of Wesley and Whitefield one man asked Whitefield whether he ever expected to see Mr. Wesley in heaven. "No," replied Whitefield, "I do not." The man was gratified with this answer, reflecting, as it seemed, upon a theological opponent, until Whitefield added, "He will be so near the Throne and I so far off that I shall never see him." (3) What a simple yet searching truth it is to realize that service for Christ constitutes the highest dignity. If we would be high, we must stoop low, as our Master did before us (Phil. 2:1–11). It is not without significance that the Prince of Wales' motto is "Ich dien," "I serve," for royalty is never more royal than when it places itself at the disposal of others. James and John little knew what was before them. One of them was to be the first martyr of the Twelve, and the other to live the longest in an age of ostracism and persecution. And yet in both cases it was genuine service, as they drank of their Master's cup, and were baptized with his baptism. It is well for us to remember this glory of service, whether it involves patient suffering or active work. "They also serve who only stand and wait." There is nothing more noble than following the example of him who came "not to be ministered unto, but to minister." As the terse

Latin of the Collect so beautifully says: "Whom to serve is to reign" (*cui servire regnare*); "Whose service is perfect freedom."

VII

DEEPENING IMPRESSIONS

As we proceed we cannot help noticing that the lessons taught by our Lord to his disciples were almost always twofold, about himself and about them. This is invariably true of the believer's life, for we need to learn more of Christ and to know more of ourselves. The two act and react upon one another. The more we know of Christ the more we become conscious of ourselves in contrast to him. And the more we become conscious of self, the more we are led to feel our need of Christ and his grace. If, therefore, the Apostle John was to be and do what his Master intended, he had to learn in an ever-increasing way some of the deeper truths about Christ and his purposes.

I. BEFORE THE PASSOVER

When the time had come for the celebration of the last Passover before the Crucifixion, Peter and John were selected for the special work of preparation (Luke 22:8–13). The association of these two is interesting, and is found several times in the New Testament. It is pretty certain that they represent a blending of age and youth, or at least of maturity and youthfulness. There does not seem much doubt that Peter was approaching middle age, if he had not arrived there, while John was the youngest of the disciples, and, perhaps, as we have seen, not much more than a youth at this time. As we ponder this work of preparing the Passover, we must concentrate our attention on what it meant to those two disciples, and to the younger man in particular. The episode would doubtless convey very little at the time, but in the light of Pentecost it would shine forth as one of the occasions on which some of the truest and deepest lessons were taught.

1. *The Master's Complete Knowledge.*—When Peter and John asked where he wished the preparation made, he gave them clear directions. "Behold, when ye are entered into the city, there shall meet you a man bearing a pitcher of water, follow him into the house whereinto he goeth" (v. 10). This detailed acquaintance with what would befall them is a striking instance of our Lord's foresight. Perhaps there was a special point in the man bearing the pitcher of water, since this was usually the work of a woman. It may be that this exceptional experience would enable them to know where to go as they followed him into the house. But be this as it may, the statement was a revelation of their Master's thorough and detailed knowledge of the situation. It is hardly possible to doubt that this knowledge impressed John, for it was so exact and complete. At any rate, the Gospel which bears John's name is pre-eminently marked by its emphasis on "knowledge," while the First Epistle of John has as its fundamental thought the various truths associated with the word "know." This complete knowledge of Christ is at once a comfort and a warning. It is an unspeakable satisfaction to realize that "He knows," and when the disciple is able to say with reverence and satisfaction, "Lord, thou knowest all things," he has experienced one of the deepest and most precious privileges of life. At the same time, this knowledge is a warning, for it is a reminder of what the Psalmist said, "He knoweth the secrets of the heart" (Psalm 44:21; cf. 94:11; 139:1, 2, 4). We are accustomed to quote "Thou God seest me" to our children to remind them of God's all-seeing eye, and although the original context of this passage was not intended for warning, but for comfort, it is well to realize that God's thorough knowledge of us is at once a joy and a reminder.

2. *The Master's Absolute Authority.*—Peter and John on entering the house were to say to the master of it, "The Teacher saith unto thee, Where is the guest-chamber where I shall eat the Passover with my disciples?" And he would show them a large, upper room, furnished, where they were to make ready (vs. 11, 12). It is clear that the master of the house was a follower of Jesus Christ, for the claim to be "the Teacher" and the assurance that the room would be placed at their disposal implies the authority of Christ. This lordship is in some respects the crown and culmination of the Divine purpose and plan, "that God may be all in all" (1 Cor. 15:28), and it can only be reached in one way, by the Lordship of Christ, "that in all things he might have the pre-eminence" (Col. 1:18). The result is that the New Testament makes very prominent the thoughts of Christ as Master and of ourselves as his servants. There are some eight words associated with Christ's lordship, each of which suggests some aspect of the truth.

(1) He is our Possessor. The Greek word rendered "Lord" occurs hundreds of times and implies ownership, and therefore perfect control (Rom. 14:9; Eph. 6:9). (2) He is our Leader. This comes only twice (Matt. 23:8, 10), and means a guide, one who goes in front, suggesting capability, and therefore our perfect acceptance of his wisdom. (3) He is our Prince. This is represented by two words, one of which is found four times (Acts 3:15; 5:31; Heb. 2:10; 12:2), and the other only once (Rev. 1:5). The thought is of primacy of position, for our Prince is our principal. (4) He is our Superintendent. This is expressed by a word found six times, and only in Luke (5:5; 8:24, 45; 9:33, 49; 17:13). It indicates overseership, one "standing over" us, giving close inspection and therefore calling for watchful obedience. (5) He is our Master. The word is used by Simeon (Luke 2:29), by the early Church (Acts 4:24), by the Saints (Rev. 6:10), and it is also associated with apostates (2 Pet. 2:1; Jude 4). It suggests absolute and uncontrolled power, unrestricted domination, with the necessity of unquestioning submission (Titus 2:9; 2 Tim. 2:21). (6) He is our King. The usage of this word in relation to Christ is important and striking (John 1:49; 19:19; Acts 17:7; 1 Tim. 1:17; Jas. 2:8; 1 Pet. 2:9). It declares his reign, rule, and glory with our corresponding position and duties. (7) He is our Potentate. This is found only once (1 Tim. 6:15), and involves ability as well as authority, power as well as position, and

suggests both warning and comfort. (8) He is our Teacher. In the Gospels this is very frequently translated Master, and implies school*master*. He can only *teach* in so far as he is *Master*. And so this searching and dominating thought of Christ's absolute authority and lordship enters into every part of our life.

3. *The Disciples' Perfect Obedience.*—Peter and John at once went, and since they found everything exactly as their Master had told them, they made ready the Passover. This prompt and complete response to the orders of Christ is another element in the life of a true disciple. The Lord's Prayer is that his will may be done on earth "as it is in heaven," and just as there are eight words associated with Christ's lordship, so there are eight more expressive of our loyalty. (1) We are his bondservants. This word is found frequently, and may be said to be the Apostle Paul's favorite designation of himself as the "slave of Jesus Christ" (Rom. 1:1). It indicates that we are not free or independent, that we belong to him in everything, "a living chattel." It implies the devotedness and thoroughness of our service. (2) We are his ministering servants. This represents the Greek word from which we derive our "deacon" (Matt. 20:26; 2 Cor. 6:4). The true "deacon" or "minister" is a servant. The derivation of the word is uncertain; it may come from a Greek word meaning to "pursue," and if so it suggests the activity and celerity of our service. A "deacon" is one who *pursues* his task. "The King's business requireth haste." (3) We are his household servants (Luke 16:13; Rom. 14:4). This seems to suggest the inwardness and homeliness of our service in the household of God (Gal. 6:10; Eph. 2:19; Acts 10:7; 1 Pet. 2:18). (4) We are his subordinate servants. The original word means under-rower (John 18:36; 1 Cor. 4:1). We are "underlings," and, like rowers, must work hard. In an orchestra there must be "second violins," and in a boat not every man can be "stroke" (Luke 1:2; Acts 13:5). Thus we see the subordination and strenuousness of our service. (5) We are his confidential servants. This is only used of Moses (Heb. 3:5), and is connected with medical service. It perhaps suggests tenderness and privilege. (6) We are his public servants. The word indicates duty done in some public capacity (Acts 13:2; 2 Cor. 9:12; Phil. 2:17, 30). Our work for Christ extends in influence, and is not confined and contracted in sphere. Thus we see the value and importance of our service. (7) We are his temple servants. The word is used in connection with the tabernacle and temple (Luke 1:74; Heb. 9:1), and suggests the sacredness and dignity of our work for God. (8) We are his responsible servants. This is the thought of stewardship, for the "steward" is the head servant, responsible for the provisions and general life of the household (cf. Skeat's Dictionary; Luke 12:42; 1 Cor. 4:1, 2; 1 Pet. 4:10). It points out the opportunity and faithfulness of our service.

As we contemplate these three thoughts of complete knowledge, absolute authority, and perfect obedience, we realize something of what it means to be a true follower of Christ. A class is said to have been asked how God's will is done in heaven, so that we may do it in the same way. A child responded that the angels do God's will "without asking any questions." This is one of the simple and yet searching secrets of everything that is worth knowing, having, and enjoying in the Christian life. In a cemetery there is an inscription on the tomb of a young girl of eighteen. " 'Who plucked this flower?' said the gardener. 'I,' said the Master. The gardener was silent."

II. AT THE SUPPER

When the work of preparation was over and the Lord and his disciples were assembled in the upper room, again we are reminded of the Apostle John (John 13:23–25). Limiting ourselves to him in relation to the Master we are able to see something of what subsequently he must have realized as a blessed truth and experience.

1. *The Disciple's Special Position.*—We are told that at the table "there was reclining in Jesus' bosom one of his disciples, whom Jesus loved." There is no doubt that the reference is to John, and it is probable that the absence of jealousy of the other disciples was due to his extreme youth. This emphasis on our Lord's love for him is particularly striking. It is found in five passages, four having one and one the other Greek word translated "love." The former word implies unselfish love, a love which does not seek for any return (John 13:23; 19:26; 21:7, 20), and in each case it is particularly interesting that the literal rendering is "whom Jesus kept on loving." His interest and affection for his young follower went out continually and showed itself in a variety of ways for the benefit of John. But the other passage has its own beautiful suggestion (20:2), for it gives us the idea of our Lord's perfect humanity in desiring the return of love from his follower. There was nothing unworthy in this yearning for a return of love, but everything that was pure and true in the desire to find himself loved by his disciple. Here, again, the reference is equally suggestive, "whom Jesus kept on loving" (with a clinging love). Years afterwards this Apostle was able to say "We love, because he first loved us."

2. *The Disciple's Special Opportunity.*—While he was reclining in the bosom of Jesus, the other disciples were in perplexity about our Lord's announcement that one of them would betray him, and they doubted of whom he spoke. Simon Peter at once thought that John would be able to discover the one to whom our Lord referred, and therefore asked him to find out. Then we are told that "he, leaning back, as he was, on Jesus' breast saith unto him, 'Lord, who is it?' " (v. 25, R. V.). It was this position of privilege that enabled him to ask the question. His nearness to Christ enabled him to have this opportunity of full knowledge. The nearer we are to Christ the more we know of his truth, "the secret of the Lord is with them that fear him, and he will show them his covenant" (Psalm 25:14). "The Lord God will do nothing, but he revealeth his secret unto his servants the prophets" (Amos 3:7; Gen. 18:17; Jer. 23:22; Dan. 9:22). If, then, we would know we must "abide," for those who are following afar off are never made partakers of the secrets of their Lord.

3. *The Disciple's Special Privilege.*—This position and opportunity at the Last Supper enables us to understand the New Testament truth of "fellowship." Perhaps it was this truth that more than anything else enabled John to say in his Epistle, "truly our fellowship is with the Father, and his Son Jesus Christ" (1 John 1:3). Fellowship is the crown and culmination of everything in Christianity. We commence with sonship. We experience discipleship. We proceed to worship. We exercise stewardship. But beyond and above all we enjoy fellowship. The word always means "partnership" or joint possession, and it is interesting to observe that it is associated with each Person of the Holy Trinity, Father, Son, and Spirit (1 John 1:3; 1 Cor. 1:9; 2 Cor. 13:14; Phil. 2:1). There is nothing higher than this, because we are made "partakers of the Divine nature" (2 Pet. 1:4). Thus the Holy Communion is a remarkable expression of this fellowship, or partnership, especially as it is the occasion and opportunity of partnership in relation to our Lord's atoning sacrifice (1 Cor. 10:16).

As we look over these two occasions on which John stands out so prominently we see once again that the greatest need of the disciple is a fuller knowledge of his Master, and thereby a completer knowledge of himself. The more we know of Christ the better for our lives, and the more we know of self the more thorough will be our consciousness of the need of our Master. This mutual knowledge is only possible by means of close fellowship with Christ. "In thy light shall we see light." It has often been pointed out that sympathy is the gateway of knowledge. The scientific man like Darwin or Huxley must have sympathy with his subject if he is to learn. The student of literature will never enter into the depth of his authority unless he is, as the French say, *en rapport* with his author. In the same way, only those who are willing to enter into the closest possible oneness and friendship with Christ will ever learn his deepest truths and enjoy the most blessed experiences of his grace. There must be fellowship with Christ (Phil. 3:10; 1 Pet. 4:13) if we would know, enjoy, and practice the Will of God and realize his glory in our life.

VIII

GREAT MYSTERIES

In an Italian picture gallery there is a striking picture of an angel near the Cross from which our Lord's body has just been taken down. The angel is holding in his hands a crown of thorns. He feels it, notes its protruding sharp points, and shows on his face his surprise and astonishment. To his pure nature that suffering was a mystery. It must have been something like this in the case of Christ's disciples. When the Cross was first mentioned, Peter turned from it with shrinking, and even rebuked his Master, saying, "Be it far from thee, Lord; this shall not be unto thee" (Matt. 16:22). And as the time drew nearer with revelation after revelation of the approaching death, there must have been a greater perplexity, until at length, on the eve of the crucifixion, matters were hastening to a crisis. We do not for a moment suppose that the disciples had any real conception of what it all meant until after the illumination of Pentecost, but it is not too much to think of them as perplexed by these statements and actions of their Lord, coming after all the marvelous words and equally marvelous works of his Galilean ministry. We must now endeavor to put ourselves in the place of the twelve apostles, and in particular of the Apostle John, as they were associated with the suffering of Christ.

I. IN THE GARDEN

As we endeavor once again to ponder the story of Gethsemane, we must remember that we are indeed on holy ground, and yet it is not too sacred for our meditation, because it is one of the things "written for our learning." Dr. Matheson has said that "it will not do to throw a veil of mystery over this prayer. Christ has asked us to watch with him. But watching implies sympathy, and sympathy implies an understanding of his sorrow." Taking with him Peter, James, and John, our Lord entered the familiar garden after the wonderful conversations in the upper room (John 13–16). What may we say of Gethsemane as we try to look at it from the standpoint of the disciples?

1. *The Master's Weight of Sorrow.*—In some way or other the Lord was already entering upon his unique work of redemption. Nothing else can account for the circumstances in the garden. As he prayed earnestly, he asked that "this cup" might pass from him. Various meanings have been given to "this cup." Some think it means our Lord's suffering in the garden, from which he prayed to be delivered. Others consider that he meant his death on the cross, from which he prayed to be saved. Yet again, others explain it to mean his death then and there in the garden from which he prayed to be saved, in order that he might reach the Cross. The last of these views, although not the usual one, may possibly be correct, since it is closely in accord with other Scriptures, gives a quite reasonable interpretation of the prayer, and appears most consistent with the character of him who came to this earth to die. Some great scholars do not hesitate to translate our Lord's prayer as "*since it is possible, let this cup pass from me,*" urging that such is the meaning of the original Greek, and also that there is an emphasis on "*this* cup," to distinguish it from another "cup" to be given him by his Heavenly Father. The latter he is ready and even eager to drink; the former he desires to pass from him. If this be so, may we not think of Gethsemane as the last conflict of Satan? The great enemy of Christ knew well that the death on the Cross would be the end of his power, and he resolved, if at all possible, to prevent it. He had tried through Herod in Christ's infancy to destroy it, and again and again, from the wilderness onwards, he had endeavored to divert him from the Cross. Having hitherto failed in every attempt, he now makes the last assault upon the suffering Redeemer. Dr. Maclaren points out how nearly fatal Christ's agony in the garden was, and another writer remarks that the words "My soul is exceedingly sorrowful, even unto death" indicate that it was a

veritable death struggle. It hardly seems possible, in view of all that had happened before, to think of our Lord shrinking from the Cross. On the contrary, he steadfastly set his face towards Jerusalem (Luke 9:51). It seems to some, therefore, that the weight of sorrow was not fear of impending death on the Cross, but that his physical strength would not be sufficient to endure the agony, so that he might reach the Cross. According to this interpretation, which is favored by a few writers, the cup from which he prayed to be delivered was premature death then and there in the garden. There are few more beautiful things in Scripture than the indications of the mutual love of our Lord and his Father, a love which was constantly and closely associated with the Cross (John 10:17), and we are told that he endured the Cross and despised the shame because of "the joy that was set before him" (Heb. 12:2). If this is the true meaning of Gethsemane, then we know that our Lord's prayer was answered. Not long before he had said, "Father, I know that thou hearest me always," and the perfect calm with which Christ came forth from the garden to meet the armed soldiers clearly showed that, as the Epistle to the Hebrews said, "He was heard by reason of his filial submission" (Heb. 5:7, Greek).

2. *The Master's Need of Sympathy.*—The fact that he took these three disciples apart from the others shows his need of sympathy. He was perfectly human as well as perfectly divine, and just before, when in the upper room, he had expressed his appreciation of the way in which they had been with him, "Ye are they that have continued with me in my temptations" (Luke 22:28). As Maclaren says in his perfect outline of this passage, we have here (*a*) the tempted Christ; (*b*) the lonely Christ; (*c*) the grateful Christ.

3. *The Master's Purpose of Training.*—We may feel pretty sure that these three disciples were taken by Christ apart from the rest, not only on his account, but also on theirs. It would be a fine opportunity for training them for future life and service. Two of the three had expressed their ability and readiness to drink of their Master's cup, and to be baptized with his baptism (Matt. 20:22), and this provided an occasion for entering, as never before, into his sorrow and suffering.

4. *The Master's Disappointment at Failure.*—But all his efforts proved fruitless, for when he returned from his lonely prayer, he found the three men asleep, and naturally expressed surprise that they could not watch with him even one hour (Matt. 26:40). When he returned from the second prayer again he found them asleep, and left them in order that he might pray once again to his Father. The opportunity of rendering him help by showing him sympathy was now past, and so far as he was concerned they might sleep on and take their rest; but the betrayer was at hand, and it was essential for them to be aroused and face what lay before them. We are told that these disciples did not know "what to answer him" (Mark 14:40), as he lovingly rebuked them for not watching with him, though we are also told that sorrow was the cause of their sleep (Luke 22:45). The Master's words were doubtless heeded by them later on when they understood their meaning, "Watch and pray that ye enter not into temptation; the spirit indeed is willing, but the flesh is weak" (Matt. 26:41). He knew exactly and entirely their desire to serve him, and at the same time the limitations of their power. The physical had for a time overcome the spiritual, and for this reason it was essential for them to "watch and pray." These two counsels, "watch and pray," are often associated. We are never told in the New Testament anything about the object of watching. It is pretty certain that we are not to watch Satan, who is too elusive for us. Nor can we watch our circumstances, because they are so variable and complicated. Then, again, it is quite impossible to watch our sins, because we have no conception of their number, character, and power in the sight of God. Once more, we cannot for a moment conceive of watching ourselves, because self is utterly beyond our powers of understanding and control. It is, therefore, probable that the absence of any object of watching is intended to suggest our watching Christ, "looking off unto Jesus," for in occupation with him we are sure of being guarded against Satan, circumstances, sin, and self. Then together with watching comes prayer, so that as we are told of the danger, we are enabled to meet it by the strength that comes through prayer.

II. THE TRIAL

Gethsemane was soon followed by the betrayal and seizure, and although Simon Peter endeavored to defend his Master, the Lord Jesus would not do anything to prevent capture. And so he was led into the High Priest's house to be examined and tried. At this point we have another picture of the Apostle John which calls for special attention (John 18:15–17). As John was known to the High Priest, he entered in with Jesus Christ into the High Priest's court without any hesitation or difficulty. But Peter remained outside until John spoke to the maid who kept the door and brought in Peter. There seems to be a special point bearing on the Apostle John in the words addressed to Peter by the maid, "Art thou *also* one of this man's disciples?" The force of "also" is significant, for, of course, it means "in addition to the other disciple." There was no need to inquire about John, who had boldly entered into the court with his Master. He was well known, and it was not necessary to ask him or about him in regard to discipleship. All this implies and clearly teaches the importance of a bold confession of Christ. If only Peter had been courageous enough to take his stand with his fellow disciple, things might have happened differently. John seems to have had no difficulty, for even though we may rightly make allowance for his being known to the High Priest, we also observe that apparently he made no secret of his association with Christ. Confession of our Lord is at once the simplest, the safest, and the most satisfying attitude for a disciple to take, and those who for any reason fail to acknowledge him will never find their life safe nor their experience satisfactory. Great stress is laid in the Gospels on the confession of Christ and the absolute necessity of not being ashamed of him (Matt. 10:32; Luke 12:8). We know how the Jews were afraid to confess him (John 9:22; 12:42), and the effect of fear and shame is always the same in its moral and spiritual weakness and disaster. John did not hesitate to let it be known that he was "one of this man's disciples," and thereby he was saved untold trouble. Whether, therefore, for our own satisfaction, or as a means of blessing to others, the Word is clear and unmistakable, "Confess with thy mouth the Lord Jesus" (Rom. 10:9). When this is our attitude, we know something of what Paul meant when he said, "I am not ashamed" (Rom. 1:16; 2 Tim. 1:12). There is scarcely anything more beautiful than the assurance that, if we are not ashamed of Christ, he will not be ashamed of us (Mark 8:38). It was because men of old were full of courageous faith that we read, "God is not ashamed to be called their God" (Heb. 11:16).

III. The Cross

After the trial before the ecclesiastical and secular authorities, it was not long before the actual crucifixion took place, and once again we have a picture of the Apostle John (John 19:26, 27). There was a special work to be done. Mary, the mother of our Lord, was standing near the Cross, and, desiring to provide for her after his death, Jesus said to his mother, "Woman, behold thy son," as he handed her over to the care of the disciple whom he loved. Then to the disciple he said, "Behold thy mother." From that moment John took charge of Mary. We are inclined to wonder why she was not placed in the care of those who were (almost certainly) her own sons. This was doubtless because of their attitude to Jesus Christ, for at that time his brethren did not believe on him (John 7:5). Spiritual fitness called for the influence of the Apostle John, for the truest bond between men is sympathy with Christ. We are accustomed to say that "blood is thicker than water," but we may add to this that "spirit is thicker than blood." Our relation to Christ is the strongest element in life, and love to him is the determining factor which brings into play the truest human sympathies. Then, too, we may well imagine that this special work would give John something to do in his grief. Service at such a time is the best anodyne.

The incident is also important as a reminder of the nature of true friendship. A thoughtful essay by Dr. H. Clay Trumbull is entitled "Love Grows Through Serving," and there can be no doubt that true friendship consists in being rather than in having a friend; in loving, not in being loved. Thus, the opportunity provided to John to manifest his interest and love on behalf of his dead Master would be of great value to the development of his character. Friendship of the right sort means a constant outlay of love and a ceaseless expenditure of self-sacrificing effort.

IV. The Death

The end was now at hand, and when everything had been finished and fulfilled, our Lord "bowed his head and gave up his spirit" (John 19:30). But once again the Apostle John appears, and in connection with a matter of great importance. In order that the bodies should not remain on the Cross over the Sabbath Day, the request was made that the legs of all these three men might be broken, and that they might be taken away. It was soon seen that Jesus was dead already, and so his legs were not broken, though one of the soldiers pierced his side, "and straightway there came out blood and water." According to Dr. Stroud's interesting medical theory, our Lord died (literally) of a broken heart. It is at this point that the Apostle John is important, for we have the record in these words: "He that hath seen hath borne witness, and his witness is true; and he knoweth that he saith true, that ye also may believe" (John 19:35). Thus, he bore testimony to the reality and certainty of Christ's death, and this for the purpose of belief by others. Christianity is a fact, and is based on testimony. The disciples were told that they should bear witness, because they had been with our Lord from the beginning (John 15:27), and the fourth Gospel closes with another assurance to the same effect, "This is the disciple that beareth witness of these things, and wrote of these things, and we know that his witness is true" (John 21:24). The word "witness" is one of the characteristic features of this Gospel, and there are no fewer than seven forms of evidence included. There was the witness of John the Baptist (John 5:33); the witness of Scripture (John 5:39); the witness of the Father (John 5:37); the witness of Christ himself (John 8:14); the witness of Christ's works (John 5:36); the witness of the Holy Spirit (John 15:26); and the witness of the disciples (John 15:27). Thus, the Gospel of the person and work of Christ comes to us on the basis of assured testimony, and bids us believe and live (1 John 5:7–11).

As we contemplate these various incidents connected with our Lord's death, we see that everything centers in the Cross. We are told of the crucifixion that Jesus was "in the midst" (John 19:18). So must it ever be. As Denney well said, in the New Testament the center of gravity is not Bethlehem, but Calvary. Christ was "in the midst" when he was first seen (Luke 2:46). Indeed, ages before he came it was prophesied that the Prince should be "in the midst" (Ezek. 46:10). After the resurrection our Lord came and stood "in the midst" (John 20:19, 26), and one of the pictures of the future is the Lamb "in the midst" of the throne (Rev. 7:17). And yet all this centrality of Christ and his Cross was only made real when illuminated by the Day of Pentecost. So is it always. Even the Cross and Resurrection, with all their glory, are only made vital to the soul by the Holy Spirit of God.

Though Christ a thousand times in Bethlehem be born,
If he's not born in thee, thy heart is still forlorn;
The Christ on Golgotha alone can never save thy soul,
The Christ in thine own heart alone can make thee whole.

IX

GREAT REVELATIONS

Like the lifting of a fog came the Resurrection of our Lord after his Crucifixion, and among the changes made by his rising from the dead there are few more striking and impressive than the transformation effected in the lives of his disciples. The Apostle John is seen to bear a special part in connection with the Resurrection, just as he had done in connection with the death. There are two events with which he was specially associated.

I. AT THE TOMB

The news of the empty tomb came to Peter and John early on that first Easter morning through Mary Magdalene. It is probable that Mary felt drawn to these two by their interest and sympathy, as well as their close association with Jesus Christ. Moreover, the mother of our Lord was staying with John. The announcement at once prompted the two disciples to go to the tomb (John 20:1–10). They both ran together, but John, as the younger man, outran his companion and arrived first. Yet although he stooped down, looked in and saw the linen cloths (not clothes) lying, something made him hesitate, and he did not actually enter the tomb. Up to this moment he, of course, had no idea of the Resurrection. When Peter reached the tomb he at once entered with characteristic ardor, and his fixed gaze (v. 6, Greek) at the linen cloths evidently led to a good deal of thought and perplexity as to what had happened. Then John, the younger man, was emboldened to enter, and it is interesting and significant to observe what they saw in the tomb. Special mention is made of the napkin, or "turban," that had been upon Christ's head, not lying with the linen cloths, but rolled up in a place by itself.

What does this mean? Why is it singled out for such prominent attention? An old explanation, which is still heard from time to time, is that our Lord's Resurrection took place with perfect ease and calm and the entire absence of hurry, so that time allowed him to wrap up the napkin and put it in a place by itself. But although there may be no doubt as to the absence of haste, the original word does not naturally suggest this interpretation. The term as rendered in the American Revised Version is "rolled up"—that is, twirled or shaped like a turban—and there does not seem to be much doubt that the reference to "a place by itself" simply means separate from the rest of the linen cloths which were used for the body. What Peter and John saw as they continued to gaze were the linen cloths in the actual shape of the Body, the turban of the head naturally being where the head had lain, and the other cloths still remaining in the exact shape of the Body. Our Lord had evidently been raised from the dead by the power of God, and had left the linen cloths (in which were the spices) exactly as the Body had been placed by Joseph and Nicodemus. It was this manifest evidence of the Resurrection that led to John being the first to believe that our Lord had been raised (v. 8).

This view of the passage gives a satisfactory proof of the reason why John was able to believe. It was the sight of the cloths in the form of the Body that first led him to think, and then to believe in what had actually happened. The interpretation now favored has been held by some of us for a long time, and it was with great interest and no little satisfaction that so able a championship was found for it a few years ago in that interesting book, "The Risen Master," by Latham. The evidence was ample so far as John with his greater insight was concerned. And yet we are told definitely that up to that moment "they knew not the Scripture that he must rise from the dead." Facts are always the foundation of faith, although faith means very much more than believing facts. "Religious faith is rather the first fruit of life than the last blossom of thought." There was something else required besides this belief in the fact of the Resurrection. That faith had to be associated with Scripture, and again in turn with the Person of our Lord as living. As Pearson, in his great work on the "Creed," says, "Divine faith founded on Scripture gives infallible certainty." Faith in the true sense of the word is trust, confidence, reliance, and this is only possible in relation to a person. And so we are not surprised to read that both Peter and John went away from the tomb to their own home. They had not yet realized the force of what they had seen, and its bearing on their future life and work. Peter seems to have returned, still wondering what had happened (Luke 24:12), while John probably went to tell the mother of Christ what he had seen, and perhaps also the conviction that filled his mind, however inadequate his faith was at that moment (John 20:8),

II. ON THE LAKE

We are not told in detail any result to the Apostle John of the personal revelation of the risen Christ. We only know that he was among those who had the Easter message of "Peace be unto you," who felt gladness that once again the beloved Master was seen, and who received the commission with the gift of the Holy Spirit (John 20:19–23). We next find John with other disciples in Galilee, whither their Master had told them to go. While waiting for his appearance, Peter, with his characteristic impulse, proposed a return to their work as fishermen (John 21:1–7). Some writers think that they ought not to have engaged in this work, but simply waited in Galilee until their Lord should appear. Others are of opinion that poverty alone naturally suggested the necessity of work for a livelihood until Christ should come. Yet, again, others think that the very best thing for these disciples was to do some work while they were waiting, since work is one of the finest preservatives against either depression or indifference. It is particularly noteworthy that there are seven of these disciples, including John and his brother James. Five of them are described and two are nameless. It is no fancifulness to think of the seven as symbolizing the Church as a whole, there represented in the work of fishing, and, if so, it is particularly encouraging to think of the two unnamed disciples standing for the rank and file of God's people who do not occupy prominent positions. All are required in the service of their Master.

After a night of fruitless toil, Jesus stood on the beach, though he was not recognized by the disciples, and when, in answer to his inquiry, they confessed the fruitlessness of their work, he told them what to do, and the immediate result was a multitude of fishes. At this moment the Apostle John, with remarkable insight, said unto Peter, "It is the Lord." He is rightly described in this connection, as in others, as "the disciple whom Jesus loved," for love is the great perceptive power. Love is not blind, as some would have us believe, for "the secret of the Lord is with them that fear him, and he will show them his covenant." We all know how in science there is an imperative need of sympathy, if we would discover the secrets of Nature, and it is the same in things spiritual; to know, we must love. Love, too, is the great penetrative power which sees God in everything. Christ was realized in the course of daily toil, and the soul that is in close fellowship with God will soon go past all second causes, and say, "It is the Lord." Love to Christ will make the eye single, and thus the whole body will be full of light.

We must pass over the eager enthusiasm shown by Peter in his effort to reach the shore, and also the practical service of the other disciples, as they did the more humdrum work, though equally necessary, of dragging the fish to shore. The disciples were soon at their morning meal provided by the Master, and then came the solemn restoration by a threefold question of the disciple who had three times denied his Lord.

When this was over and the word came, "Follow Me," Peter naturally wondered what would happen to his young companion and friend, and, seeing John following, he asked the Lord Jesus, "What shall this man do?" It was not jealousy, but genuine interest and affection that prompted this question. "Lord, what about this man?" The answer of Christ was in the form of a slight and yet definite rebuke: "If I will that he tarry till I come, what is that to thee? Follow thou me." The supreme requirement was that each disciple should feel himself in direct relation to the Master, and the following of Christ is the sum and substance of true living. To follow means to trust and obey; this, and this only, but this is all. Meanwhile, there seems to be the suggestion that John's part was that of waiting. The idea went abroad that John was not to die, but in reality our Lord only referred to the possibility of John's waiting till the coming of the Master. Not that it meant absolutely that he should do this, but that there was a sovereignty over his life as well as that of Peter's, and the issues were kept in the hands of the supreme Master. "If I will." This is the secret of all true discipleship. We are subject to the will of Christ, and we know that, as Dante says, "In His will is our peace." Each man has his own place, his own individuality, his own time, and his own attitude and to his own Master he stands or falls.

The last testimony to John in the Gospels is probably borne by some disciple of his or some disciples who were aware of what he had been, had seen, and had done. "This is the disciple that beareth witness of these things and wrote these things, and we know that his witness is true." These words read very like a postscript by another hand or other hands, assuring us of the reality of the man whose Gospel from the very first has been the treasure of the Church in its revelation of her Lord and Master. And as we close this record we can endorse with thankfulness the fine words of Godet:

"For my part, I rejoice to be able to say that the renewed study of this inimitable work has been the certainty of its authenticity shining before my view with ever more irresistible clearness. It is proved, as it seems to me, above all, by the luminous transparency with which there is revealed in it the self-consciousness of Christ. A Divine life, humanly lived, Jesus offers himself to the world as the bread of life, come down from heaven, that whosoever eats of it may realize through him the sublime destination of our race: man in God, God in man. This conception bears within it the seal of its origin."

As we review the story of the Apostle thus far in his career, we cannot help noticing the individuality of his life and witness. Although one of twelve, he stands out from the rest, because he possesses his own personality, lives his own life, bears his own witness, does his own work, and waits patiently his Master's will. This is always the true secret of Christian living, "to every man his work."

It is so sweet to know
My whole life long
Thy loving plan for me
Cannot go wrong.

I know that thou wilt choose
The best for me,
And I can be at rest
And trust in thee.

X

AFTER PENTECOST

The Day of Pentecost was a watershed between two dispensations, and at the same time made remarkable changes in the lives of the Apostles. John, as the youngest of the twelve, does not stand out prominently in the record in Acts, though there are hints from time to time that Pentecost had influenced him and enabled him, like the rest, to serve his Master in the power of the Holy Spirit. And even if he thus takes a subordinate place in the early Church, we may well ponder the various hints given of him in order to discover what we can of his life and character.

I. WHAT PENTECOST WAS

It is impossible to look at the story of Acts without recalling an important passage in the fourth Gospel which anticipated and really prophesied what would happen. On the last day of the Feast our Lord invited people to come to him and satisfy their thirst, and then this interpretation is added, "This spake he of the Spirit, which they that believed on him were to receive; for the Spirit was not yet given, because Jesus was not yet glorified" (John 7:39). Under the symbol of water, this was a promise of the bestowal of the Spirit on all believers. The main thought seems to be that as long as Christ was bodily present there was no real need of spiritual presence. It is equally clear that "not yet" is not equivalent to "unknown before," but must be understood as referring to a time before Pentecost, because Christ was not yet ascended. In some way or another the descent of the Holy Spirit was associated with and depended on the ascension of Christ, for when Pentecost actually came the Spirit was given to disciples alone, and was bestowed as a gift of the ascended Lord (Acts 2:33). As Dr. A. J. Gordon once said, "The Spirit of God is the successor of the Son of God in his official ministry on earth. Until Christ's earthly work for his Church had been finished, the Spirit's work in this world could not possibly begin."

The difference between the time before Pentecost and that day can also be seen in the results of the Holy Spirit's work in and through those who were disciples of Christ. Whatever activity they had shown before was as nothing compared with what they were enabled to do as the result of that gift (John 14:12).

It is inevitable to notice that the Day of Pentecost was the occasion on which, according to the Master's promise, the disciples were "baptized with the Holy Spirit" (Acts 1:5). Much has been written on the subject of "the baptism of the Holy Ghost," though it may be worth while to remember that as it stands the phrase is not found in Scripture. There are seven passages which speak of people being baptized with or in the Holy Spirit, and this "baptism" is clearly stated to be the actual experience of every Christian without exception, and not the special privilege of a certain number (1 Cor. 12:13). As the term "baptism" when used of water refers to an initial act which is never repeated, it seems in every way best to interpret the phrase "baptized with or in the Holy Spirit" as referring to the initial work of the Holy Spirit in uniting believers to Christ, and to one another in him (Acts 2:33; Gal. 4:6). If this is the true meaning, then the idea of "the baptism of the Holy Ghost" as a second distinct work of grace is not warranted by Scripture, especially as these words are not strictly Scriptural. But while this is so, we must be careful to use and to emphasize the important New Testament teaching on a Spirit-filled life as the privilege and duty of every believer. So that Pentecost meant the initial and never-repeated "baptism with the Holy Spirit" as the occasion of constituting the new community in union with the ascended Lord and as equipping them for his service. Thenceforward the disciples were not baptized afresh, but "filled" with the Holy Spirit for special needs as occasions arose. This distinction between the "baptism" and the "filling" of the Spirit is in exact harmony with New Testament phraseology in Acts and elsewhere, and, to put it in well-known words, we may say that there is "one baptism, but many fillings."

II. What Pentecost Did

Limiting ourselves to the effects of this gift of the Holy Spirit on the disciples and concentrating as far as possible on the Apostle John, let us try to see something of what happened.

In Acts 1:13 we find John with the rest in the place of prayer and expectation, and it is a point of some interest that while in the other lists of the Apostles contained in the Gospels (Matt. 10:2–4; Mark 3:16–19; Luke 6:14–16) John's name is third and fourth, here (in R. V.) it is found second, immediately after that of Peter. With the rest, he was waiting the fulfillment of the Master's promise, and they were "with one accord" expressive of that perfect oneness of desire and hope which showed that they were in the true line of blessing. This emphasis on "one accord" is particularly noteworthy in Acts, and calls for study by all who desire to know the secret of united intercession and life (Acts 1:14; 2:1, 46; 4:24; 5:12; 7:57; 8:6; 12:20; 15:25; 18:12; 19:29). There seems to be no doubt that the unanimity of the disciples was one reason why their Lord could and did bless them.

In Acts 2:14 we read of "Peter standing up with the eleven," so that on this occasion Peter was the spokesman not only for himself, but for the others, in proclaiming to the crowd his Master's message, and telling them frankly what had been done. The difference in the one who had denied his Lord is particularly striking, for the gift of the Holy Spirit had transformed him into a new man. There does not seem to have been the same temperamental weakness in John, though we feel sure that the gift of the Spirit must have made a decided difference in him as well.

In Acts 3:1 we read of Peter and John going to worship in the temple. The association of these two is particularly interesting in view of what we have already seen of them (Luke 5:10; 22:8; John 20:3, 4; 21:20–22). It has been suggested that this was due to the fact that they were the leaders among the Apostles, and we find them together on other occasions (4:13; 8:14). Mr. Walker, of Tinnevelly, in his fine commentary, speaks of them as "an admirable combination of strenuous activity and thoughtful love." Once again Peter is the natural leader, no doubt because of his greater age and experience, though he associates John with him in what he does, and the man who was healed clung to both apostles in his newborn gratitude (Acts 3:4, 11). This was another opportunity for testimony on behalf of Christ, and after the disclaimer of his and John's own power and holiness, Peter again gave testimony to their Master as the One who had made the man strong (3:11–26).

In Acts 4:3 John begins his life of suffering, for with Peter he is apprehended and put in prison. The testimony for Christ was particularly annoying to the Jewish authorities, especially because the resurrection from the dead was associated with it. Then on the next day Peter and John were brought before the Jewish Council, and were asked "by what power or in what name" they had done this miracle. With remarkable boldness the two men bore their testimony, and this attitude was a cause of astonishment to the Jewish leaders (4:13). Something had evidently happened, for there was no hesitation and no fear, as these two spoke frankly about their Master. The result was all the more surprising, because neither Peter nor John had received any technical training in Jewish theology. They were what we should call "plebeians," without professional knowledge, and, of course, this meant that in the opinion of the Council they were "ignorant," in the sense of ill-informed men. But, nevertheless, many of these leaders began to recognize that the men had been seen in company with Jesus of Nazareth, and it would appear as though they thought that this courage was somehow connected with their association with him. This was indeed the secret of what had happened, for by the power of the Holy Spirit they had been enabled to maintain their fellowship with Jesus Christ and to bear testimony to him and to his grace.

In Acts 4:19 we have a further illustration of the courage of Peter and John, for on being threatened and charged not to speak again in the name of Jesus, these fine men replied, "Whether it be right in the sight of God to hearken unto you rather than God, judge ye; for we cannot but speak the things which we saw and heard" (4:19, 20). Thus they showed what has been well called "the moral imperative of grace." The Holy Spirit has wonderful power to transform ordinary and uneducated individuals into able, courageous witnesses for the truth (Luke 12:12).

In Acts 8:14 John is again mentioned with Peter as being sent by the Church in Jerusalem to Samaria, consequent upon the remarkable work done by Philip. Peter and John were to go down to bestow upon the baptized the unique gift of the Holy Spirit. It is impossible to avoid recalling the former attitude of John to the Samaritans (Luke 9:54) when he wished to bring upon them the fire of Divine judgment. Now he is to be the means in God's hands of conveying to them the gift of the Holy Spirit. Prayer is associated with this laying on of hands, and it is important to remember that this gift on the part of Peter and John was at once unique and personal. There is no suggestion in the New Testament that they were able to transmit this power to others. As apostles, they occupied a position which did not admit of any strict succession (Acts 1:22). Then, too, it must never be forgotten that these unique gifts of the Spirit in the early Church were not limited to the Twelve, because an ordinary Christian layman, Ananias, was enabled by the laying on of hands to bestow spiritual blessing on the new convert, Saul of Tarsus (Acts 9:17, 18). The action of laying on of hands in the New Testament, and indeed throughout Scripture, is clearly that of benediction and commission rather than transmission (Sanday, "Conception of Priesthood").

In Acts 12:2 we have the last reference to the Apostle John in the Acts, where he is referred to in connection with the martyrdom of his brother James. Perhaps this description of "James, the brother of John," is a reminder of that memorable day when both James and John expressed their ability to drink of their Master's cup of sorrow (Matt. 20:20–28). James was the first to be executed, while John, his much younger brother, was destined to remain for many a year and to endure much suffering before he was called hence.

In Galatians 2:9 John is described with James, the brother of our Lord, and Peter as one of the "pillars" of the Church. This shows quite clearly the important and conspicuous position which he held at this time. The metaphor "pillar" is also interesting from the spiritual standpoint. It suggests something which rests on a foundation, and we know that John was indeed firmly fixed on the foundation of Jesus Christ (1 Cor. 3:11; Eph. 2:20). Then a pillar is intended to give support to a building, and we are sure that the Apostle John, by his intimate association with his Master, his knowledge of Christian truth, his gift of the Holy Spirit, and his disposition of genuine love, must have been of the greatest possible help in the Church of that day. We may also think of a "pillar" as a mark of beauty, for a pillar in a building undoubtedly adds to the attractiveness of the structure. The Apostle John was assuredly a "pillar" in this sense. The reality of his character and life must have been a witness to the "beauty of holiness" (Psalm 29:2). Whatever may be our position as Christians, it is for us first of all to behold and then to reflect "the beauty of the Lord" (Psalm 27:4; 90:17).

As we review these various instances connected with the life of the Apostle John after Pentecost, we are reminded of the work of the Holy Spirit in every believer. Indeed, without that Spirit no one can be regarded as a Christian at all (Rom. 8:9). The Holy Spirit is associated with three special features of Christianity in relation to the individual. The first of these is Conversion, including all the various aspects of the believer's initial spiritual experience. It is the providence of the Holy Spirit to convict of sin, to reveal the grace of God, to bestow the gift of life, to assure of acceptance in Christ, and to introduce us to the Presence of God. The second is Communion with God, for everything is intended to lead up to fellowship. The Holy Spirit alone makes this real, for after being introduced to God we have "access by one Spirit unto the Father," whereby communion with God begins and continues. Everything in connection with prayer and the other means of grace is associated with the Holy Spirit as the medium of communication and the guarantee of blessing. The third is Character, for life must be expressed in practice, and grace is needed to produce this effect. Here, again, the Holy Spirit makes character possible and real, for he abides in the soul, producing "the fruit of the Spirit," and by constant revelation of Christ strengthens the believer in the inner man, and transforms him into the image of the Son of God. There is scarcely anything clearer or more emphatic in Scripture than the Holy Spirit's relation to the individual, for his action covers our whole life. So it was, we are perfectly sure, with the Apostle John, and so it must be with each of us today.

XI

DARK DAYS

Our Lord said that James and John should drink of his cup of suffering, and as James had the first sharp, short form of it (Acts 12:2), so it fell to John's lot to experience a long, protracted suffering, extending over many years, until at length all the other apostles had passed away (John 21:22). We see something of this in that part of his life connected with the

Book of Revelation. Although this is the last Book of the Bible, it is probably not the last in chronological order; and yet we have no information about the actual life of the Apostle later than what is found here. Without attempting to obtain any idea of the Book itself, we will concentrate on the various hints that are given about John himself, in order to discover all that is possible about his character.

I. The Seer

To John was given the privilege of receiving "the Revelation of Jesus Christ," the "unveiling" of some of the deepest truths concerning the present and future of the world in relation to Christ. This revelation came from God through an angel to John, and it is worth while to remember that as in the Gospels he gives the fullest, clearest picture of Christ, so here it was his privilege to receive, and then pass on, some of the most important aspects of Christian truth concerning the future. A seer is "one who sees," and the emphasis on this thought and word all through this Book is particularly interesting and important. John received and reproduced the messages given to him from God concerning his Master. There are few, if any, positions in the Christian Church more important than those connected with insight into truth, and one remarkable feature is that spiritual insight is often dissociated from ordinary intellectual power. Paul makes a special point of "knowledge" in his later Epistles as one of the outstanding features of a mature Christian life, and in one passage he associates this with perception (Phil. 1:9).

In another instance the ripe Christian, as contrasted with the elementary believer, is described as one who has his "perceptions permanently exercised" (Heb. 5:14). No wonder, then, that John was selected for this special work. In this he was akin to the Old Testament "seer," whose spiritual vision was so important in connection with Divine revelations. The true "seer" is the one who has "visions of God" (Ezek. 1:1), and then reports these visions to others for their guidance, instruction, and warning. The influence of the Holy Spirit upon the mind of the believer is one of the most vital truths in Christianity, and is frequently emphasized by Paul (Rom. 12:2; Eph. 4:23).

II. The Witness

The Apostle was not only a seer; he was called upon to testify what he saw, and the earliest witness he bears in this Book is particularly striking, because it reveals some of the fundamental realities of the Christian Gospel (Rev. 1:4–8). (1) First of all, he bears witness to the great truth of the Divine Trinity—Father, Spirit, and Son. The Father is described in language equivalent to the Old Testament word "Jehovah," as the One "Who is, and Who was, and Who is to come"; eternal, unchangeable, and therefore, dependable. The Spirit is described in all his fullness by the phrase, "the seven spirits that are before his throne" (see also Rev. 3:1; 4:5; 5:6). Jesus Christ is then spoken of as "the faithful witness, the first-born of the dead, and the ruler of the kings of the earth." This seems to suggest his threefold work as Prophet, Priest, and King. He witnesses to truth; he bestows life as "the first-born from the dead"; and he gives power as the "ruler of the kings of the earth." Thus, as Prophet, he reveals; as Priest, he redeems; and as King, he rules. (2) Then comes the assurance of "grace" and "peace" from this Divine source.

Grace is one of the greatest words of the New Testament. It is found at least a hundred times in Paul, and while only seen six times in John, yet the references are decidedly characteristic (John 1:14, 16, 17; 2 John 3; Rev. 1:4; 22:21). Grace brings salvation, and thus deals with the past; it bestows sufficiency, and thus meets the present; it ensures satisfaction, and thus guarantees the future. Peace is the effect of grace, and this again is a great Biblical conception.

There seems to be a twofold peace suggested by the Apostle John (John 14:27; 16:33; 20:19, 21, 26). There is the peace of relationship restored and the peace of restfulness realized. These include peace of conscience covering the past, peace of soul providing for the present, peace of heart assuring the future. Or we may think of the peace of pardon, of power, of purity, of provision, of perception, of promise, and all because of the indwelling presence. (3) Then follows the outburst of praise based on these realities. The Apostle expresses himself in one of those doxologies of which the Epistles have so many. Christianity is essentially joyous, and necessarily calls for a song. There is a twofold doxology here, and it is interesting to observe the threefold doxology in Chapter 4, the fourfold in Chapter 5, and the sevenfold in Chapter 7. Our experience of Christianity ought to be a growing joy expressed in a growing song. The reason given here for praise is the Saviour's love as shown in his grace and power. He "loveth us" (R. V.), showing that his death did not exhaust his affection, and the proof of this is that he has "loosed us" from our sins. The Authorized Version, in using the word "washed" (Greek—louo), thus differs from the R. V. "loosed" (Greek—luo). Whichever reading we adopt, both are true. The Authorized Version thinks of sin as a stain; the Revised Version as a chain.

Our Lord's power follows from his grace, because in making us "a kingdom" and "priests," he assures us of authority and access, as we do him service. Thus, the song is called forth by his compassion, his cleansing, his crowning, and his consecration of us. No wonder the Apostle poured out his soul in saying, "To him be the glory and the dominion forever and forever. Amen."

III. The Sufferer

After this outburst the Apostle soon reminds his readers of his own position. He was in the island of Patmos, and was already experiencing some of those troubles which were the inevitable lot of the primitive Christians. But he does not emphasize any uniqueness in this respect, for he speaks of himself as their "brother, and partaker" of these sufferings. It is also interesting to notice that he speaks of the tribulation, kingdom, and patience as "in Jesus," for they were all associated with his relation to Christ. From the very first it was through much tribulation that believers could enter the kingdom (Acts 14:22), and yet although tribulation was their portion, it could not affect the blessed fact that they possessed a "kingdom," which, because it was "in Jesus," made them safe from all harm. Meanwhile, the "patience" or "endurance" which enabled them to meet these sufferings also came from the same source, and the Lord Jesus Christ gave them grace sufficient for every need. The Apostle's earthly location might be "in Patmos," but his spiritual position was "in the Spirit." Thus he, like Paul, is able to show the two aspects of the believer "in Christ" and "at Colossæ" (Col. 1:2). This was exactly what his Master had said many years before: "In Me … peace; in the world … tribulation" (John 16:33). All this suffering was, of course, due to the "Word of God and the testimony of Jesus." It has always been impossible to be faithful to Christ for very long without incurring opposition, and even raising hostility, but notwithstanding these troubles, the believer has the source of comfort and strength in his communion with his Heavenly Master, and he knows that "greater is he that is in us than he that is in the world" (1 John 4:4).

IV. The Worshiper

Before the Apostle John could bear witness to the world of the great truths God had to reveal to him, it was necessary for him to see in all his Divine glory the Master whom he had long loved and served (Rev. 1:10–20). The call came to him to write what he saw in a book, and send it to seven churches, and when he turned to see who it was that was speaking to him, he had a vision of his Master in his exaltation. The various items mentioned are symbolical of our Lord's functions, and all seem to come from the Old Testament, where they were associated either with the priest or the king. There were also seven symbols of his character, expressive of what he was to his people. It is impossible to dwell in detail on this vision, and it must suffice to notice its effect on the Apostle as he fell at the feet of his Master as one dead. Then came the threefold response. First, assurance in the touch of the hand and the voice, which said, "Fear not." Next the word of authority, telling John that his Master was not dead, but alive for evermore, and possessor of the keys of death and of Hades. And then, arising out of this, assurance and authority came the appointment to do his work and tell others what he had seen and what he was to be told. Thus the Apostle had a vision of Christ as loving, watchful, active, and helpful. He is not dead, but alive; he sees and knows what his people need; he is walking amidst the churches, and is ready to cheer the despondent: to send messages of grace, and thus to inspire with his constant presence, power, and peace.

V. The Servant

All through this Book John is seen as a faithful worker for his Master, and this position is particularly clear when on two occasions he comes face to face with the angel who was revealing to him the truth. From the purely natural point of view it was not surprising that he fell down before the feet of the angel to worship (19:10; 20:12), but at once he was corrected, and reminded that the angel was only a "fellow servant." The ministry of angels is an important feature in the Christian religion. In the Old Testament they brought Divine messages and performed Divine services, but to-day they do not do the former of these, for with the gift of the Holy Spirit and the completion of revelation, our intercourse with the unseen has passed into the "fellowship of the Holy Ghost." But the angels still exercise their ministry on our behalf, and are ministering spirits sent forth to minister for them who shall be heirs of salvation (Heb. 1:14). Yet although they are so, we are not aware of them, otherwise it would be as easy for us to worship the messenger as it was for the Apostle John. Where he almost stumbled we should not be likely to stand. This reference to angels as "fellow servants" is a helpful reminder of the true position of the believer as a worker for God, and there is scarcely anything more significant than the title, "His servant John" (Rev. 1:1). Angels, prophets, apostles, and Christian brethren are all in one way or another workers in God's vineyard. There are varieties of gifts, but the same God, the same Lord, the same Spirit (1 Cor. 12:4–7).

VI. The Watcher

It is in this position of Watcher that the Apostle John specially comes before us in connection with the "unveiling." To him it was given to see and to tell the future, and the three words continually found together through this Book, especially in its earlier chapters, are "I saw," "I heard," and "write." And while not concerning ourselves with any precise interpretation of this remarkable Book, it may be said that the vision included at least four things: (1) A vision of Christ in all his majesty; (2) a vision of the Church in all its reality; (3) a vision of the world in all its hostility; (4) a vision of eternity in all its glory. The Apostle declares who the Lord Jesus Christ is, as the hope of his Church and the ruler of the universe. Then we are told of God's victory over sin, God's kingdom, God's city, and God's presence. Whatever else this Book records, there is no doubt that it reveals the Lord Jesus Christ in all the glory of his grace and rule in time and eternity. The Apostle was permitted to reveal the first position between Christ and the world, and then the inevitable victory of his Master in that day "when the kingdoms of this world shall have become the kingdom of our Lord and of his Christ, and he shall reign for ever and ever."

Thus we see the Apostle in this latest record of his life as "suffering, serving, shining." His life was lived in Christ. His love was constantly centered on his Master. His labor, whether in suffering or in service, was always done for his Master's glory, and all the while he was inspired with the hope that, notwithstanding every adverse circumstance, his Master would and must reign until every enemy should be vanquished (1 Cor. 15:25). It is for us to occupy the same position, maintain the same attitude, endure, it may be, the same suffering, and endeavor to do the same work. It is not enough that we should be nominally Christians; there must be in our life the same practical reality as we find in the Apostle John's, if we would witness to our Master and win souls for his kingdom.

> Lord, when we pray, "Thy kingdom come!"
>   Then fold our hands without a care
> For souls whom thou hast died to save,
>   We do but mock thee with our prayer.
>
> Thou couldst have sent an angel band
>   To call thine erring children home;
> And thus through heavenly ministries
>   On earth thy kingdom might have come.
>
> But since to human hands like ours
>   Thou hast committed work Divine,
> Shall not our eager hearts make haste
>   To join their feeble powers with thine?
>
> To word and work shall not our hands
>   Obedient move, nor lips be dumb,
> Lest through our sinful love of ease
>   Thy kingdom should delay to come?

XII

REVIEW

It is now necessary to look back over the various records of the life of the Apostle John and to note, so far as is possible, the development of his character. We shall find slight, but quite definite indications of his growth, which will enable us to see something of what Divine grace accomplished in him. In order to look at this subject in detail, we will consider the revelations of the Apostle's personal life in the various Books that bear his name.

I. THE GOSPEL

While naturally the Gospel as a whole is impersonal, because it is concerned with, the revelation of Christ, yet there are three significant hints of the writer which seem to show a little of his character in* relation to his Master.

(1) The question of the young disciple (John 1:38). When Andrew and John left their old master to follow the new One, they naturally asked our Lord, "Where dwellest thou?" This was the simple, but obvious, question of one who wished to know something more of the new Teacher to whom they were going. This is still the inevitable desire of the newborn soul. He wishes to know more of his Master, for having realized that he is the "Lamb of God" (1:36), and having followed him (1:37), the instinctive craving of the recently enlightened heart is to have further knowledge and experience.

(2) The inquiry of the growing disciple (John 13:25). At the Last Supper John, leaning on the breast of his Master, asked the question in response to Peter's request, "Lord, who is it?" This expressed the attitude of one who had enjoyed a good deal of experience, and who was in the natural place for receiving still further knowledge. It is a mark of a growing disciple to hold fellowship with the Master, and, concerning this or that which may perplex and prove difficult, to say, "Lord, who is it?"

(3) The insight of the mature disciple (John 21:7). After the Resurrection when the seven were at work in the early morning, it was John who first recognized his Master after the command about the net. This insight is characteristic of the true and mature disciple who is able to understand what is often hidden from less instructed followers. In the midst of troubles, surrounded by problems, pressed down by sorrows, and almost overwhelmed by difficulties, the growing disciple can, nevertheless, say, "It is the Lord."

These three stages of John's experience are interesting, because they express what is found elsewhere in Scripture. Thus, it would seem that the best reading of the well-known incident when Peter was restored indicates this threefold growth of the disciple of Christ (John 21:15–18). The first call was to feed the "lambs," referring to those who had just commenced the Christian life. The next call was to tend the "sheep," a word which seems to imply the fullest discipleship. And then, according to some texts, there is another word, "feed my *growing* sheep" (v. 17), expressive of a stage between the "lambs" and the "sheep." If this is correct, it certainly agrees quite literally with the stages in another writing of the Apostle John, where he describes Christians as, respectively, "little children," "fathers," "young men" (1 John 2:12–14). Comparison may also be made with other passages. In Psalm 5:11, we have a threefold joy: (*a*) the joy of trust, illustrating the commencement of the believer's life; (*b*) the joy of protection, marking its progress; (*c*) the joy of love, indicative of the culminating experience of the godly. Then, too, we recall that the Apostle Paul, in addressing the elders of Miletus, spoke first of the "grace of God," referring to the elementary teaching; then, "the Kingdom of God," expressing full instruction; and, last of all, "the whole counsel of God," meaning thereby the complete revelation of God for his mature people (Acts 20:24–27). But whether we may use these passages or not, there seems to be no doubt that the Christian life is characterized by stages of ever-deepening desire for more knowledge of Christ and an ever-widening experience of what he is to the soul.

II. THE ACTS

As we have seen, the position of the Apostle John curing the period covered by the Book of Acts is quite secondary and subordinate, and yet we feel sure that he was truly faithful to whatever calls were made upon him. The New Testament picture of the believer after Pentecost is that of an individual filled with the Holy Spirit, and whatever had been the case previous to that time, it was nothing compared to the spiritual life then and afterwards. The dispensation of the Holy Spirit ushered in at Pentecost was signally marked in a threefold way. It was characterized by (*a*) a rich personal experience: men were full of faith (Acts 6:5), wisdom. (Acts 6:3), joy (Acts 13:52), and hope (Acts 7:55). Then it was noteworthy for its (*b*) great personal courage, both of speech (Acts 4:31) and of action (Acts 13:9). And as the outcome there was (*c*) splendid personal service in preaching (Acts 2:4) and living (Acts 9:31). There is scarcely anything more outstanding or more striking in the story of the primitive Church recorded in the Acts than the association of the Holy Spirit with every part of the life of the disciple and of the community. Not only are men like Peter, Stephen, and Paul filled with the Holy Spirit (Acts 4:8; 7:55; 9:17), but ordinary disciples have exactly the same experience (Acts 4:31; 13:52), and almost every Christian grace is associated with the Holy Spirit, including wisdom (Acts 6:3), comfort (Acts 9:31), power (Acts 10:38), faith (Acts 11:24), and joy (Acts 13:52). All this, we are confident, was the experience and life of the Apostle John.

III. THE REVELATION

Without unduly repeating what has been already said about the indications of the Apostle's life in the Apocalypse, one thing in particular may be emphasized. It is clear that all through the Book what he saw and heard he wrote, neither more nor less. The exact correspondence between the revelations he had from God and the response he made to them by putting them in writing is a wonderful testimony to his loyalty and faithfulness. It is a reminder of what he himself had recorded years before about his Master. In a striking passage we are told that "the Son can do nothing of himself, but what he seeth the Father do; but what things soever he doeth, the Son also doeth in like manner" (John 5:19). To the same effect were other of the Lord's words, "I can of myself do nothing; as I hear, I judge." This precise agreement between what the Lord saw and heard from the Father and what he said and did in the world was beautifully imitated by his follower John, and we know that the visions he received in the island of Patmos were all reproduced with exactness for the benefit of God's people in all ages. Obedience is the organ of knowledge, for in proportion as we fulfill the Master's words, we receive the Holy Spirit and are enabled to understand still more of his truth and grace (John 14:15–17).

IV. THE EPISTLES

It is generally thought that the three Epistles which bear John's name were written towards the close of his life, and, although they are concerned with general instruction on Christian truth, they reveal certain aspects of the Apostle's own life which we shall do well to ponder.

1. *Strong Testimony.*—In the introduction to his first Epistle (1–3) he lays a strong foundation by his reference to our Lord and the substance of the Gospel. He places the greatest possible stress on the fact that he had heard, seen, and handled "the Word of Life," and on the basis of this personal experience he was ready to bear witness and declare to others what had been so precious to him. Thus, Apostolic experience led to Apostolic testimony and Apostolic communication. John was a man of strong convictions, due to his consciousness of the Divine, human, life-giving, and unique Christ, and on this account was ready to pass on to others what he himself was finding so full of blessing and power.

2. *Personal Experience.*—This is seen by the frequent use of the word "we" throughout his Epistles. He thereby associated others with himself, and did not hesitate to speak in these terms. A careful consideration of such phrases as "we say," "we walk," "we know," "we ought," and many more, bears testimony to this aspect of his life and work.

3. *Definite Appeal.*—We observe this in the almost constant use of the words "I write" and "we write" (1:4; 2:1, 8, 12). The Apostle had a message, and it was essential that he should pass that on to others. The great frequency with which he uses the words "I write" points beyond all question to the definiteness of what he had to say. He knew the truth of which he wrote, and he wished others to understand it also.

4. *Absolute Assurance.*—It is well known that the word "know" is in some respects the keynote of the First Epistle, but it is perhaps scarcely realized how prominent the thought is. Thus "we know" occurs fifteen times; "ye know" six times; "ye have known" three times; "we have known" once; and "he that knoweth" once. Then, too, he tells us that his Epistle was written "that ye may know" (5:13). All this shows beyond question the confident assurance of the Apostle. To him Christianity was no question of mere assumption or simple hopefulness; it expressed itself in assurance. While faith possesses, assurance knows that it possesses, and as the Gospel was written that his readers might "have" (20:31), so the Epistle was written that they might "know they have" (5:13). Knowledge in regard to things spiritual is not concerned with intellectual attainment or capability, but with spiritual insight and experience. Indeed, it is frequently associated with what would be regarded by the world as great ignorance, and yet those who possess it are frequently full of profound insight into the truth of God in Christ.

5. *Loving Interest.*—If we may assume that the Apostle wrote his Epistles at the end of his life, great point is thereby given to his frequent personal appeals to his readers. The most frequent of these is his address as "my little children" (2:1, 18, 28; 5:21). Then, too, he appeals to some of them as "young men" and "fathers" (2:14). They are also regarded as "brethren" (3:13), and perhaps beyond all others as "beloved" (2:7; 3:2; 4:1, 7). It is probable, as Westcott suggests, that each of these titles has some special point in connection with the precise appeal made. In any case, it shows the keenness of the interest of the old disciple in those who were coming after him.

6. *Perfect Satisfaction.*—We are told that this Epistle was written for the purpose of fellowship similar to that which the Apostle himself enjoyed, and that in the fellowship there would be the fulness of joy (1:3, 4). This reference to their joy being "full" is also mentioned in connection with the "elect lady" of the Second Epistle (v. 12), and it is interesting to note that the same phrase is found four times in different connections in the Gospel. When all these passages are put together, they give the explanation of how our joy in Christ may be complete. Then,

too, three times over the Apostle speaks of God's love being made perfect (2:5; 4:17, 18). This seems to mean that love to God had reached its height and crown in the experience of the believer, and there is perhaps nothing higher than this in the New Testament. Thus, we see something of the life the Apostle lived, and of the life he recommended to those to whom he wrote. When our joy is full and our love perfected, we know what fellowship means and what Christianity is intended to do for human life.

7. *Holy Severity.*—It might appear from what has been said that the Apostle in his old age had become somewhat weak and tender, not to say sentimental, in his devotion to his Master and in the experience of Divine love, but a moment's consideration will suffice to show the falsity and impossibility of this idea, because love in Scripture is never merely emotional and sentimental, but is always associated with truth and righteousness. The Apostle of love is, therefore, ready to speak in the plainest tones of the "liar," who denies that Jesus is the Messiah, and even describes him as "Anti-Christ" (1 John 2:22, 23). This view of our Lord is more than once emphasized, doubtless in the face of the errors that were already rife in his day. Those who were not prepared to acknowledge the true Incarnation of Christ were frankly said to be "not of God," and were showing an anti-Christian spirit (4:3; 2 John 7). In this connection the words of the Apostle concerning Diotrephes in his Third Epistle are very significant. Although John was able to rejoice in much that was true of Gaius, the beloved, yet with equal plainness he speaks of Diotrephes as one who loved to have the pre-eminence, who would not receive the Apostle himself, but spoke against him with malicious words, who would not receive the brethren, and forbade those who were ready to do so and actually cast them out of the Church. All this seems to show that Diotrephes must have been very like one of those Nicolaitanes (Rev. 2:6, 15), and the Apostle was quite ready to deal severely with him, if they should meet. Thus, John shows the most perfect congruity between devoted love to Christ and genuine hostility to those who did not follow the truth. He divides men very plainly into two classes: the children of God and the children of the devil (1 John 3:10), and speaks of the way in which men are either marked by "love" or "hate." False doctrine is of vital importance, because it inevitably leads to false living. Character and conduct, doctrine and duty, necessarily go together as cause and effect.

As we take leave of the Apostle of love, it is fitting to observe two things in his life which are as true today as ever. (1) What Grace can do. Originally, John seems to have been an impulsive, perhaps also a sharp-tempered man, and yet through the influence of the Lord and his Spirit, his life was altogether changed. He illustrated the transformation of Grace. "Instead of the thorn shall come up the fir tree, and instead of the briar shall come up the myrtle tree" (Isaiah 55:13). Grace is still ready and able to transform lives and to change the "lion" into the "lamb." But Grace has its intensifications as well as its transformations. It does not take away from human nature anything that is right and true, but increases, deepens, intensifies all our natural force. So it was with the Apostle John.

All the powers which he possessed before his conversion were taken up by his Master and used in Christian service. It has been well said that the Christian needs two births in his Christian life. He must first of all be changed from the natural to the supernatural by the New Birth of the Spirit. Then he must be born once more by being changed again into the natural, so that the supernatural may express itself in ordinary natural ways, as the man surrenders everything to God and places himself at his Lord's disposal.

But in order that all this may come about, it is important to remember (2) what Grace needs. If God is to work in us "to will and to do of his good pleasure" (Phil. 2:13), he requires from us just two things: Faith and Faithfulness. We must trust and then obey. Faith appropriates the Divine grace into mind, heart, conscience, and will, and then faithfulness expresses that grace in love, loyalty, and labor for Christ. So it was with the Apostle John, and so it will be with every disciple today, if only we receive of our Master's fullness and then reproduce that grace in daily living. We shall show in our lives what Christ is and what he is willing to be to others, and then everything in us will reflect his image, reproduce his character, and bear testimony "to the praise of the glory of his grace."

II

THE GOSPEL

I

THE PURPOSE AND PLAN

It is often said, and it can scarcely be said too often, that many people know about the Fourth Gospel who are not as familiar as they ought to be with the Gospel itself. There is a world of difference between knowledge of what men have said concerning this Gospel and acquaintance with its actual contents. The object of these outline studies is to call attention to the Gospel as it is, to examine its contents, and thereby to see something of its meaning and message. Taking it just as it stands, an attempt will be made to discover what its author believed, and how he regarded his Master, who is admittedly the theme of the writing. There is nothing to compare with a personal impression resulting from a personal study of the actual document.

The purpose of the writer is given at the end (20:30, 31), as though to suggest a reading through first, to get the proper impression, but whether we look at the purpose in the light of the Gospel or the Gospel in the light of the purpose, we shall see that the entire writing possesses a unity based on a definite object, and every section appears to be selected with direct reference to its specific purpose. Jesus Christ is central, and each incident, even when he himself does not appear, is associated with him. It is an argument in the form of a narrative, an argument for Christ arising directly out of the account given of his life and work. A new revelation is shown to have been given to the world, and in the revelation a new power is offered every human life.

The existence of a purpose does not detract in the least from the reality of the record. Even a novel written with a purpose is valuable, whether the purpose is actually stated or not, for as some one has said: "A novel without a purpose is like a life without a career. In order to be a story it must have something to say." The same is true of history, for it is obviously impossible for genuine history to be uncolored. Mere annals are of no further value than as a record of facts, and it is the historian's imagination in reconstructing the life and purpose of the period that makes his work so valuable. "It is imagination that must take data and rebuild the past." It is the same with a religious work, as we see from the Old Testament history, which was written with a special purpose by prophetic men, though their object never affects the historical character of what record. In like manner the purpose of the Fourth Gospel is in no sense derogatory to the facts which form the substance of the writing. Indeed, not one of the Books of the Bible can be properly understood unless we endeavor to arrive at a clear idea of what the author meant, and it is this definiteness and distinctiveness of purpose that give the Gospels in particular their real value.

Four Gospels and one Christ. Four records and one aim. Four pictures and one Person. Four methods of recording impressions of that Person. Matthew may be said to demonstrate; Mark to depict; Luke to declare; John to describe. Matthew is concerned with the coming of a promised Saviour; Mark with the life of a powerful Saviour; Luke with the grace of a perfect Saviour; John with the possession of a personal Saviour. Each Gospel has been given a keynote from the Old Testament: Matthew, "Behold, Thy King" (Zech. 9:9); Mark, "Behold, my Servant" (Isa. 42:1); Luke, "Behold, the Man" (Zech. 6:12); John, "Behold, your God" (Isa. 40:9). It is therefore important that, whatever may be the relations between these four records, each should be studied alone, first of all, to obtain the definite impression intended by the writer.

I. THE PURPOSE

Unlike Matthew and Mark, Luke and John both give the reason why they wrote their Gospels (Luke 1:1–4), and John's definite statement bears so closely on the composition and contents of the whole of his Gospel that it must be considered with all possible minuteness. "But these are written, that ye may believe that Jesus is the Christ, the Son of God; and that believing ye may have life in his name" (20:31). This shows that the writer had a definite purpose: "These are written that"—and that the purpose is twofold: (1) to lead to personal belief in the historical "Jesus" as "the Christ" or Messiah (for the Jews) and as the "Son of God" (for the Gentiles); (2) to lead, by believing, to the possession of life in his name.

There are seven terms in this verse which are characteristic of the entire Gospel. They can be tested by a good concordance, or else by reading the Gospel through and marking the references.

1. "Believe": Ninety-eight times in John as compared with Matthew eleven times, Mark fifteen, and Luke nine. This keynote of faith is struck in the earliest chapter and is found everywhere until it culminates in the message to the Apostle Thomas (20:29).

2. "Jesus": The historic name, and nowhere are the true humanity and historic character of our Lord more clearly set forth than in John's Gospel.

3. "The Christ": This term, signifying the Jewish Messiah, is a special point, more particularly in relation to the Jews, in the first great section 1 to 12.

4. "The Son of God": Another title of Christ found in the first chapter and illustrated all through. There is perhaps no title which is found more frequently than "the Son" with its correlative "the Father."

5. "Have": This word is peculiarly characteristic of John and always implies *conscious* possession of spiritual things, having and holding, obtaining and retaining.

6. "Life": The Greek word (ζωή) always refers to the inward and spiritual reality as distinct from the outward and visible expression (βίος). This distinction (and contrast) may be seen in our words "zoology" and "biology." The word "life" occurs in John thirty-six times as compared with Matthew seven, Mark four, and Luke six.

7. "His name": A phrase wholly characteristic of John (1:12; 2:23; 3:18) and occurring no less than eleven times in chapters 14 to 17. The "name" always means the revealed character and "in his name" means in union with what we know of him.

The whole Gospel is built up on the truths associated with these seven terms, and when we thus study carefully the purpose of John, we find the two ideas of fact (5:30) and faith (5:31); the revelation and the record; the work and the writing. Our Lord's life is intended to be the basis and inspiration of our faith. Every fact in him is to be a factor and a force in us. We must therefore study the Gospel along the lines of this purpose as expressed in these ideas, and the more closely we do so the more we shall see that everything from beginning to end is deliberately and definitely included in the special object here so clearly set forth.

II. THE PLAN

This purpose (20:31) is built up and realized by means of a definite plan. Everything in the Gospel subserves the purpose, and careful study shows that nothing is superfluous. What is this plan? Can we discover it? It is the presentation of Jesus Christ in those aspects of his revelation which drew forth faith in him. This is not done by argument or by philosophy or even by theology; it is set forth as the manifestation of a Life. Thus we have a definite, though comprehensive picture of Christ himself as a personal, practical Gospel for man. While the materials used are all historical, such a selection of facts is made as to adapt them strictly to show the way in which Jesus revealed himself to men and also the way in which he was received by them.

Yet side by side with this manifestation of Christ to faith, there is the obvious and sorrowful fact that not all did receive him, and so the Gospel reveals a growing unbelief, which culminates in Christ's rejection and crucifixion. This unbelief is shown to be due to the deep-seated sinfulness of man and his consequent alienation from God.

These two aspects of Faith and Unbelief are strikingly shown by the recurrence of one phrase, "His own," in two places (1:11; 13:1). We are told first of those who were "His own" people who did not, because they would not receive him (1:11). Then we are shown the other class, "His own" who did receive him (13:1).

Thus three elements may be said to run through the Gospel: Revelation, Reception, Rejection. They are found in the prologue, and in one way or another they are the substance of every chapter from first to last.

III. THE PLAN OUTLINED

With the purpose of the Gospel (20:31) clearly in mind and the plan realized, it is now necessary to consider the way in which the plan is developed and the purpose at every point shown. The chief main division has already been given, consisting of two parts: First, 1 to 12, "His own"; second, 13 to 21, "His own." Then we find that the Gospel is further divided into seven great sections.

1. *The Prologue* (1:1–18).
   (1) The Revelation (1:1–4).
   (2) The Rejection (1:5–11).
   (3) The Reception (1:12–18).

2. *The Revelation of the Messiah* (1:19 to 6:71). The beginnings of faith and unbelief. At each stage a selection of scenes is given in which Jesus manifested himself, and in the discussions on which the true meaning and twofold consequence of his revelation were brought out, sometimes resulting in faith and at others in unbelief.
   (1) Faith begins in the disciples (1:19 to 2:12). This is due to the threefold testimony of John the Baptist, the first disciples, and the first miracle.
   (2) The first public manifestation (2:13 to 4:54). This includes Judæa, Samaria and Galilee, the three main sections of the land.
   (3) The crisis of the manifestation (5:1 to 6:71). This is seen first in Jerusalem (5) and then in Galilee (6).

Every part illustrates the growth of faith and unbelief, and the seven points of 20:31 are all illustrated and developed in this section.

N. B.—Some writers prefer to end this section with Chapter 4, but as Chapters 7 to 12 form a unity of place, time, and circumstances, it is better to regard the latter section as the beginning of the end, rather than the end of the beginning.

3. *The Great Conflict* (7 to 12). The development of unbelief into active hostility and the growth of faith in the true followers.
   (1) The commencement of the conflict (7, 8). This is seen in three stages: before, during, and after the feast.
   (2) The course of the conflict (9, 10). This includes the Sign and its consequence (9), the Shepherd and his claim, and the Son and his consciousness (10).
   (3) The culmination of the conflict (11, 12). This is shown in the great miracle (11) with the differing results (11:47 to 12:19), followed by the closing scenes (12:20–36).

Then comes a concluding comment on the public ministry (12:37–50), giving first the evangelist's and then the Master's judgment. There was no need of further testimony, for Christ's public work was over. So this epilogue is given, showing that Isaiah's explanation was true and that the manifestations of Christ were quite sufficient. The outcome was seen in the two sides of light and darkness.

4. *The Development of Faith* (13 to 17). We are now to give special attention to our Lord's manifestation to his disciples with reference to their faith.
   (1) The education of faith (13).
   (2) The instruction of faith (14 to 16).
   (3) The encouragement of faith (17).

5. *The Culmination of Unbelief* (18, 19). The Betrayal, Trial, and Crucifixion.

6. *The Culmination of Faith* (20). The Resurrection.

7. *The Epilogue* (21).
(Personal Conclusion, vs. 24, 25.)

The prologue and epilogue should be compared and contrasted, the former dealing with Christ before his Incarnation and the latter with him after his Resurrection; the former treating of his First Coming and the latter of his Second.

Thus on the foundation of the manifestation of Jesus Christ are built the two great facts and factors of faith and unbelief. In some respects the prologue contains the whole Gospel:

   (1) 1:1–4 correspond to 1:19 to 6:71.
   (2) 1:5–11 correspond to 7 to 12.
   (3) 1:12–18 correspond to 13 to 21.

As we review the Gospel, we can see how the record is gradually and significantly concentrated. In the first twelve chapters (the first part), dealing with the public ministry of Christ, his work is connected with all three provinces of Palestine and covers practically three years. In the last nine chapters (the second part), our Lord's ministry is confined to one city and covers only a few days. Then, too, we observe how the three outstanding lines of thought are shown by characteristic words and expressions from beginning to end (1) Christ's revelation is noticeable all through and is indicated by such words as "glory," "manifested," "sign," "works," "light," "word." An important part of this revelation is the relation of the Father to the Son and the Son to the Father. The phrase, "He that sent me," occurs over forty times, and our Lord often repeats the significant assertion, "I am," with its obvious claim and meaning. (2) Then we also observe the twofold result of this revelation, sometimes in unbelief and at other times in faith. There are three statements in which it is seen that the manifestation of Christ makes a very distinct separation between those who accept and those who reject him. The word "division" indicates this (7:43; 9:16; 10:19). On the one side is the solemn result of unbelief and rejection as indicated by such words and phrases as "world," "blind," and "ye will not come to Me." This process of unbelief is seen almost everywhere in the public ministry recorded in the first part. Then the element of reception is equally clear and is indicated by such words and phrases as "sheep," "his own," and by the attitude of faith that marks the true disciple. While unbelief is a wilful rejection of truth, faith is based on and is a response to what is declared as true. One of the most striking words in the Gospel is "witness," which occurs almost fifty times, and the direct response to this is seen in the word "believe" which, as we have seen, occurs nearly one hundred times. All through the Gospel the testimony of various witnesses is given, and the outcome is either belief or unbelief, according to whether the testimony is received or rejected. (3) The issues of this faith and unbelief are also clearly seen in the Gospel in "eternal life" on the one hand and "judgment" on the other. It is interesting and perhaps significant that the idea of death is practically non-existent, but, instead, we find emphasis on the solemn thought of judgment as an act or attitude that commences here and culminates in the life to come.

The more thoroughly the details are studied, the clearer it will be seen that every part in some way subserves the purpose and is part of the plan of the Gospel.

IV. A SPECIAL FEATURE

It has frequently been pointed out that there is one element in the plan which runs through every part of the Gospel. This is the personal factor, which is often clear, sometimes only hinted at, but is always real. It is as though the selection of material was due to the personal experience of the Apostle himself, and the Gospel, as it stands, is a progressive record based on his own life. It is, as some one has well said, the story of "how I came to believe and how you also may believe." If this be true, John's Gospel is intended to elicit experiment in others and thus lead in turn to further experience. This personal element is certainly seen in the minute details of Chapter 1 and the personal touches of such passages as 13:23–26; 18:25–27; 19:25–27, 31–37; 20:5, 8; 21:7, 22.

It has also been noted that only three times in the Gospel have we any direct hint or suggestion of the writer himself, but when the three passages are put together, they seem to indicate three stages of his progressive experience: 1:38, the desire of the young believer, "Where dwellest thou?" 13:25, the inquiry of the growing believer, "Lord, who is it?" 21:7, the insight of the mature believer, "It is the Lord." This seems to correspond with John's own division of Christians into children, young men, and fathers (1 John 2:12–14).

And so, when we review the Gospel and pay special attention to its purpose, plan, and progress, we see how every part helps to carry out the writer's intention of recording the Divine manifestations of Jesus Christ and the twofold result in some being hostile and others loyal to him. His claim to reveal the Father and his call to men, "Follow me," lead either to rejection, which culminated in the crucifixion, or to reception, which culminated in the adoring cry, "My Lord and My God" (20:28).

In proof of what has now been said, it is interesting to read that Dr. H. Clay Trumbull on one occasion, being met by an exceptionally intelligent student who had imbibed Agnostic views, advised him to study the Gospel according to John for the purpose of examining with all possible fairness the strongest presentation of Christian truth. The man read it through from beginning to end, taking it simply as a book without examination of outside evidence of its genuineness. When he read it through, he said: "The One of whom this book tells us is either the Saviour of the world or he ought to be," and it is interesting to know that, because of what the Gospel told the Agnostic of Jesus Christ, he was ready to heed the call of our Lord so frequently uttered throughout the Gospel. It is not surprising to know that this testimony has been endorsed by other leading Christian workers who are convinced that any man who is determined to know and do the truth cannot study this Gospel without becoming a Christian.

It is a familiar story, but one well worth repeating, how the venerable Bede had for his last labors the translation of this Gospel of John. We are told that he wrote while age crept upon him, and as he drew near the end of his work, his strength failed him. His disciples urged him on and cried, "Master, Master, there is but one chapter more." He wrote on until his strength was gone, and his disciples said, "There is but one verse more." Summoning his failing strength, he translated the remaining verse and said, "It is finished." They answered, "It is finished," and then as he lay where he could fix his eyes on the place where he used to pray he passed away to be with that Saviour whom he loved, served, and glorified.

It is no wonder that in all ages this has been regarded as the most remarkable of our four Gospels. Testimony after testimony to this could be quoted from leading minds through the centuries. Luther's words are often quoted: "This is the unique, tender, genuine, chief Gospel.... Should a tyrant succeed in destroying the Holy Scriptures and only a single copy of the Epistle to the Romans and the Gospel according to John escape him, Christianity would be saved." And coming down to our own time, the late Bishop Ellicott well said: "If the heart studies the Christ as protrayed in this writing it will need no other proof of his Divinity."

II

THE DIVINE REVELATION

We have taken a general view of the Gospel as a whole, and in proceeding to look at it in detail, it is important to keep in mind the Purpose (20:31). Then we should recall how the Purpose is fulfilled by the Plan already given. The great division of the Gospel into its two parts (1–12; 13–21) is the best general division, and this will follow the sevenfold outline before mentioned. Our present study will be concerned with a portion of the first main division, or sections one and two of the sevenfold outline.

I. The Prologue (1:1–18)

The Person whom the Gospel is to unfold is first declared and it is interesting to notice that theory is given first and then the record follows to prove it.

1. *The Word revealed* (1:1–4). The Apostle first describes the Word in his being (vs. 1, 2), and then in his working (vs. 3, 4). The term used by John, *Logos*, was doubtless familiar during the Apostle's life, and as Paul did not hesitate to use the philosophical and religious language of his day without adopting current ideas, so the Apostle John does the same, though giving the terminology a specific Christian meaning. "John is not so much concerned with the abstract philosophical conceptions, though he does outline a real philosophy of religion in these verses as he deals with the revelation of the nature of God in Christ the Logos and Son." The three statements concerning Christ in verse 1 are most embracing: (1) His eternal subsistence; (2) his eternal relation to God; (3) his eternal oneness with God. Nothing could well be plainer or more impressive than this foundation. This Divine. Word is also the Creator, all things having been called into existence by his almighty power. And not only so, but since he was life, the life was the light of men.

2. *The Word rejected* (vs. 5–11). Very soon the gloom of conflict is seen, but at the outset comes the assurance that the darkness cannot overtake and overcome the light. Then after this wondrous Being is conceived in terms of Divine personality, creative agency, spiritual life, and moral light, suddenly a Divinely-appointed man is seen to appear (v. 6), selected for the purpose of bearing witness to the Divine light, in order that man through faith might receive the life and enjoy its light. But notwithstanding the Divine profession of both Christ and his Forerunner, men did not know the Lord, and when he came did not, because they would not, receive him. Thus at the very outset attention is called to the solemn fact of refusal and rejection which we know runs through this Gospel to the very end.

3. *The Word received* (vs. 12–18). There were some, however, who did not refuse, for when he declared himself they received him and thereby obtained "authority" to become what they had not been before, "children of God," whose spiritual life was due to nothing human, but solely to the Divine will. Then the Word of verse 1 is identified with the human Christ (v. 14), and it is interesting to notice the parallels between the three statements of the former and the three of the latter verses: (1) (v. 1). In the beginning was the Word: (v. 14) and the Word became flesh. (2) And the Word was with God: and dwelt among us. (3) And the Word was God: full of grace and truth. Already some of the characteristic words of the Gospel have been used, such as "life," "light," "darkness," "witness," "believe," "world," "faith." In verse 17 we have for the only time in the record of the history the "great historical Name," Jesus Christ, and it has been suggested that grace is associated with him who is "Jesus," and truth with him who is "Christ." We must also consider the four chief titles of our Lord here found: The Word; the Light; the Life; the Son. The meaning of each is important, and their order of usage is significant and suggestive.

II. The Revelation of the Son of God (1:19 to 6:71)

It is essential to note with all possible care and at every stage the selection of scenes in which Jesus Christ manifested himself and the discussions during which the true meaning and solemn issues of his revelation were brought out.

1. *Faith begins in the disciples* (1:19 to 2:12). John had spoken of the Baptist as the "witness," and now he proceeds to say what the witness is.

(1) The testimony of the first preacher (1:19–37). When the committee from Jerusalem visited the Baptist they learned with clearness the true meaning and relationship of him with the One whose way he prepared. It is fitting that his testimony should commence the work, because his knowledge fits him for the special service. He first speaks of himself as not the Messiah, but only the one sent to prepare his way, and say that One infinitely greater than himself is among them. The deputation must have been puzzled at these remarkable statements; and then on the next day the Baptist identifies Jesus Christ as the Messiah by declaring him to be "the Lamb of God that taketh away the sin of the world." Thus early is the thought of sacrifice for sin brought forward. But Christ is more than this, for he is the One who baptizes with the Holy Spirit. These two offices, indicating Redemption and Holiness, are inseparable, and they are based upon the fact that Christ is none other than "the Son of God" (v. 34).

(2) The testimony of the first disciples (1:38–51). This section is of particular interest on two main grounds. First, it shows the remarkable variety in our Lord's disciples, for the six men here mentioned or implied are seen in the sequel to be men of remarkably different temperaments and capacities. Then, too, the section is particularly interesting because of the varied methods by means of which these men came to Christ. Two of them came as the outcome of the Baptist's testimony. The next two came as the result of the personal influence of their brothers. The next came as the outcome of Christ's direct appeal. And the last came through the personal invitation of his friend who urged the necessity of experience as the one way of getting rid of prejudice.

(3) The testimony of the first miracle (2:1–11). In the Prologue the Apostle depicts the eternal Son of God becoming man in order to reveal the Father. Then follows the witness of the Baptist to the majesty, grace and holiness of the Son of

God. Next comes, as we have just seen, the entrance into fellowship with Christ of the first band of believers, based on the conviction that he is their Messiah. Now follows the first manifestation of power on the part of Christ, showing that he is prepared to act like God and thereby reveal his Deity. The Apostle's designation of what we call miracles is "sign," indicating that what our Lord did was not merely a marvel but symbolical of something higher. This first miracle or "sign" was thus a manifestation of Christ's glory. He asked both from his mother and from the servants trust and obedience, and as a result he put forth power on behalf of the assembled company. The outcome was that his disciples believed. They were deeply impressed by what they had seen, by his evident supremacy over nature as he had already shown it over man. Authority, eliciting trust and obedience, will always result in joy, and the outcome will be the manifestation of glory.

2. *The first public manifestation* (2:13 to 4:54). The season of private and personal preparation is over, and it is necessary for Christ to present himself to the Jewish nation. We may think of Israel at this time as socially barren, ecclesiastically formal, and morally weak, and it was, therefore, as necessary as it was important for Christ to offer himself to his people.

(1) In Judea (2:13 to 4:3). In Jerusalem our Lord claimed authority (2:13–22). He had already exercised it over human nature and over physical nature, and now he is brought face to face with the religious life of the people, and again asserts the right and power to deal with the most sacred realities of the national life. This, naturally, raises difficulties and even opposition, and again we see the two streams, or Rejection and Reception, which invariably marked his approach to the people. But even of those who believed, it could only be said that they were shallow even if sincere, and for this reason Christ did not entrust himself unto them (2:23–25). Thus the chapter shows the threefold authority of Christ over nature, religion, and the human intellect. But there was one man of those who were impressed by the miracle who, though like them, shallow and sincere, was evidently capable of receiving deeper things. And so we are told first of the "earthly thing," regeneration (3:1–10), and then of redemption, "the heavenly thing" (3:12–21). In the country of Judea John the Baptist's second and closing testimony to Christ was given. He repeated and completed his witness, speaking of himself as the friend of the Bridegroom, and rejoicing to know that while he himself would continually be decreasing, the Bridegroom, coming from above, would be constantly increasing because of what God was to him in the fulness of life and power (3:22–36).

(2) In Samaria (4:4–42). After the south in Jerusalem and Judea, the next public revelation of Christ was given in the center of the land, Samaria. It may only have been a geographical necessity for him to go through Samaria (4:4), but it is more probable that a moral and spiritual obligation is to be understood. The episode of the woman is another remarkable contrast with that of Nicodemus, showing the truth of the words: "There is no difference, for all have sinned" (Rom. 3:22); "there is no difference, for the same Lord is rich unto all who call upon him" (Rom. 10:12). Our Lord's interview and conversation with the woman show how carefully he planned his approach to her, first winning her heart with his request for water, then impressing her mind with his teaching concerning himself as the living water, then probing her conscience by a reference to her past life, and at last revealing himself to her soul by the clear, full declaration of his Messiahship, which he would not tell the Jews.

(3) In Galilee (4:43–54). Then followed the interesting episode of the nobleman's faith which appropriately follows the faith of the Samaritan in Christ (4:42). "It is this fact of Christ in the realm of faith which is the golden thread upon which the incidents described in the Gospel are strung. It is illustrated in every chapter and it brings them all into a wonderful unity." The nobleman's trust is seen to develop along three clear stages. At first he only believes because of miracles. Then he rises higher and believes on the bare word of Christ. Then, highest of all, he and his house believe as he has the consciousness that his son was alive. Thus Christ at once elicited and trained his faith.

3. *The crisis of manifestation* (5:1 to 6:71). At this point the healing of the impotent man raised the entire question between Christ and the Jews, and it is particularly interesting to note with a thoughtful author, Dr. H. W. Clark, in his "The Christ from Without and Within," that at this point the Gospel enters upon an entirely new method. Up till now Christ has been considered from the spectators' standpoint, as though contemplating him from outside and coming to the conclusion that he must be divine. But at this stage the line of treatment changes, and from the beginning of Chapter 5 to the end of Chapter 10 John dwells "not in the consciousness of the spectators of Christ, but within the consciousness of Christ himself. He has been speaking about Christ before: now Christ speaks for himself." This is a very important point in the development of the thought of the Gospel, for instead of calling attention to what men saw and heard, these chapters reveal the inner mind and feeling of Christ, and instead of the impression of greatness made by his work, we are called upon to consider the greatness of his Person as revealed in his consciousness (Clark, p. 118). The miracle served to bring to a head the opposition, and it is noteworthy that the controversy about the Sabbath was only the occasion of the infinitely greater controversy due to the claim of Christ implied in this alleged breach of the Sabbath (5:18). The entire relation of the Father to Christ was thus raised, and in his controversy with the Jews our Lord claimed perfect oneness with the Father, perfect love between him and the Father, and perfect submission of his will to God. There was not only the claim to this personal relation to the Father (5:19–23), but arising out of it came the claim to a personal relation to man (5:23–29), and last of all a claim connected with his own personal character (5:30–47). The whole chapter is concerned with the great subject of life. The thought of "witness" also becomes particularly clear and definite in this section (5:31–40). We find included the witness of John, of the miraculous works, of the Father, and of the Scriptures, all being united in their

definite and unmistakable testimony to Christ as the Son of God.

This opposition in Jerusalem (Chap. 5) is soon followed by similar experience in Galilee (Chap. 6), where again a miracle becomes the occasion of discourses which accentuate the great hostility. The leaders of the nation at the capital had evidently been endeavoring to influence the people of the north in Galilee, and the feeding of the five thousand, the only miracle recorded in all four Gospels, is thereby seen to be a turning-point in the ministry. Once again the thought is of life, but there is a progress and development of the idea for, as in Chapter 5 Christ is the source of life, so here he is the sustenance. The discourse, or more correctly discourses, at Capernaum (6:25–71) are best understood in connection with the dialogues with the Jews, and when the subject is considered in this way the gradual growth of the opposition is seen. (1) The first stage was that of *discussion* (6:25–40), which ended with the claim by Christ to be the Heavenly bread. (2) This led at once to *dissatisfaction* (6:41–51), for the Jews murmured at this claim in view of what they believed they knew of his earthly origin and circumstances. But Christ in reply did not mitigate but intensified his claim by saying that the bread was his flesh. (3) The outcome of this was *dissension* (6:52–59), for the Jews now strove with one another, being horrified at the very thought of "flesh to eat." Again Christ maintained and more than maintained his position by elaborating the thoughts, and telling them once again of himself, his life and work, and the assurance of the eternal consequences to those who were united to him. (4) This was too much for many of his nominal disciples and the outcome was *defection* (6:60–66), for they could not possibly continue with One who had been saying such difficult, mysterious and impossible things. (5) It was then that our Lord turned to the twelve and sought the proof of their *devotion* (6:67–71), and was assured by Peter, speaking for them all, that notwithstanding everything, they were convinced that he had the words of eternal life, as the Holy One of God.

In the light of this developing conversation it is not difficult to understand the true meaning of the chapter. It is sometimes wondered why there is no institution of the Lord's Supper in this Gospel, and the true answer is pretty certainly that the purpose of the Evangelist "was to interpret a Person rather than to record that Person's deeds" (Holdsworth, "The Life Indeed," p. 80). As Westcott and other great commentators have pointed out, this chapter does not refer to the Lord's Supper, but to the Cross, or rather perhaps, as the Bishop of Durham in his booklet has so well said, both this chapter and the Lord's Supper refer in different ways to the Atoning Sacrifice of Christ.

At this point we must stop for a while, and it is essential to master the details of the various incidents, watching at each point the growth of faith and unbelief. From the very beginning, section by section, different men and women are taken as types of faith, while side by side there is the ever-deepening dissatisfaction and hostility of "the Jews." The seven points stated in the purpose (20:31) are also all illustrated and developed in the sections now before us.

III

THE GREAT CONFLICT (Chaps. 7–12)

As we proceed we cannot help noticing the remarkable development in our Lord's relations with those around him. We have already considered something of his revelation of himself and the commencement of faith and unbelief which was the twofold result. Now we shall observe the development of the opposition which deepened into conflict and culminated in his seizure and death.

I. THE COMMENCEMENT OF THE CONFLICT (Chaps. 7, 8)

These two chapters are concerned with events associated with the Feast of Tabernacles. It is significant and appropriate that Christ's conflict with the Jews should be at the capital, Jerusalem, and at one of the Feasts when so many people were present. A careful study of the section reveals the following main points.

1. *Before the Feast* (7:1–13). We observe here the relation of our Lord to his brethren. They wanted him to give public proofs of his claims, but that was not his way, and he reserves to himself perfect liberty.

2. *During the Feast* (7:14–39). Here we see the relation of our Lord to the Jews, and almost every verse reveals different attitudes of the people and their leaders to him (7:7, 15, 20, 25, 30, 32, 35, 40, 41). Meanwhile, he claimed to be the Water of Life (7:37–39), as he had already claimed to be the Bread of Life (6:48).

3. *After the Feast* (7:40 to 8:59). It is profoundly interesting to notice the effect of the company of officers who were sent by the leaders to apprehend Christ. They came under the wonderful spell of his truly fascinating personality and teaching, and returned without him (7:32, 45, 46). We also see the apparently nervous fear of Nicodemus, who desired to be faithful and yet had not sufficient courage to carry the matter through to the end (7:50–52). At this time there was a new claim made by Christ, to be the Light of the world (8:12). It is more than probable that the symbol was suggested by the lamps which formed a special feature of the Feast of Tabernacles. As the Light of man's life we can see how he convicted of sin (8:1–11), guided human existence (8:12), and reproved unreality (8:13–59).

II. THE COURSE OF THE CONFLICT (Chaps. 9, 10)

It is probable that this section is to be associated with the Feast of Dedication (10:22) which fell in the month of December, about two or three months after the Feast of Tabernacles. But in any case there is a close connection and a real unity throughout.

1. *The Sign and its consequences* (Chap. 9). This is an illustration of our Lord as the Light of the world (8:12 and 9:5). He was a light for the blind eyes of the body, and also for

spiritual blindness (9:35–39). To the man and to Christ himself the consequences of this action were profound and far-reaching.

2. *The Shepherd and his claim* (10:1–21). There is a close connection between this and the preceding chapter, and in 10:21 there is a distinct reference to the healing of the blind man. The allegory is really a continuation of the discourse which our Lord began (in 9:39–41). It was necessary to rebuke the Pharisees for their treatment of the man, and at the same time to encourage the man in his new-born faith. The Pharisees claimed by their excommunication of the man to hold the keys of the kingdom, but in that action they had clearly forfeited the right to be regarded as true spiritual leaders because their sentence on the man did not express the judgment of God. And then in this section our Lord contrasts them as false guides with himself as the true Guide. Here we see the last symbol used by Christ to describe himself, and there are three figures, or perhaps three scenes, showing him as the Leader (vs. 1–6), the Door (vs. 7–10), and the Shepherd (vs. 11–18). The thought of the Shepherd runs through the whole, and is expressive at once of his superior power and his considerate love.

3. *The Son and his consciousness* (10:22–42). Matters were rapidly approaching a climax, and it is interesting to observe the way in which our Lord's words, action and attitude led to division concerning him (10:19). They demand a proof that he was indeed the Messiah, and when he replied, telling them plainly that they were not of his sheep, they proceeded to stone him. To this Christ made the rejoinder, asking which of the good works was the one for which they were stoning him, and with another claim to be uniquely related to God he went away, escaping out of their hands.

III. THE CULMINATION OF THE CONFLICT (Chaps. 11, 12)

At this point it must be again noticed that a break is made in the narrative and the writer resumes the method of writing which marked the first four chapters. As we have already seen, from Chapter 5 to Chapter 10 inclusive the record is given from the standpoint of Christ himself, while before the fifth chapter and after the tenth the story is told in the third person; about Christ, instead of Christ speaking for himself. "Now John begins to speak about Christ once more," and we shall see "what a human estimate would term the sad ending of his life" (H. W. Clark, "The Christ From Without and Within," pp. 183, 184). Once more we see clear marks of unity in this section, and also the signs of the development of hostility culminating in the determination to put Christ to death.

1. *The great miracle* (11:1–46). Here we have the last of the "signs" recorded in connection with our Lord's public ministry, and, as with the first one (2:11), so with this, it was worked for the glory of God (11:4, 40). As it has been helpfully pointed out, the miracle shows Christ as the Master of death, even though he was himself about to die.

2. *The differing results* (11:47 to 12:19). The restoration of Lazarus was the immediate occasion for the decisive judgment of the Jewish leaders against Christ (11:53), and it is noteworthy that in this section we have in turn (1) the attitude of the leaders, (2) the attitude of the disciples, and (3) the attitude of the people.

3. *The closing scene* (12:20–36). With the visit of the Greeks, followed by the last expression of hostility on the part of the people, our Lord's public ministry closed, and as his time had not yet come, he left them with a warning (12:36).

Then the record of the public ministry is closed with a twofold epilogue. Nothing more was needed, for our Lord was already firmly fixed in the hearts of his disciples (12:1–9); was a subject of great interest on the part of popular opinion (12:12–19), and was also the object of attention from a far wider circle represented by the Greeks (12:20–28). This epilogue is deserving of very close attention as a summary of the whole of the public ministry.

(1) The Judgment of the Evangelist (12:37–43). In solemn words it is pointed out that Isaiah's explanation was true, that the manifestations had been sufficient, and that the people would not accept Christ because they were afraid of the leaders, because they thought more of human commendation than Divine praise.

(2) The Judgment of the Master (12:44–50). In these words we have Christ's own conclusion with reference to his ministry among the Jews. There were two sides, light and darkness, and if only he had been accepted as the light there would have been salvation not judgment. As it was, darkness necessitated the solemn result of judgment on sin. This contrast between light and darkness is particularly interesting as seen in the continuance of the teaching in First John.

Again we must observe how all through this section the purpose of 20:31 is developed in detail. Although chief attention is naturally given to unbelief and opposition, the work of faith was going on and disciples were being impressed and influenced towards that culmination of faith which we shall see later on (10:42).

IV. SUMMARY OF THE PUBLIC MINISTRY

We must pause here to review the entire section from 1:19 to 12:50 with special reference to some of the outstanding features.

1. *The phases of the glory of Christ.* (1) Consider his various titles as seen from the very beginning and in almost every chapter, but especially in chapter 1. (2) Consider his five presentations of himself to the Jews as seen in this section: 2:12 to 4:54; 5:1 to 6:71; 7:1 to 10:21; 10:22 to 12:11; 12:12–50. (3) Consider his consciousness and claims, especially as seen in chapters 5 to 12. The Divine title "I am" will naturally be observed in various forms, but particularly in 8:58. Three great revelations of himself call for special notice (5:17, 18; 8:58; 10:30).

2. *The phases of the life of faith.* (1) Consider Christ's presentation of himself as the object of faith. In almost every chapter he is seen in relation to human life and needs. From the very beginning in Chapter 1 he offers himself for trust, and in every place he is seen in one form or another as the Saviour,

Lord, and Friend of man. From his earliest manifestations to the disciples (chap. 1) and his public appearance in Jerusalem (chaps. 2, 3), Samaria (chap. 4) and Galilee (chap. 4), he is seen as the Source of life (chap. 5), the Sustenance of life (chap. 6), the Satisfaction of life (chap. 7), the Guide of life (chap. 8), the Lord of life (chaps. 9 to 11). It has also been suggested that in chapters 1 to 6 he is revealed as Life; in chapters 7 to 9 as Light, and in chapters 9 to 11 as Love. (2) Consider the attitude of faith in those who responded, and how it was elicited. In every chapter there are illustrations of this wonderful truth. Whether it was on the part of disciples or Nicodemus or the woman or the nobleman or those of the Jews who were ready to accept him, trust is the one element in which life finds its perfect realization. To quote again some words of a recent writer: "It is this effect of Christ in the realm of faith which is the golden thread upon which the incidents described in the Gospel are strung. It is illustrated in every chapter, and it brings them all into a wonderful unity" (Holdsworth, "The Life Indeed," p. 57).

It is also interesting to notice that our Lord is recognized in this Gospel first by pious Israelites (chap. 1), then by Samaritans, a mixed people (4:39), and then by Gentiles from afar (12:20), the three together representing the whole world. And thus while in Nicodemus, the woman of Samaria and the Roman nobleman we may think of the way in which God's grace to the world is illustrated, we also see in them the proof of the world's response of true homage to the Lord Jesus Christ.

3. *The phases of the working of unbelief.* (1) Consider the character of the hostility. As we notice this ever-deepening from point to point we see something of its persistence and bitterness. If it were not so true to human nature we should be inclined to wonder whether man could maintain and increase such an attitude of enmity to a Being like Christ. (2) Consider the grounds of the rejection of Christ. Why were they so hostile? The answer is that they fully recognized the claim that he made, and as they were not prepared to acknowledge it, there was nothing else to be done but to refuse it and reject him. This shows that the hostility went far deeper than any mere act of doing beneficent works on the Sabbath day. It was due to the stupendous claim involved in these "signs," the claim to be nothing less than Divine.

And so we notice the record of division in the record of Christ (7:43; 10:19). Thus it is always, for men cannot be neutral; they have to take sides either for him or against him.

IV

THE REVELATION OF THE MASTER
(Chaps. 13–17)

A new section, the second part of the Gospel, commences here, and we notice the transition from the public manifestations of the Messiah to the spiritual revelations of the Master to the disciples in preparation for their great future. As we proceed, it is important to keep the earlier sections well in mind, including the purpose and plan of the Gospel with the three great truths which underlie the whole: Revelation, Rejection, and Reception. We shall now see how the Lord manifested the glory of his love to those who loved him.

I. THE EDUCATION OF FAITH (Chap. 13)

To educate is to elicit, to draw out, and our Lord thus "educated" or elicited the faith of his disciples by showing them his love in deed and word. Up to this moment he had been concerned "with his own" (1:11) who did not receive him, but now he was to give himself wholly "to his own" (13:1) who did receive him. The hour had come for him to return to the Father; a return to be accomplished through the treachery of one of the disciples and the opposition of the world. He thereupon, conscious of his own Divine mission and dignity, manifests his love for his disciples, and the chapter is easily divided into sections which show the ways in which Christ drew out the faith of his followers.

1. *Humility* (vs. 1–20). We are impressed at the outset with the wonderful consciousness of Christ, a consciousness including his human and Divine nature, and of the relationships, Divine and human, which were involved in his redemptive work. Notwithstanding, or rather because of this supreme dignity as man's Redeemer and God's representative, he condescends in lowliness to do menial service. As the Redeemer of man he knew that his hour had come for departing from the world. In relation to evil, he loves his own to the uttermost, knowing that they would be entirely alone after his departure. In regard to God the Father, he knew that all things had been given into his hands, and that as he had come forth from God so he was now returning to his Father. Thus in this full consciousness of his greatness he expresses his humility and then inculcates it on his disciples.

2. *Faithfulness* (vs. 21–30). But even at this moment there was the consciousness of trouble, for the treachery of one of the circle was announced. It would seem as though this constituted the last pleading of love, and after the expression of our Lord's deep grief, the traitor, undisclosed except to John, departed, leaving the Master alone with those who truly loved him.

3. *Freedom* (vs. 31–38). With the alien element gone there came a change in the spirit and teaching of Christ. He realized that the time had come for him to be glorified, and as he said the words he inculcated a new commandment that they were to "love one another." The newness seems to have lain in the object of the affection, for there had been every kind of love before this time, with the one exception of love to our fellow-Christians simply because they and we belong to Christ. Herein lay the newness.

Reviewing this chapter, it has been helpfully pointed out that our Lord in educating or eliciting the faith of his disciples gives three proofs of his permanent love for them (v. 1). The first was connected with the future of his disciples, for he washed their feet, indicative of the service he would still do for them when he should be on high in order to keep them clean. The second proof was his prediction of the treachery of Judas, so that when the events should reveal themselves their faith would be strengthened instead of weakened. The third was the gift of the new Commandment which, when properly observed, would enable the fellowship between the disciples to continue unbroken. Thus "the disciple whom Jesus loved" presents to us these proofs of the love of the Master (Stuart, "Tracings from the Gospel of John," p. 294).

II. THE EDIFICATION OF FAITH (Chaps. 14–16)

To "edify" is to build, and edification here means the building up of that faith which had already been elicited. In this process it is particularly striking to notice that not once does our Lord refer to his death.

1. *Consolation* (chap. 14). It is evident that the disciples were deeply concerned with what lay immediately before them, and so the Master struck the keynote, urging them not to fear. As this exhortation is repeated (v. 27), it seems clear that some reasons must have been given why they should not be troubled and afraid, and it has been most helpfully suggested that the chapter is really occupied with seven reasons for this consolation. (1) Verses 1–3, the future home. (2) Verses 4–11, the perfect way. (3) Verses 12–14, the guaranteed life. (4) Verses 15–17, the coming Helper. (5) Verses 18–24, the personal Lord. (6) Verses 25, 26, the Divine Teacher. (7) Verse 27, the abiding peace. Then in conclusion the Lord tells them of the true conception of his departure as a reason for joy rather than sorrow, and gives the assurance that it was intended to emphasize his union with the Father (vs. 28–31).

2. *Communion* (chap. 15). This discourse seems to have been delivered on the way from the upper room to Gethsemane (14:31), and our Lord reveals a threefold relationship in regard to the disciples. (1) Their relation to himself in a life of union and communion (vs. 1–11). (2) Their relation to one another in a life of love and service (vs. 12–17). (3) Their relation to the world in a life of enmity and persecution (vs. 18–27).

3. *Anticipation* (chap. 16). These discourses appropriately close by a reference to the ultimate triumphant life of the disciples through the Holy Spirit. (1) The Holy Spirit and the world, emphasizing need (vs. 1–11). (2) The Holy Spirit and the disciples, indicating power (vs. 12–15). (3) The Master's own presence, promising victory (vs. 16–33).

A thoughtful writer has endeavored to distinguish between these three chapters by suggesting that in chapter 14 we have personal religion with special reference to the relation of believers to Christ; in chapter 15, social religion with special reference to the relation of believers to one another; and in chapter 16, universal religion with special reference to the relation of the believer to the world.

III. THE ESTABLISHMENT OF FAITH (Chap. 17)

In this prayer we have the faith as educated (chap. 13) and edified (chaps. 14–16), confirmed and established. This chapter is the record of the true "Lord's prayer," which enabled the disciples to obtain a fuller revelation of their Master than they had ever had before.

1. *Christ and the Father* (vs. 1–5). The keynote is "glorify," and is a prayer for his own glorification because he had finished the work given him to do.

2. *Christ and the Apostles* (vs. 6–19). Now he prays for his disciples, and the main thought is suggested by the word "keep." They belong to Christ and the Father, and as they were in a hostile world, alone and without their Master, it would be necessary for them to be kept from evil and consecrated to true service.

3. *Christ and the Church* (vs. 20–26). Then the prayer widens out for those who would believe through the word of the disciples, and the main idea seems to be indicated by the word "be." They were to be one as the Father and the Son were one, that the world might believe. And then the prayer closes with a request that all those whom God had given Christ might be with him in his glory.

In this prayer we can see how wonderfully the Lord restates in the form of petition the various thoughts of chapters 14–16, and as such it is no mere addition, but the culmination and ground of the entire section.

Thus, we may think of chapters 1–12 as the revelation of the Messiah, and chapters 13–17 as the revelation of the Master.

Another way of looking at these chapters has been suggested as follows: chapter 14, Consolation (Faith); chapter 15, Instruction (Love); chapter 16, Prediction (Hope); chapter 17, Intercession (Glory). No wonder these chapters have been called "the holiest of all."

V

THE TWOFOLD ISSUE (Chaps. 18–21)

From the private and personal talks with the disciples we turn to the closing chapters, in which the two movements of faith and unbelief find their crown and completion. Chapters 18–20 seem at first to be merely historical, as though the inner thought had been set aside for simple narrative. But this is only apparent, for, although the characteristic words Life, Light, and Glory are not found, and even other words which were formerly emphatic lose a good deal of their characteristic significance, yet the glory of our Lord shines at every point, and in dying and rising from the dead, life, light, and love are abundantly evident. The one thought that runs through the whole section is the twofold issue of unbelief and faith. In chapters 18 and 19 the emphasis is placed on unbelief with only a slight reference to belief, while in chapter 20 belief is seen at its full height. All through the section the Father is glorifying the Son (12:31–33; 17:1). Thus the record is not merely historical and external, but expressive of the manifestations of our Lord's love in word and deed. From beginning to end he is the Divine Redeemer, and what is now recorded is seen to be absolutely consistent with all that precedes. The supreme test is triumphantly endured, and the record has a perfect unity in the uniqueness of his sufferings followed by the uniqueness of his victory.

I. THE CULMINATION OF UNBELIEF (Chaps. 18, 19)

1. *The Betrayal* (18:1–11). In this story we are impressed with our Lord's calm dignity, and the two lines of man's sin and God's plan are kept in view throughout.

2. *The Trial* (18:12 to 19:16).

(1) Ecclesiastical (18:12–27). This Jewish trial is twofold, and again the majesty of the Sufferer is seen. With this are included the denials of Peter, revealing his unfaithfulness as against the faithfulness of John. Then, too, we cannot help observing unscrupulous unbelief set on murder contrasted with the calmness of Christ in reply and his love in protecting his disciples.

(2) Civil (18:28 to 19:16). This trial before the Roman Governor is in many respects the most noteworthy feature of this section, especially in its revelation of Pilate's character. The narrative is far fuller than those of the Synoptic Gospels. Four charges were laid against Christ: That he was a malefactor (v. 30); that he made himself a king (vs. 33–37); that he claimed to be the son of God (19:7); that he had spoken against Caesar (19:12). It has been pointed out that the scene before Pilate is subdivided into a series of seven acts or sections. The events occur alternately from the outside to the inside of the Pretorium. Outside (18:28–32); inside (vs. 33–38); outside (vs. 38–40); inside (19:1–4); outside (vs. 5–7); inside (vs. 8–11); outside (vs. 12–16) (Whitelaw, "The Gospel of St. John," p. 383). A close study of the material as here given reveals in a most remarkable way the character of Pilate, and the narrative is made all the more impressive by the sevenfold "therefore" in 19:1–21. The contrasts seen here are between the unbelief of the Jews, the vacillation of the Governor, and the glory of our Lord in his words and silence, his calmness and patience.

3. *The Crucifixion* (19:17–42). Much at this point is omitted by John, and yet he gives his own incidents. We see the culmination of everything in the sacrificial death of Christ. And in addition to the actual crucifixion (vs. 17–22) we have the two groups, consisting of four enemies and four friends (vs. 23–27); the two words (vs. 28–30); and the two requests (vs. 31–42). The love of Christ continues to the end (13:1) and the love of his followers grows stronger in the darkest hour as believers come forth to pay the last offices of respect and affection.

II. THE CULMINATION OF FAITH (Chap. 20)

Now in marked contrast we see the climax of belief as the former chapters revealed the climax of unbelief. It is a revelation of the glory of Christ in his new and victorious life, and a selection of facts is made to prove this.

1. *The revelation of the fact of resurrection* (vs. 1–10). Peter and John saw the empty tomb and the grave cloths, and John was the first to arrive at belief in what had taken place.

He saw the cloths "rolled round" in the exact shape of the body as it had lain in the tomb, and the position of these cloths led John to believe that his Master had been raised from the dead.

2. *The revelation of the Person raised* (vs. 11–25). (1) The revelation to an individual (vs. 11–18). This was a manifestation to love, and Mary's sorrow was turned into adoring faith. (2) The revelation to the community (vs. 19–23). This was a manifestation to fear, for the Ten were enabled to obtain peace and joy through the appearance of their Master.

3. *The revelation of Person and fact* (vs. 24–29). This was a manifestation to doubt, and shows how the last among the Eleven came to believe and utter the supreme declaration, "my Lord and my God." Thus, while Thomas went down the lowest, he rose to the highest and "my Lord and my God" is the crown and culmination of the Gospel to which the Author has intended to lead up from the very commencement. The disciples through their experience of their Master came at last to believe not only that he was the Word made flesh (1:14), but that he was the Word in the beginning, with God and God (1:1). Thus the Gospel may be said at the end to return to its beginning, and everything that is between is said to be understood in the light of the opening and the close.

The final statement of the purpose of the Gospel is here given to which reference has already been made in detail (20:30, 31), and in these verses we find all the characteristic and significant words, phrases, and ideas of the entire Gospel.

III. THE EPILOGUE (Chap. 21)

This is usually thought to be an appendix, but it is an appropriate close to the Gospel. As the Prologue dealt with the pre-Incarnate Christ (1:1–18); as the Gospel itself is the record of the Incarnate Christ (1:19 to 20:29); so we may think of this Epilogue as giving us the picture of the post-Incarnate Christ, and in this, the interpretation of his Personality as realized throughout the entire Christian dispensation. This record very appropriately shows how the scattered disciples were gathered again, and how their Lord was related to them and they to their Lord. Thus, while the material is entirely historical, there is no doubt that the chapter is full of deep spiritual meaning.

1. *The Lord and the Church* (vs. 1–14). The thought is that of *Work*. At first the disciples, seven in number, representing the whole Church, go forth to work of their own will and pleasure, but when they fail they learn to obey their Master and thereby obtain their reward. Work for God must always be marked by faithfulness to our Lord's directions or else failure is inevitable. When we thus carry out his directions we shall find him by and by on the eternal shore preparing us a welcome (vs. 12–14).

2. *The Lord and the Christian* (vs. 15–19). The thought is that of *Witnessing*. The disciple is reinstated and his new work is allotted to him.

3. *The Lord and the Future* (vs. 20–23). The thought is that of *Waiting*. The statement about John was misunderstood and was therefore corrected; while the thoughts of the followers

of Christ were directed to that "blessed hope," his glorious appearing.

The Gospel closes with the personal attestation, identifying the writer of it (vs. 24, 25). And so the end matches the beginning, and the same ideas are found here as in the Prologue. Just as that spoke of his pre-Incarnate work, so this tells of his post-resurrection work. Just as that recorded his rejection, so this tells of his reception. Just as that narrated his First Coming, so this anticipates his Second Coming.

VI

SPECIAL TOPICS

After mastering the contents of the Gospel as a whole, it is necessary and important to proceed to the definite study of details. This method is of great value and is capable of almost indefinite explanation because of the fulness of matter in the Gospel. The following points are only intended to be suggestive of further study, and at the same time illustrative of similar possible themes.

I. THE DOCTRINE OF THE GODHEAD

1. His existence (1:1). 2. His spirituality (1:18; 4:24; 5:37; 6:46). 3. His manifestation (1:18). 4. His nature (3:16). 5. His life (1:14; 6:57). These are only a few of the aspects of the doctrine of God scattered through the Gospel, calling for careful consideration and arrangement.

II. THE PERSON AND WORK OF CHRIST

Through the Apostle we are to arrive at the mind of the Lord Jesus, for his purpose beyond all else is to reveal his Master. Every part of the Gospel keeps this idea in view, and looking first at the Gospel as a whole we may think of it as giving a threefold manifestation of Christ. 1. As the Divine Messiah (chaps. 1 to 12). 2. As the disciples' Master (chaps. 13–17). 3. As the world's Redeemer (chaps. 18–21). Thus we may say that Christ is seen (1) as the Word revealing the character of God and his purpose for man; (2) as the man revealing God's ideal for human life and the chasm made by sin; (3) as the Saviour accomplishing God's will and restoring man to union and communion with God.

But beyond these general aspects we may look still more closely at the detail given of Christ's Person and work. 1. His relation to God; (1) as the Word (1:1); (2) as the Son (1:14). 2. His revelation of God; (1) God in himself (4:24); (2) God in relation to man (1:12). For this point special study should be devoted to the discourses in each chapter. 3. His Divine claims: (1) In acts (2:15); (2) in word (8:58). "Either he is God or he is not good." 4. His perfect humanity; (1) Subject to our physical conditions (4:16); (2) submitting to our moral conditions (5:19, 20). 5. His relation to the Jews (as Messiah). See especially chapters 1–12. 6. His relation to all men: (1)

Light (1:4), (knowledge); (2) life (1:13) (power). See especially 1:14, 17. "Grace (love) and Truth (light)." 7. His relation to the Church. See especially chapters 13 to 17.

III. THE REVELATION OF THE HOLY SPIRIT

This is another of the important features of the Fourth Gospel, especially when considered in the light of the Synoptic Gospels, and the fuller revelation in the Acts and Epistles.

1. *The first stage* (chaps. 1–7). The figure of water is seen, symbolizing (1) the incoming Spirit (chap. 3): (2) the indwelling Spirit (chap. 4): (3) the outflowing Spirit (chap. 7). It is also to be noted that 1:32, 33 and 3:34 associate the Spirit with Christ as at once the Receiver and Giver.

2. *The second stage* (chaps. 14 to 16). The remarkable revelation of the Spirit on the eve of our Lord's departure, giving the new name Paraclete and various new offices with the strong emphasis on the Spirit's Personality ("He").

3. *The third stage* (chap. 20). The Easter gift of the Spirit is the culminating point of our Lord's earthly manifestation and was perhaps intended as an anticipation of and preparation for Pentecost.

IV. THE REVELATION OF "LIFE"

As this is the specific purpose and main characteristic of the Gospel (20:31; 10:10), it seems to call for fuller attention, though at best this can only be fragmentary. Beyond and above all else Christianity is the religion of life. Eternal life is "the gift of God" (Rom. 6:23); this gift is intended for "justification of life" (Rom. 5:18); the believer is to "walk in newness of life" (Rom. 6:4); the Holy Spirit is called "the Spirit of life" (Rom. 8:2); and Christ is our priest "after the power of an endless life" (Heb. 7:17). In harmony with this we read in Bunyan's immortal allegory that the cry of Christian as he left the city of destruction was "Life! Life! Eternal Life!" John's Gospel is pre-eminently the Gospel of life. Matthew speaks of righteousness; Mark of service; Luke of grace; but John may be said to include all these and very much more by his emphasis on life. While life is mentioned in each of the Gospels it is far more fully treated in the Fourth than elsewhere, and in particular it is regarded both as a present blessing (6:47) and also as connected with a future state (5:29). At times we find the mention simply of "life"; at others of "eternal life," but between these there is no difference (3:36). Life is found in almost every chapter under various aspects.

1. *The Nature.* First of all, we must inquire as to the precise meaning of life as depicted in the New Testament, and especially in John. It is very much more than existence, and always implies and involves the thought of union. Indeed, every reference to life will be found to mean union. Thus, physical life is the union of the soul and the body; spiritual life is the union of the soul and God; while everlasting life in the fullest sense is the union of body and soul forever with God. And so life spiritual, here and now, means the possession of the Divine nature, the union of the soul with God in Christ and

the consciousness of fellowship resulting from it (John 17:3). It is impossible for even the ablest man to *define* life; it can only be *described* in its effects; and the one sufficient description of "eternal life" is union and communion with God. This is what Paul meant when he spoke of Christ as "our life" (Col. 3:4).

2. *The Source.* This is seen in the opening words "in him was life" (1:4). This is the fount and starting point (1 John 5:20). Life is so important and prominent in nature that it needs an adequate explanation, and nothing material or mechanical or human can account for it. Life always comes from life. God is the Source.

3. *The Beginning.* We see this in connection with the new birth (3:7), where our Lord emphasizes first the fact and then the method, the "what" and the "how." First, the fact of regeneration is shown and its necessity emphasized, and then, the way of its attainment is seen in the requirement of faith in Christ (3:15). The opposite of life is said to be death (3:16), and just as life in all its aspects means union, so death in its various elements means separation. Physical death means the separation of soul and body; spiritual death means the separation of the soul from God; everlasting death means the separation of body and soul from God forever. Those who disbelieve are said not to "see life" (3:36). Thus we are reminded that Christianity is the introduction of a new power, and not merely the provision of new knowledge. Knowledge cannot save; there must be life.

4. *The Indwelling.* Reception will necessarily be followed by realization, and the soul that has received God's life and is born again will be conscious of it as "living water" (4:11). This realization will in turn be followed by satisfaction, for in union and communion with Christ, our Life, we "never thirst," but find in him "a well of water springing up unto eternal life" (4:14).

5. *The Possession.* A new thought about life is suggested in almost every chapter, and as we contemplate the next section of John's Gospel we are reminded that the Lord Jesus Christ has been appointed by the Father to give us life (5:21), and that this life is at once a present possession (5:24) and a future promise (5:25). The cause of all this is Christ himself who has this life (5:26), and who is, therefore, able to communicate it to those who receive him. The word "eternal" here and elsewhere is particularly important, because it implies quality rather than duration. We possess the life now, and it is simply because of its Divine quality that it necessarily lasts forever.

6. *The Sustenance.* It is very striking that, after Christ claims to be the Source of life (chap. 5), he uses various symbols or metaphors in the following chapters to prove this possession of "life in himself." Thus in chapter 6 he is shown to be the support of the life of which he is the source. As in physical life it is essential to absorb and assimilate matter, so in things spiritual Christ is the Living Bread and the chapter is full of the most striking expressions about eating him and eating his flesh and blood (6:35, 51, 53, 56, 57, 58). Nothing could be more significant and impressive than this almost constant reiteration and increased intensity in regard to the appropriation of Christ.

7. *The Overflow.* It is interesting to observe the three uses of the symbol of "water" in these chapters. In chapter 3, "born of water" symbolizes the incoming of the Spirit. In chapter 4 the "living water" indicates the indwelling Spirit. In chapter 7:38, "rivers of living water" suggest the overflowing Spirit. That which we receive and possess is to be passed on to others, and from within us will flow rivers of life, giving blessing to those around. This is taken on the usual interpretation that it refers to believers, but there is much to be said for the suggestion made in the Companion Bible, under chapter 7:37, that the reference is to the Lord Jesus Christ as the Giver rather than to the believer as the receiver. But in either case the thought of "living water" clearly implies a constant, perennial and absolutely unfailing source of supply.

8. *The Power.* When the Lord Jesus Christ spoke of himself as the Light of the World, he said that his followers should not walk in darkness, but "have the light of life" (8:12). This seems to refer back to the opening statement that "the life was the light of men" (see also 9:5; 12:46). It is the possession of life that gives light, for, when we receive into our hearts the Lord Jesus Christ as our Saviour, Friend, and Master, the result is such an access of spiritual experience that perception, insight, knowledge become ours as we follow our Master. There is perhaps nothing more striking in Christian life than the way in which the follower of Christ obtains light on many a dark part of his circumstances.

9. *The Abundance.* The Lord Jesus did not come to bestow life only, great though that is, but that the believer might have it in abundance (10:10). We are not to be content with anything less than this. And the difference is often the difference between a poor, weak, and anæmic Christianity and one that pulsates with freshness, vigor, and energy. It is unfortunately only too possible for us to have merely a little warmth or a little heat when we ought to be thoroughly energized, and it is only too possible to be just saved instead of having the enjoyment of Christ's abundant salvation.

10. *The Condition.* In two successive chapters Christ teaches the solemn yet blessed lesson that life is possible only through death. In connection with Lazarus, Jesus Christ is the Resurrection and the Life (11:25). And when the Greeks came to see him he at once spoke of the grain of wheat dying in order that it might produce life and fruit. So, even though Christ was to be put to death, the raising of Lazarus showed that he had the power to guarantee victory; and in the same way, even though the disciple of Christ loses his life in this world, he finds and preserves it unto life eternal (12:25).

11. *The Outcome.* While the message about abiding and fruitfulness (chap. 15) does not specifically mention life, the thought is there all through, implying that only as we are united in life to Christ can we produce fruit that will abide. Then in the great prayer our Lord seems to sum up everything by the thought of the Father having given him authority to give eternal life to all believers, a life that is defined as knowing God and Jesus Christ (17:3). This constitutes the essential glory of life, that we are one with Christ and one with the Father in

him. There is nothing higher, truer, nobler than this thought of union with God in Christ (17:21–23).

12. *The Secret.* The Apostle reminds us in the statement of his purpose that this life is possible only "in his name" (20:31). The "name" always stands for the revealed character, and "in" inevitably and invariably means union. So that our "life" is found in fellowship through believing. Faith links us to Christ and thereby produces that union, the outcome of which is communion, which necessarily lasts forever and ever.

V. The Teaching on "Faith"

We have already seen that the whole Gospel is intended to elicit faith, and the mere occurrence of the word "believe" shows the importance of the material of the Gospel in this respect. In Matthew we find the word eleven times; in Mark fifteen; in Luke nine; while in John it occurs about a hundred times. A great American teacher, the late Dr. Dwight, of Yale, used to base his exposition of John on the discovery that the main purpose of the Gospel was to create faith, and yet more faith in the hearts of the disciples. One of his disciples recently remarked that Dr. Dwight showed how successive passages end with sentences recording the growth of faith in the little band around our Lord. "His disciples believed on him" (2:11). "Many believed on his name" (2:23). "Many of the Samaritans believed on him" (4:39). "The man believed" (4:50, 53). "Many believed on him there" (10:42). This is seen in one way or another to the very end. But it is important to try to analyze this faith by looking at some of its features as here recorded.

1. *Its Source* (1:36, 37). It was elicited through personal contact with Jesus Christ based on testimony.

2. *Its Elements.* These may be said to be two, marking the stages of growth: (1) believing the message (5:47); and (2) trusting the Person (14:11).

3. *Its Manifestation.* This is seen in two ways. First, by devotion to Christ (1:49), and then by confession of him (6:69).

This is only a little of the wonderful wealth in this Gospel in connection with faith, and special attention should be given to the personal types of faith here recorded. From the very outset to the close men and women are seen exercising a faith and manifesting it in a wonderful and beautiful variety of ways.

VI. The Teaching on Unbelief

We have already observed how the revelation of Christ invariably led to a twofold attitude being taken up, the one involving reception through faith, and the other expressing itself in an exactly opposite direction. It is this contrast between belief and unbelief that constitutes one of the most vital and impressive features of this remarkable Gospel. Here again we must endeavor to analyze unbelief and see what it really means.

1. *Its Nature.* It consists in one simple but all embracing fact, the rejection of Christ. Whatever may have been the causes or explanation, unbelief is simply the unwillingness to recognize and receive Christ in his claim to be Saviour and God.

2. *Its Phases.* As we study the Gospel we notice the gradual development of this unbelief. (1) It commences with murmuring at something that Christ said or did (2:18). (2) Then follows hatred as the outcome of this murmuring (5:16; 6:41). (3) The culminating point was hostility (7:1). It is always so with the attitude of unbelief. It starts with some objection involved in the claim of Christ, and if this unwillingness to surrender continues, animosity and deadly opposition are the inevitable outcome.

3. *Its Destiny.* The outcome of unbelief is death, understood as separation from God, just as the outcome of faith is life, understood as union with God (17:3).

As the Gospel is studied carefully for the various elements of unbelief, it is important to look at the record of personal types like Caiaphas, Pilate, and others. All of them united in rejection of Christ, though they reached their goal by various ways.

It may perhaps be asked why so much space is given to this topic, and the answer is probably that the revelation of Christ could not be understood historically in any other way. Thus unbelief leading to rejection may be said to solve the problem of the Jewish attitude to Christ which was such a stumblingblock to the early Church. It shows that they were unreasonable and wicked and had no excuse (5:39, 40). Their rejection was hostility to light (3:20); enmity to truth (8:45) and at heart, hatred of God (15:24).

VII. The Miracles

These constitute a special feature of John's Gospel and demand the closest attention.

1. They are always called "signs," that is, tokens of something higher than themselves. In the other Gospels they are described as "wonders," expressive of the effect on the beholders, and as "powers," indicative of the conclusion that those who saw them came to as they endeavored to account for them. But John goes higher still in speaking of them as "signs," that is, symbols, proofs, messages, object lessons of spiritual truths, embodied in the works themselves.

2. There are eight recorded, seven before and one after the Resurrection.

3. Each one should be studied with all possible care for its revelation of some specific manifestation of the glory of Christ (2:11).

VIII. Other Studies

The Gospel is so varied in its material that it is only possible to touch in the briefest way on some of the other topics included. Perhaps the following may be suggestive both on their own account and also of other elements to be found in this remarkable portion of Scripture.

1. The teaching on sin: its nature, aspects, and end.

2. The seven conversions recorded: Each with its aspect of Christ's revelation and the corresponding response.

3. Some characteristic and important words like: "Witness," "truth," "judge," "darkness," "light," "glory," "world," "death," "My Word," "in that day." As an illustration of what can be derived from a study of these and similar words we may concentrate on the term "witness," which is found some fifty times. In 5:31–47, there are four witnesses, one human and three Divine (vs. 33, 36, 37, 39). Then Christ himself is spoken of as a witness, and these, with the witness of the Holy Spirit and believers (15:26, 27), constitute the sevenfold testimony which is intended to elicit and assure faith.

Other ideas, words and phrases can easily be found like "manifested," "I am," "world," "verily, verily," and the various present participles in the Greek. These characteristic expressions are all the more remarkable because of the comparative absence of other words found frequently elsewhere. Thus "repentance" and "repent" are found in the three Synoptic Gospels, but not once here; and "righteousness" and "righteous" found nineteen times in Matthew, twice in Mark, and eleven times in Luke, are only found three times here. On the other hand, the Divine Fatherhood is referred to in Matthew forty-four times, in Mark five times, in Luke twenty times, and in John a hundred and twenty-one times. The proportion in regard to such terms as "world," "truth," "light," and "love," is also noteworthy. In Matthew "world" occurs nine times, in Mark three, in Luke three, in John seventy-nine. In Matthew "truth" occurs once, in Mark three times, in Luke three times, in John twenty-five. "Light" is found in Matthew seven times, in Mark once, in Luke six, in John twenty-two. And "love" is seen in Matthew seven times, in Mark four times, in Luke six times, and in John thirty-six. In view of the bitter hostility of the Jews, as recorded in this Gospel, these figures are also noteworthy. Matthew mentions the Jews five times, Mark seven, Luke five, and John seventy-one.

4. The sevenfold gifts in the one gift in 3:16. Christ himself is said to be God's gift, and he himself then gives in turn his flesh (6:27), his life (10:28), his example (13:15), the Comforter (14:16), his peace (14:27), his Word (17:8), and his glory (17:22).

5. The five manifestations of Christ to the Jews as seen at various times and under various circumstances in chapters 1 to 12.

6. The relation of the Gospel and the Epistle. The one intended to lead to faith (20:30, 31), and the other to knowledge (1 John 5:13).

As we review these outline Studies of the Gospel according to John it is only too clear that the merest fringe of the subject has been touched. Reference has already been made to that great scholar and truehearted Christian, Dr. Timothy Dwight, who felt that in the Fourth. Gospel we have an absolutely trustworthy reflection of the experiences of an immediate follower of Jesus Christ, and he never swerved from the conviction that the mind of the disciple named John was the creative mind behind this book. One day when discussing the incident of Mary's anointing the feet of our Lord, he pointed with evident satisfaction to the little mark of authenticity found in the third verse of the twelfth chapter which says, "and the house was filled with the odor of the ointment." One who was present said that looking round the class with a characteristic twinkle in his eye, he remarked "myths don't smell that way." On another occasion when his class was lingering on that significant verse, "he that eateth my flesh and drinketh my blood hath eternal life," Dr. Dwight said quietly, "Gentlemen, the Lord's Supper will in time convert the world." He was not thinking of the Sacrament itself but of the steady power of the life and death of Christ as they are received in the disciples and expressed through them.

Some utterances of another scholar, Professor Riggs, of Auburn, New York, may fitly close our consideration.

"Our study of this noble Gospel has come to an end. To that study which makes experience, life the chief interpreter, there can never be an end. It calls us to go on to know the Lord through all the profound realities of communion and obedience which involve the ultimate depths of life. The deeper we go by this way of interpretation the surer shall we be that this is no fabricated portrait of the Master. It is rather the picture of one who saw not merely the scenery of Galilee and Judea, nor simply the external forms of that memorable group now known as Master and Disciples, but whose profoundly religious spirit, touched, illumined, guided by the Spirit of Truth, grasped the eternal significance of him to whom his life had been given. Is there a subjective element in John? Of course there is, but it is the subjectivism of one whose insight was directed to the inner, eternal meanings of Jesus. Rightly has it been said that John saw Jesus and his truth *sub specie eternitatis*. Does that make the Gospel less true? Evidence enough there is of its historicity. No other Gospel is more faithful to historical situations; no other Gospel is more keenly alive to psychological presentations. Its portraiture of Jesus, different as is its setting from that of the Synoptics, is thoroughly consistent with theirs. What they exhibit constantly in action and now and then by word is here completely interpreted in that blaze of glory which casts a noonday clearness upon the person and character of the Messiah."

VII

OUTLINE STUDIES

CHAPTER 1:1–18

1. *The Divine Word.—Godhead.*
   (1) His position.
   (2) His relationships.
   (3) His activity.
2. *The Divine Light.—Glory.*
   (1) His witness.
   (2) His coming.

(3) His reception.

3. *The Divine Son.—Grace.*
   (1) The condescension.
   (2) The reality.
   (3) The message.

Out of eighteen verses Christ is distinctly mentioned in sixteen, and even the other two relate to him. Thus at the outset we are reminded that "Christ is all." There are three chief names here which should be taken in order, for the purpose of realizing their meaning, truth, and power.

1. *The Word.* Christ is God's thought made audible and his will made intelligible. It is for us to listen and learn, because the message is for all men, at all times, and in all things.

2. *The Light.* When we receive Christ as the "Word," we begin to see the Light of Life. He reveals sin, self, and God; he gives life, mental, moral, and spiritual; he purifies our character and conduct; he beautifies life and the world; and he gladdens all who accept him.

3. *The Son.* Having received Christ as "Word" and "Light," we become sons of God (v. 12), which means restoration to the position lost by sin; nearness to God; character, obedience and dignity.

It is important to remember that all this is due to our (1) receiving "*him*" (not it), a living, loving, Divine Person. (2) And it also means that we "receive" him, which is resting entirely upon him by simple trust (v. 12). (3) Most important of all is the solemn limitation of this opportunity, "*to as many as.*" It is for us to ask ourselves whether we have thus "received him."

CHAPTER 1:19–34

The great word here, characteristic of the entire Gospel, is "witness."

1. *The Testimony to the Messengers.*
   (1) The man.
   (2) The message.
2. *The Testimony to the Multitudes.*
   (1) The ministry.
   (2) The meaning.

After the introduction, 1:1–18, Christ is attested by John the Baptist, and two main thoughts stand out with prominence.

1. *The Work of Christ.* The Baptist uses three titles, and when they are put together they represent almost everything that Christ is to us. (1) He is the Lamb of God, who removes sin, bestows forgiveness, and guarantees acceptance by his sacrifice. (2) He is the One who baptizes with the Holy Spirit, bestowing new life, new purity, new power, and blessing. (3) He is the Son of God, thereby guaranteeing to us the right to become sons of God (v. 12). These three are to be kept together, and we must never think of Christ as the Lamb of God without at the same time remembering that he bestows the Holy Spirit and makes us God's children. Observe the order of these three blessings. We cannot have the second and the third without the first.

2. *The Work of the Baptist.* He calls himself a "voice," thereby showing his humility. And yet, although only a "voice," the fact that he *was* a "voice" shows that he had an important work to do. Much depends upon the tones of a voice, and we are sure that the Baptist's witness to Christ was expressed in the very best and most attractive way. A voice may be harsh and forbidding and give a wrong impression of the character behind it. So our witness for Christ may give people a false idea of his grace and glory. But if we are a "voice" in the true sense of that word, we shall at once realize that we are only his witnesses, and at the same time shall witness truly, lovingly, our lips and lives speaking for him. The Baptist was not long at work, but what he did all through was to bear witness to Christ, to point others to him.

CHAPTER 1:35–51

After the attestation of Christ by the Baptist, he is acknowledged by several men, who become his disciples.

1. *The First Two Disciples.*
   (1) The message.
   (2) The hearers.
   (3) The Master.
   (4) The result.
2. *The Second Two Disciples.*
   (1) The effort.
   (2) The effect.
   (3) The announcement.
   (4) The assurance.
3. *The Fifth Disciple.*
   (1) The mission.
   (2) The appeal.
   (3) The claim.
   (4) The response.
4. *The Sixth Disciple.*
   (1) The testimony.
   (2) The objection.
   (3) The advice.
   (4) The outcome.

In going from New York to Chicago, or from London to Liverpool, or Toronto to Vancouver, a choice can be made of several ways. The goal is the same in each case, but the journeys vary. Here we have four ways to Christ in the life of these early disciples:

1. *The Preached Word* (vs. 35–39). The testimony to the Lamb of God attracted the two disciples.

2. *The Personal Influence* (vs. 40–42). Andrew brought his brother to Jesus by the power of his own invitation.

3. *The Direct Appeal* (v. 43). Christ approached Philip direct without any human instrumentality.

4. *The Personal Testimony* (vs. 45, 46). Philip bore witness to what Jesus had been to him, and invited Nathanael to do likewise. Thus, while each man came his own way, they

all arrived at the one goal of a personal experience of Christ. Everything is intended to lead up to this, and it is for this reason that the Golden Text emphasizes our Lord's words: "Follow Me," which, when properly understood, include Trust and Obedience. We are first to "come *unto*" him and then to "come *after*" him.

CHAPTER 2:1–11

The Apostle uses the word "sign" to describe our Lord's miracles, and the terms found in the other Gospels, "wonder" and "power," are never employed by John. This usage indicates that the miracles were intended to have some meaning above and beyond themselves, a special significance. There are eight altogether and it is often thought that the grouping of seven *plus* one suggests that each miracle or "sign" has some specific meaning. Bishop Westcott does not hesitate to say that "the sequence of these 'signs,' these living parables of Christ's action, these embodiments of truth in deed can hardly be mistaken."

One way of considering them (Hutchison) is to regard the first as introductory of the Divine kingdom as a whole; the second and third to have special reference to the individual; the fourth and fifth to the Church; the sixth and seventh to the world; while the eighth is considered as the crowning event. Another suggestion is that these miracles correspond with each other by a system of introversion; the first corresponding to the eighth; the second to the seventh; the third to the sixth; and the fourth to the fifth. This method certainly indicates some striking parallels. Westcott thinks that the first two give the fundamental character of the Gospel its nature and condition. The next five are signs of the manifold working of Christ, while the last symbolizes the future in regard to corporate and individual work for Christ. Thus, it may be said that each miracle displays some special "rays" of our Lord's "glory." Westcott thinks that the correspondence and connections of these miracles with the different parts of the Gospel as a whole can be easily followed out in other directions and in fuller detail.

It is therefore suggested that, guided by various commentaries and other books, the special meaning of each "sign" and the particular aspect of "glory" manifested should be carefully considered. The following books deal with this subject:

"Our Lord's Signs in St. John's Gospel," by Hutchison, published by T. and T. Clark (valuable for detailed exegesis and doctrinal teaching).

"The Seven Signs," by Brockington, published by Elliott Stock (a spiritual treatment with analogy suggested with the seven songs of the Apocalypse).

"The Eight Signs of John's Gospel," by Madeley, published by Digby, Long & Co. (much useful, spiritual teaching, though unfortunately blended with a somewhat pronounced advocacy of conditional immortality).

"The Miracles of St. John's Gospel," by T. W. Gilbert, published by Longmans (specially teaching on eternal life).

CHAPTER 2:13–22

Christ's private ministry was over and his public work was commencing. It was, therefore, suitable to start at the capital, Jerusalem, and at the most familiar feast, the Passover. The importance of this incident cannot be overestimated in understanding Christ's ministry, because it was a definite offer to the nation, and when it was rejected, Christ had nothing to do but to gather and separate his disciples.

1. *Authority claimed.*
   (1) The need.
   (2) The preparation.
   (3) The action.
   (4) The Word.
2. *Authority confirmed.*
   (1) By Scripture.
   (2) By challenge.
   (3) By miracles.
   (4) By wisdom.

The one thought running through the whole passage is the authority and Lordship of Jesus Christ, and what he did in Jerusalem is a symbol of his attitude to the soul (Mal. 3:1).

1. *Lordship claimed.* We see that Christ is regarded as sent by the Father to be the Messiah and Saviour, and all through the verses this claim is to be noted.

2. *Lordship proved.* This is indicated in three ways: (1) By his oversight (vs. 13–17); (2) by his foresight (vs. 18–22); and (3) by his insight (vs. 23–25).

3. *Lordship exercised.* We see this in the (1) cleansing of the temple, (2) working of miracles, (3) teaching. It is very significant that while the miracles were "signs" to the disciples and impressed them (v. 11), the "sign" for the outside (v. 22) was the resurrection. Miracles continually impressed those who were already Christ's followers, just as spiritual experience confirms our faith today, but for the world the one supreme "sign" or miracle or proof is the resurrection.

4. *Lordship accepted.* In contrast with the Jews, it is for us to yield to Christ and to recognize his authority over us. We shall do this along familiar lines expressed by four words: (1) submit, (2) admit, (3) permit, (4) commit. When this is all true, then we shall (5) transmit.

CHAPTER 3:1–21

In the first part of this Gospel (chaps. 1 to 12) five manifestations of Christ are recorded, each beginning at Jerusalem. The first of these is in 2:13 to 4:54 and included Jerusalem (2:13 to 3:21), Judæa (3:22–36), Samaria (4:1–42), and Galilee (4:43–54). So that we are now concerned with Jerusalem, including a manifestation to the rulers (2:12–22) recording the first national rejection of Christ; to the inhabitants (2:23–25) recording the first beginning of faith; and then the interview with Nicodemus in the present passage, giving the first instance of Christ's dealing with an enquirer. It is also important to notice carefully the connection between chapters 2 and 3 and the remarkable emphasis on "men" and "man" (2:24 to 3:1). It would seem as though Nicodemus were one of the people referred to in the earlier verses, those to whom Jesus did not trust himself, because of their superficial, though sincere attitude. This needed to be deepened, and the process is seen in connection with Nicodemus.

1. *Regeneration.*
    (1) Its necessity.
    (2) Its nature.
    (3) Its effects.
2. *Revelation.*
    (1) Divine truth illuminated.
    (2) Divine testimony given.
    (3) Divine love declared.
    (4) Divine light emphasized.

This is a study of contrasts between earthly and heavenly aspects of life. We have the teacher of Israel (v. 10) and the Teacher come from God (v. 2). There are also the two "excepts," "except God be with him" (v. 2) and "except one be born anew" (v. 3). Then also there are the earthly and heavenly things (v. 12). All this constitutes the passage one of supreme importance in regard to spiritual life.

1. *The Necessity of Life.* Christ used the word "must" (v. 7), and the absolute necessity of a new start is thereby seen. Many reasons support this contention, including the awful effects of sin and the absolute impossibility of living the true life here or enjoying the true life hereafter without this regeneration. We should, therefore, emphasize in the strongest way our Lord's "must."

2. *The Possibility of Life.* Our Lord uses another "must" in referring to himself (v. 14), and this shows the way in which the new life becomes possible. This is one of the "heavenly things" in contrast with the "earthly," for it is because of the Divine redemption through the Cross that we obtain the new life of the Spirit in the soul. The absolute necessity of Atonement is thus added to the absolute necessity of the new birth.

3. *The Condition of Life.* This is seen in the reference to faith, for our Lord emphasized the importance and necessity of believing in him (vs. 15, 16, 18). Faith is the link of connection between the soul and Christ, between two "musts," for the moment we look we live, and when our faith is centered on Christ "lifted up," God's new life of the Spirit comes into our souls.

Thus, we see how Jesus is "the Saviour of the world." Nicodemus had said "we know," but our Lord showed that it is not a question of what we know, but what we *are*. Not knowledge, but life, is needed.

So the passage emphasizes Life, Love, and Faith. The life of the soul is provided by the love of God and faith is the link of connection.

CHAPTER 4:1–29

This is part of Christ's first public manifestation, beginning at Jerusalem (2:13 to 4:54). After Jerusalem (2:13 to 3:21), having been rejected there, he went into the country, the district near Jordan (3:22–24). Then came a dispute between the disciples of John the Baptist and some Jews, and this provided the occasion for John's last testimony to Christ (3:25–36). There was no rivalry, because John fully recognized his inferiority to the Messiah (3:30). Then Christ left Judæa for Samaria. The Pharisees had heard of his success, and in going through Samaria to Galilee he would be free from this Pharisee spying.

1. *Opportunity seen.*
    (1) Offered.
    (2) Used.
    (3) Blessed.
2. *Offer made.*
    (1) God's gift declared.
    (2) God's gift described.
    (3) God's gift desired.
3. *Obstacle put.*
    (1) The request.
    (2) The reply.
    (3) The reminder.
4. *Opposition shown.*
    (1) The rejoinder.
    (2) The requirement.
    (3) The revelation.
5. *Object attained.*
    (1) The despairing response.
    (2) The definite revelation.
    (3) The delighted realization.

Here we see how the Lord approached and captured this woman for himself by four steps.

1. *Attracting the heart* (vs. 4–9). By a simple request for a drink of water, he broke down the barriers of prejudice and predisposed her for anything else he might have to say.

2. *Arresting the mind* (vs. 10–15). Then he made her think by a reference to the "living water" and the "gift of God," which, as she pondered, made her desire something of which he spoke (v. 15).

3. *Arousing the conscience* (vs. 16–24). But there was something in her life which had to be put right before she could have this "living water," and notwithstanding her attempt to evade the pressure, our Lord drove home the arrow of conviction to her conscience, until at length she seems to have admitted the truth of his sayings, and yet in hopelessness thought that it would not be possible to know these things until some future day (v. 25).

4. *Assuring the soul* (vs. 25–30). Then our Lord revealed himself to her as a personal and present Saviour, telling her that she need not wait for any "far-off Divine event," inasmuch as he was there at that moment as her Saviour and Friend. Thus there was a revelation of love for the heart, truth for the mind, sin for the conscience, and grace for the soul.

Chapter 4:43–54

Christ at length reached Galilee on his return from Jerusalem through Samaria (4:3, 4) at the close of his first visit to the capital (2:12, 13). There is a clear connection between the first and second miracles (4:46, 54), and though this may be only chronological, marking the opening of the Galilean ministry and the return thither, it is possible that there is a deeper connection, the first miracle or "sign" being connected with marriage, and the second with home; the first with the joy of a wedding, and the second with the sorrow of a family. Christ and life's gladness, and then Christ and life's sadness. The nobleman was some officer of the royal household of Herod Antipas, the ruler of Galilee, who was sometimes called king, and it is a story of the progress of faith.

1. *The Beginning of Faith.*
    (1) Its undoubted existence.
    (2) Its unsafe foundation. "Signs and wonders."
    (3) Its unsound material. "See."
2. *The Training of Faith.*
    (1) Sincerity tested.
    (2) Belief examined.
    (3) Confidence proved.
3. *The Maturity of Faith.*
    (1) Absolute reliance.
    (2) Strong confidence.
    (3) Fuller experience.

This miracle, like others, is a parable of the Gospel of Christ.

1. *The Great Sorrow* (v. 46). This is seen (1) in a home; (2) among the rich; (3) about a child. An Arab proverb says that "grief is a black camel that kneels at every one's gate."

2. *The Great Saviour* (vs. 47–50). His aid is (1) sought (v. 47). Then he is (2) asked (v. 49), and as the outcome he is (3) trusted (v. 50).

3. *The Great Satisfaction* (vs. 51–54). We can imagine something of what the father felt as he heard the words, "Thy son liveth," and his satisfaction took three forms: (1) trustful obedience (v. 50); (2) thankful joy (v. 51); (3) thorough blessing (vs. 53, 54).

4. *The Great Secret.* Everything is associated with the man's trust, and it is this effect of Christ on human life which links together the various incidents in this Gospel, as illustrated in every chapter. After the Samaritans are brought into personal contact with Christ through faith, we see the same element in the story of this nobleman, and it will be well for us to analyze what faith really is. (1) It starts with an intellectual perception of facts. The man knew of Christ and his works and accepted them as realities. (2) Then follows a general belief in the value of these facts. The man knew what Christ had done for others, and on this account he believed that he would do the same for him. (3) Then everything culminates in appropriating trust in the Person and Word of Christ. The man took Christ at his word and rested entirely upon him.

The result of his faith was the enjoyment of (1) immediate blessing, (2) clear assurance, and (3) deeper experience. Faith, therefore, rises from the acceptance of facts to a personal trust which rests on Christ himself. We start by saying, "I may trust," and then we follow with "I must" and "I will," and then comes "I do." Slightly to alter some well-known words, we may say that Faith means: Forsaking All, I Take Him.

Chapter 5:1–15

No two people are alike, whether physically, intellectually, or morally. For this reason it is important to emphasize individuality and the chief value of these chapters is the variety they offer, showing how our Lord dealt with each case in a different way, though, fundamentally, there was the same need of the same Saviour.

1. *The Need of Healing.*
    (1) Great suffering.
    (2) Prolonged suffering.
    (3) Friendless suffering.
    (4) Disappointed suffering.
2. *The Way of Healing.*
    (1) Christ's knowledge.
    (2) Christ's compassion.
    (3) Christ's inquiry.
3. *The Condition of Healing.*
    (1) The appeal to interest.
    (2) The call to faith.
4. *The Character of Healing.*
    (1) Immediate.
    (2) Thorough.
5. *The Outcome of Healing.*
    (1) The inquiry and the answer.
    (2) The revelation and the message.
    (3) The testimony and the result.

In "Conversations with Christ," by Lucas, it is suggested that the man was not quite genuine, because his suffering had debased him. For this reason it is thought that he at once told the enemies of Christ who it was who had healed him, but whether this is correct or not, the heart of our Lord's message to him is found in verse 11.

1. *Restoration.* "He that made me whole." This healing of the man, typifying the spiritual blessing of Christ, has several characteristics: (1) It was free. The man had "nothing to pay." (2) It was full. The man was "made whole." (3) It was immediate. Christ's blessings do not take long to bestow. (4) It was permanent. The trouble never came back. These four points are true of Christ's salvation.

2. *Requirement.* "Take up thy bed and walk." Christ not only restores, but expects his followers to grow and make progress, and the man's action is a symbol of what believers ought to do. (1) There should be obedience. Christ commands us to show in our life that we are healed. (2) There should be holiness. The "whole-ness" of the body is a fit symbol of the holiness of the soul. (3) There should be testimony. By lip and

by life we should tell others of what Christ has done for us. Gratitude alone should prompt us to do this.

3. *Restoration and Requirement Inseparable.* "The same said unto me." This is an important point, showing that salvation and obedience are absolutely inseparable. We must never emphasize the one without the other. Inquirers about Christianity should be told that two things make up a Christian, salvation and obedience; not only birth, but growth. Christ lived and died and rose, first, to restore men to right relations with God; and then to bring their lives into harmony with the Divine ideal. This is also a hint to Christians for what God has joined together we must never put asunder. We are delivered in order to serve (Luke 1:74; 1 Pet. 2:9). Walking is often used as a symbol of our spiritual expression of life (Eph. 4:1; 5:2). These two combined and inextricably bound up constitute essential Christianity.

CHAPTER 5:19–29

After the miracle and the hostility arising out of it, came Christ's vindication of himself (vs. 19–47), and in verses 19–29 we see Christ's claim to authority with its threefold, "Verily, verily."

1. Christ and the Father—Position (vs. 19–23).
2. Christ and Individuals—Life (v. 24).
3. Christ and the World—Authority (vs. 25–29).

Thus we have three pictures of Christ and three attitudes of Christians: (1) In relation to the world, Christ is to be honored; (2) in relation to the individual, Christ is to be trusted; (3) in relation to the Father, Christ is to be imitated.

CHAPTER 5:30–47

In the course of his vindication, Christ spoke of certain "witnesses," and when this passage is put with others, we find no less than seven distinct testimonies to him in this Gospel: (1) Himself (v. 31; 8:14); (2) John the Baptist (5:33); (3) Miracles (5:36); (4) The Father (5:37); (5) Scripture (5:39–47); (6) The Holy Spirit (15:26); (7) Believers (15:27).

CHAPTER 6:1–21

The record of the feeding of the five thousand in all four Gospels indicates its importance as a crisis, and a careful study of the evangelists shows that the miracle introduces Christ in four different aspects: as the Messiah in Matthew; the Teacher in Mark; the gracious Man in Luke; and the Divine Person in John.

1. The Circumstances (vs. 1–4).
2. The Conversation (vs. 5–7).
3. The Confession (vs. 8, 9).
4. The Command (v. 10).
5. The Confidence (v. 11).

6. The Care (vs. 12, 13).
7. The Consciousness (v. 14).
8. The Caution (v. 15).

As every miracle is a parable, we may look at this incident as revealing some of the deepest truths of the Gospel.

1. *The Revelation.* A wonderful picture of Christ. (1) His consciousness. He knew all the circumstances and was purposing to do something, because he had the ability (v. 6). (2) His calmness. In both miracles the beautiful quiet and perfect restfulness of Christ are most impressive. We are taught afresh the truth of Bushnell's words, that the character of Christ forbids his possible classification with man.

2. *The Request.* He associates himself with his disciples, because he wishes to teach them. (1) His consultation. He took counsel with them, regarding them as his fellow-workers. (2) His co-operation. He called them to an apparently impossible work when he told them to give the people food.

3. *The Response.* The attitude of the disciples is full of spiritual meaning. (1) The surrender. They were to bring their little store to him. He always uses natural means as far as they will go. He might have worked the miracle without these loaves and fishes, but he chose to receive them, and so the men were told to bring what they had to him. This means full surrender of everything, however small, for "loaves unblessed are loaves unmultiplied." (2) The service. Then, with his blessing resting on their scanty supply, they were bidden to go and feed the multitude. Christ can make much of inadequate means if only they are fully yielded to him. All that he requires is complete surrender, perfect trust, and loyal obedience. To quote Bushnell again, "Duty is not measured by our ability." Indeed, as Prebendary Webb-Peploe has said, responsibility is "ability to respond," *our* response to *his* ability.

4. *The Result.* The outcome was complete satisfaction of the needs of the people. They were all filled by means of Christ's miracle and the disciples' work. We can also be quite sure that the disciples themselves were still more deeply impressed by their Master's influence and power, and were led thereby to deeper, stronger faith.

> "Unspeakable thy joy,
> And glorious thy reward,
> If by thy barley loaves one soul
> Has been brought home to God."

CHAPTER 6:22–40

The great discourse, or it may be the discussions, in this chapter followed immediately on the feeding of the five thousand. That event was evidently one of the turning-points of Christ's ministry, and the discussions with the Jews, followed by the departure of many professed disciples, show the vital importance of the occasion. For the moment we are only concerned with one section, before taking a general view of the whole.

1. *Inquiry* (vs. 22–25).

(1) The people.

(2) The surprise.

(3) The desire.

2. *Reproof* (vs. 26–29).

(1) Rebuke.

(2) Exhortation.

(3) Direction.

3. *Correction* (vs. 30–35).

(1) As to source.

(2) As to gift.

(3) As to character.

4. *Instruction* (vs. 36–40).

(1) The comers.

(2) The Christ.

(3) The Father.

The references to bread in this chapter are to be explained not only by the miracle, but by the fact that the Passover and the feast of unleavened bread were near (6:4). To the Jews the symbol of bread was full of spiritual meaning. The manna in the wilderness (Exod. 16:15), the bread earned by Adam (Gen. 3:19), the bread brought by Melchisedek (Gen. 14:18), the bread given by Joseph (Gen. 41:54), the unleavened bread at the Passover (Exod. 12:15), the shewbread in the tabernacle (Exod. 40:23), all occupied an important place in Jewish thought. It is therefore not surprising that Christ used this bread as a symbol of himself. When Satan met Christ in the wilderness, it might have seemed as though bread were everything, but our Lord soon showed that there was something far higher (Luke 4:4). Man is much more than physical, or else life would depend on bodily health.

1. *Christ the Source of Life.* The analogy fails here, because bread cannot give life to the body, while Christ is the life of the soul. We can do without many things, but for the repair of physical waste we must have food. Sin wastes spiritual strength, and for this reason we need life (6:53). Christ is our life, repairing the waste and giving new powers (6:51). In the Incarnation he was God *with* us; at Calvary, God *for* us; at Pentecost, God *in* us.

2. *Christ the Support of Life.* When life has been given, new strength comes and has to be maintained, for every part of our nature requires continual sustenance. Just as the manna did not last for two days, so our Lord's Prayer is "Give us this day our daily bread." Christ provides this, for he not only died to become the source of our life, but he lives to be its support. Day by day Christ is our life, and to us to live is Christ (1 Cor. 1:30; Phil. 1:21; Gal. 2:20).

3. *Christ the Satisfaction of Life.* There is such a thing as bare physical existence without enjoyment, but as bodily vigor implies far more than mere existence, so in spiritual things our needs are great and continuous. The supreme question for Christians is whether they enjoy their religion. It has been said that "some people have just enough religion to make them miserable." But Christ intends us never to hunger (v. 35) and to "live for ever" (v. 51). The New Testament has many suggestions expressed by words like "riches," "fulness," "abundance." Christ has fed millions and is still inexhaustible,

and if only we receive him in his fulness, we shall be "satisfied with favor" (Deut. 33:23; Psa. 36:8; 65:4; 103:5; Jer. 31:14).

CHAPTER 6:25–71

It will readily be seen that these discourses are the sequel of the miracle of the feeding of the five thousand, and the perfect naturalness of the subject will also be realized when looked at in connection with the dialogues with the Jews, for a careful consideration shows the gradual growth of the opposition and at the same time the true significance of Christ's words.

1. *Discussion* (vs. 25–40). (1) This was the first stage, which ended with the claim by Christ to be the Heavenly bread.

2. *Dissatisfaction* (vs. 41–51). (2) The Jews murmured at this claim in view of what they believed they knew of his earthly origin and circumstances. But Christ in reply did not mitigate, but intensified his claim by saying that the bread was his flesh.

3. *Dissension* (vs. 52–59). (3) This was the outcome, for the Jews now strove with one another, being horrified at the very thought of "flesh to eat." Again Christ maintained and more than maintained his position by elaborating the thoughts, and telling them once again of himself, his life and work, and the assurance of the eternal consequences to those who were united to him.

4. *Defection* (vs. 60–66). (4) This was too much for many of his nominal disciples, and the result was defection, for they could not possibly continue with One who had been saying such difficult, mysterious and impossible things.

5. *Devotion* (vs. 67–71). (4) It was then that our Lord turned to the Twelve and sought the proof of their devotion, and was assured by Peter speaking for them all that, notwithstanding everything, they were convinced that he had the words of eternal life, as the Holy One of God, and on this account they could not and would not go away.

As we review these conversations and discourses, we cannot help noticing three solemn lessons.

1. *The Inevitable Result of Truth.* We see this in the way in which the Jewish character was revealed and its destiny settled in relation to Christ.

2. *The Invariable Attitude of Evil.* The opposition to our Lord is seen to be associated with his death, and it is not too much to say that dislike, if not hatred, of the Atonement, together with rejection of the One who atones, constitute the predominant features of all opposition to Christ and Christianity through the ages (1 Cor. 1:18, 25).

3. *The Immeasurable Satisfaction of Christianity.* This is seen all through these wonderful chapters, revealing our Lord as a personal Saviour, who dwells in a believer, is assimilated by him, and satisfies the hunger of the soul forever (vs. 35, 51, 57, 68). So that we may say in this, as in other connections, "Christ is all."

CHAPTER 7:1–31

The third manifestation of Christ to the Jews extends from 7:1 to 10:21, during which time he shows more fully and clearly than ever his Divine claims, and side by side with this we observe the development of the controversy which eventually led to his rejection by the nation. The entire section is marked by its relation to the feast of tabernacles (7:1, 14, 37; 9:1).

1. *The Challenge* (7:1–13).
    (1) The peril seen.
    (2) The proof sought.
    (3) The purpose shown.
2. *The Controversy* (7:14–24).
    (1) Testimony given.
    (2) Testimony questioned.
    (3) Testimony confirmed.
3. *The Conflict* (7:25–31).
    (1) Resistance.
    (2) Revelation.
    (3) Result.

In the course of this discussion between Christ and the Jews, we notice in particular three solemn truths.

1. *Relationship to God.* The issue was becoming more and more definite. The Jews claimed to be preeminently the people of God, expecting a Messiah, and yet when the Messiah was in their midst, they did not accept him. This thought of their relationship to God had no meaning for them, except in relation to their past, and everything connected with Abraham and the covenant seemed to them to make all things sure. Their present spiritual condition counted for nothing; they only rested upon a relationship from ancient days which they considered sufficient for everything. But in strong and striking contrast our Lord emphasized the necessity of their proving themselves true children of Abraham (Luke 3:8).

2. *Realization of Truth.* Christ told them the simple yet sufficient way of proving the truth of his statements, "If any man willeth to do his will, he shall know of the teaching, whether it is of God or whether I speak from myself" (7:17). This shows that truth becomes known through doing or being willing to do the will of God. The passage teaches that, as we obey what we know, there comes into our lives an ever-increasing conviction that we are on the side of truth. This is one of the ways in which the Fourth Gospel emphasizes obedience as a condition of intellectual illumination. There is an objective doctrine and a subjective element in man, and when the two are united in simple obedience, the result is spiritual assurance. "There is no revelation possible to the rebellious, the half-hearted, or the apathetic; but when the whole man makes a true self-surrender of himself to God, his eyes become opened to truth and he knows the doctrine" (Holdsworth, "The Life Indeed," p. 94).

3. *Refusal of Christ.* Notwithstanding all that our Lord said, it is clear that prejudice prevented them from accepting him and his teaching. Decision has to be faced, and in this section men are evidently making up their minds with reference to Jesus Christ. Some accept, but others reject, and the conflict of thought leads to a corresponding conflict of determination with all the results later on of open and utter opposition. Unbelief is seen here, as elsewhere, to be the fundamental sin, "Ye will not come."

CHAPTER 7:32–52

It was necessary for something to be done in the face of these discussions and their differing results (vs. 30, 31). Men always have to take sides in relation to Christ. One attitude is impossible, that of ignoring him.

1. *The Hostile Attitude* (vs. 32–36).
    (1) The embassy.
    (2) The greeting.
    (3) The outcome.
2. *The Loving Attitude* (vs. 37–39).
    (1) The one condition.
    (2) The assured welcome.
    (3) The complete satisfaction.
3. *The Varied Result* (vs. 40–52).
    (1) Division.
    (2) Confession.
    (3) Hardness.

This is one of the many illustrations of the striking contrast caused by Christ.

1. *Christ and his enemies.* His clear enunciation of truth and his assurance of a loving welcome were met by a determination to oppose and reject his offer. We see all through the story the growth of that hardness which at length culminated at the crucifixion.

2. *Christ and his friends.* The wonderful testimony on the last day of the feast (vs. 37–39) is a striking instance of what our Lord is willing and able to be to those who follow him. He is the perennial source of spiritual life and the perfect satisfaction of that life. Not only so, but others are blessed through those who receive him, for they become rivers of blessing (v. 38). This reference to the Holy Spirit and the condition of his coming at Pentecost, consequent upon the glorification of Jesus Christ, has its personal and spiritual counterpart, for the Holy Spirit only comes down into our hearts when the Lord Jesus Christ is on his throne there. If we will but commit ourselves to him in simple, childlike faith and surrender and admit him into our hearts, and then permit him to be our Lord, we shall soon be enabled by his grace to transmit to others the blessings of his Divine grace.

CHAPTER 8:1–11

It is well known that this passage is disputed in so far as it is part of the present Fourth Gospel, but whatever may be said about its place here, there seems to be no doubt that it represents a true incident in our Lord's life. It has been well said that it is so marked "by the wisdom, holiness, and goodness of him to whom it is attributed that it could no more have been invented than any other feature in the inimitable life of Christ." In studying our Lord, we can look at his life as a whole, and consider its general effect, or we can confine attention to particular topics. Of the latter there is scarcely one more interesting than the present story, in which we see our Master's self-possession, insight and wisdom.

1. *Christ and the men* (vs. 1–9).
    (1) Malignant hatred.
    (2) Probing silence.
    (3) Determined wilfulness.
    (4) Perfect conviction.
2. *Christ and the woman* (vs. 9–11).
    (1) Personal contact.
    (2) Searching gaze.
    (3) Judicial decision.
    (4) Loving admonition.

In this twofold attitude of one and the same Person, we notice the different expressions of the same feature. This contrast between our Lord's attitude to the man and to the woman calls for careful attention. He was the same Christ and yet was very different to the two parties.

1. *The Twofold Attitude.* To both he showed his wisdom, justice, and love. He manifested his wisdom to the men by showing that he knew their plot and would vanquish their claim. He showed his wisdom to the woman in his careful distinction between concern for her guilt and for the salvation of her soul. He showed his justice to the men in his refusal to deal with matters outside his province, and to the woman in his strict insistence on righteousness of life. His love was shown to the men in his endeavor to awaken their conscience to a sense of their sin, and to the woman in his careful and sympathetic dealings with her, notwithstanding that she was henceforth to live a different life.

2. *The Cause of this Twofold Attitude.* The reason why the one Christ was so different in each case was due to the difference in the people before him. It is a solemn truth that God is to us what we are to him. If we come to him with idols in our hearts, he will answer us according to those idols, but if we come to him with penitence and sincerity, he will deal with us accordingly. The same sun that melts the ice hardens the clay, and God's relation to us always depends upon our relation to him.

CHAPTER 8:12–59

The discussions at the feast of tabernacles are continued, and the section of which this is a part extends from 7:37 to 8:59 and deals with the last day of the feast of tabernacles.

Four classes of people may be distinguished: The orthodox party, represented by the Pharisees, who were mainly hostile and are usually described by John as "the Jews"; the ordinary people who came up to the feast, and who were not definitely on one side or the other; the religious officials, mainly Sadducees; the disciples of Christ.

1. *Divine Testimony* (vs. 12–20).
    (1) To himself.
    (2) To the Father.
    (3) To the Jews.
2. *Solemn Announcement* (vs. 21–30).
    (1) About the Jews.
    (2) About the Father.
    (3) About himself.
3. *True Disciples* (vs. 31–36).
    (1) Abiding in Christ's Word.
    (2) Knowing Christ's Truth.
    (3) Possessing Christ's freedom.
4. *Nominal Children* (vs. 37–42).
    (1) Wicked life.
    (2) Empty boasting.
    (3) Sinful nature.
5. *Real Foes* (vs. 43–47).
    (1) Deadness of perception.
    (2) Offspring of Satan.
    (3) Rejection of Christ.
6. *Divine Claims* (vs. 48–59).
    (1) Sincerity.
    (2) Sinlessness.
    (3) Salvation.

As we review these various discussions, we are enabled to see what it is to be a true Christian.

1. *Knowing Divine Truth* (v. 32). We need truth because of our ignorance and error about God, about life, and about eternity. Christ himself is the truth (1:17; 14:6; 18:37), and now "truth is in Jesus" (Eph. 4:21), since he reveals God, life, and eternity. This truth is a power, for Christ promises it shall make us free. Our intellectual bondage, due to ignorance, error, and prejudice; our religious bondage, due to self-righteousness; our spiritual bondage, due to our sinfulness—shall all be removed.

2. *Possessing Divine Sonship* (v. 35). In time past those who were out of Christ were children of the devil (v. 44), but now we are God's children, by adoption (Rom. 8:15) and regeneration (John 1:12).

3. *Enjoying Divine Liberty* (vs. 32, 36). Freedom is one of the greatest privileges and blessings of the Gospel and includes liberty from the guilt and power of sin, from all merely human bondage (Gal. 5:1). And yet by a beautiful spiritual paradox it involves complete slavery to Christ. Liberty is not license. We are at once Christ's slaves and Christ's freemen. Liberty consists in the possession of God and surrender to his will. As the Episcopal Collect says, "Whose service is perfect freedom." And a hymn-writer remarks, "A life of self-renouncing love is a life of liberty."

CHAPTER 9:1–38

Some think this incident follows immediately on 8:59, at the Feast of Tabernacles, but it is perhaps better to regard it as happening about three months after at the Feast of the Dedication (10:22), because of certain events which seem to have taken place in Galilee between the two feasts.

1. *The Miracle worked* (vs. 1–12).
    (1) The need (vs. 1–3).
    (2) The worker (vs. 4–6).
    (3) The deed (vs. 7–12).
2. *The Miracle tested* (vs. 13–34).
    (1) The man examined (vs. 13–18).
    (2) The parents examined (vs. 19–23).
    (3) The man re-examined (vs. 24–34).
3. *The Miracle crowned* (vs. 35–41).
    (1) The demand made (v. 35). Faith.
    (2) The homage accepted (v. 38). Worship.
    (3) The work done (vs. 39–41). Judgment.

This is one of the most striking instances of the opposition to Christ shown by the Jewish authorities, and the main thought of the lesson can be seen in the contrast between the "we know" of the Pharisees (v. 24) and the "I know" of the man (v. 25).

1. *Prejudice.* "We know" (v. 24). All through the story we see (1) the official pride, (2) the utter formalism, (3) the deliberate bias, and (4) the absolute falsehood of those who were determined to reject Christ. This opposition was due to the will influenced by desire.

2. *Reception.* "I know" (v. 25). In the man we see (1) his personal humility, (2) his experimental belief, (3) his spiritual discernment, (4) his joyous confidence. All this was caused by willing obedience founded on simple trust. We can, therefore, rejoice in the assurance that comes from experience as the foundation of faith. This is invincible and unassailable, for no one can touch or set aside the reality which comes from a personal contact with Christ.

> "Whoso hath felt the Spirit of the Highest
>   Cannot confound nor doubt him nor deny;
> Yea, with one voice, O world, though thou deniest,
>   Stand thou on that side, for on this am I."

CHAPTER 10:1–18

There is a close connection between this and chapter 9. Jesus continues his remarks to the Pharisees due to their conduct in excommunicating the man who had been born blind. They claimed to be the expounders of the Divine law, and in that capacity they had dealt with the man, and, if their action was true, the man had undoubtedly forfeited his proper place among God's people. But their sentence did not reflect God's judgment, and the Pharisees were not true spiritual guides, for they did not seek God's honor. Thus, the subject of verses 1 to 21 is the contrast between these false guides and Jesus himself, the true Guide. The relations of a shepherd and his sheep are used allegorically, and the subject is unfolded in three contrasts (vs. 1–6, 7–10, 11–15). The figures of shepherd and sheep would be very familiar (Jer. 23:1–4; Ezek. 34; Zech. 11:16).

As the verses are somewhat hard to divide, because the entire subject is blended gradually through the three contrasts, it will perhaps be best to look at it under the four following figures:

1. *The Fold.*
    (1) The place (v. 1).
    (2) The intruders (v. 1).
    (3) The porter (v. 3).
2. *The Door.*
    (1) The claim (vs. 7, 9).
    (2) The test (v. 8).
    (3) The assertion (vs. 8, 10).
3. *The Flock.*
    (1) Life (vs. 9, 10).
    (2) Intercourse (vs. 3, 4).
    (3) Conduct (vs. 4, 5).
4. *The Shepherd.*
    (1) And the fold (vs. 2, 4, 9).
    (2) And the intruder (vs. 1, 5, 12, 13).
    (3) And the sheep (vs. 2, 3, 4, 14, 15, 16).

In this lesson we have the final metaphor expressive of the various relationships of Christ to his people.

1. *The Shepherd.* This was something entirely new. He had spoken in parables generally (Luke 15), but now he speaks of himself as the Shepherd. As such, he is the (1) Saviour; (2) owner; (3) friend; (4) guide of his flock. Each of these points can be seen in the lesson. And, as such, he (1) saves; (2) keeps; (3) loves; (4) leads. Each one of us ought to be able to take this home to the heart and say, "The Lord is *my* Shepherd" (Psa. 23:1).

2. *The Sheep.* Almost every verse has something to say about the relation of the sheep to the Shepherd (all of which should be noted), but we will concentrate on verse 9, which tells of three things: Safety, Liberty, Satisfaction. (1) We are saved by the Shepherd, who gives his life for our redemption (vs. 11, 15). (2) We enjoy freedom through the open door of the sheepfold, and rejoice in our liberty in Christ (Gal. 5:1). (3) The satisfaction comes from the "pasture," the spiritual food which is ours, as Christ, our Shepherd, leads us day by day.

3. *The Under-Shepherds.* The solemn contrast between the false shepherds and the true Shepherd conveys a definite lesson for all Christian workers. We are expected under Christ to be of help to his people, whether as a "porter" or in some other capacity. Let us take care that we are not like the Pharisees, hirelings (vs. 12, 13). Our position should be in Christ; our devotion should be shown for Christ's sheep; and our spiritual life should be marked by knowledge, sympathy, and love.

4. *The "Other Sheep."* Verse 16 looks forward to the future, and it is significant that Christ already spoke of them as belonging to himself, "I have." He also said, "Them also I must

bring," and yet we know that he did not, personally, in his earthly lifetime, bring a single one of them. What, then, is the meaning of this solemn "I must"? Surely, it is that they are to be brought through us, and this is the specific work of what we call missions or world-wide evangelization.

CHAPTER 10:19–30

Opposition to Christ was continually growing and ripening, until at length the utterances about himself as the Shepherd, about the hireling, the wolf and the sheep, led to the inevitable clash between him and his foes, involving a severing of the true and the false in those who heard him (vs. 19–24).

1. The serious separation (v. 19).
2. The solemn declaration (v. 25).
3. The significant explanation (v. 26).
4. The safe preservation (vs 28–30).

The entire passage shows the contrast between those whom Christ described as "my sheep," and those of whom he said, "Ye are not of my sheep."

1. *My Sheep.* In the course of Christ's statements he mentions no fewer than seven separate statements of his relation to his followers. They hear his voice, he knows them, they follow him, he gives them eternal life, they shall never perish, no one shall snatch them out of his hand, no one can snatch them out of the Father's hand. And this sevenfold relationship to man is based on Christ's unique relation to God (v. 30).

2. *Not my Sheep.* In striking contrast the Jews are told that their inability and unwillingness to believe were due to the fact that these elements of relationship were not true of them (v. 26). Nothing could be more striking than this plain and definite contrast. Men are either Christ's "sheep" or they are not. There is no other alternative.

CHAPTER 10:31–42

Now comes the close and culminating points of the great discussion. The Jews at once recognize that our Lord had asserted his deity (v. 30), and it is this claim that constitutes the reality and bitterness of the opposition.

1. The attack (v. 31).
2. The appeal (v. 32).
3. The answer (v. 33).
4. The accusation (vs. 34–38).
5. The action (v. 39).
6. The avoidance (v. 40).
7. The acceptance (vs. 41, 42).

And so the breach was complete. The Jews sought but failed to separate the good works of Christ and the Person who performed them. They would not mind accepting the works even though they were set on stoning the Worker. But Christ did not because he could not withdraw his claim, and so we have the two parties, those who would not and did not accept him, and those who would and did.

1. *The Faithless.* Four times the Jews had wished to take him (7:30, 32, 44; 10:39); twice they had taken up stones to cast at him (8:59; 10:31), while on an earlier occasion they had sought to kill him (5:18). The enmity aroused by his healing on the Sabbath day (chap. 5) had never really died out (7:1, 19, 25), but increased and was intensified, point by point, until at last it culminated in this hostility. It is sad to think that while he was welcomed in Samaria (chap. 4), and was not very severely opposed in Galilee (chap. 6), yet in the center of the nation, at Jerusalem, he was met with the most violent and virulent hostility.

2. *The Faithful.* In striking and beautiful contrast is the acceptance of him during this period of retirement beyond the Jordan, and after the effort of the Jews to take him, this acknowledgment of him and his claims must have been a delight and a true refreshment to his wearied body and mind. "Many believed on him there" (v. 42). Here again the contrast is clear-cut and definite.

CHAPTER 11:1–16

It has been well and most suggestively pointed out (H. W. Clark, in "The Christ From Without and Within") that at the end of the tenth chapter a break is made in the narrative, and the method of writing is resumed which had been dropped at the end of the fourth chapter. In chapters 1–4 the record gives various incidents about Christ, while from chapters 5–9, inclusive, Christ mainly speaks for himself, expressing his own inner life and consciousness. "Now John begins to speak about Christ once more."

At the same time we are reminded of the friendships of Christ, as we are introduced to Mary, Martha, and Lazarus.

1. *Love's Interest* (vs. 1–4). The message sent to Christ was based on his love to Lazarus. But our Lord thought first and foremost of the glory of God.

2. *Love's Delay* (vs. 5, 6). The force of the word "therefore" seems strange. How could Christ love Lazarus and yet allow him to die? It was because the death was seen to bring more glory to God.

3. *Love's Courage* (vs. 7–10). When the time came for action, nothing could stop Christ, for he was "immortal" till his work was done.

4. *Love's Purpose* (vs. 11–16). The words "friend" and "glad" are significant, for Christ was about to show what he would do. He had already raised the dead, but this would be the greatest miracle of all.

As we ponder this passage, we see the characteristics of Christ's love to Lazarus, Martha, and Mary.

1. *Personal Love.* It was concentrated on each of the three. Love is always and necessarily personal, whether it is the love of pity or of pleasure, love for the disobedient or the obedient. The realization of Christ's pitying love brings the sinner to repentance, while the consciousness of personal love brings joy and peace to the believer.

2. *Perfect Love.* Christ's love was always unselfish, self-denying, self-sacrificing. While natural affection brings pleasure and delight in the return it elicits, Christ's love was disinterested, pure, unselfish. He loved not because of what they could be to him, but of what he could be to them. True love is always ready to give itself for others. And the various references to Christ's love are inevitably and closely associated with its proof in the gift of himself (John 15:13; 2 Cor. 5:14; Gal. 2:20; Eph. 5:2).

3. *Particular Love.* Christ loved Lazarus and yet allowed him to die (v. 4), because love could see far ahead and knew that the death would result in greater blessing to all. He loved Martha in an entirely different way, as is seen by the conversation (vs. 17–27). A strong and robust woman, with more strength than pathos, the conversation was characteristic of her nature, as understood by Christ. No pathos was used, because none was necessary. The supreme thought was that of instruction, and in this the wisdom of Christ's love was shown. His love for Mary was again quite different, because she was overwhelmed with her sorrow, and it may be that this fact is the explanation of the truly remarkable and mysterious words used of Christ's feelings at this time, which were, for some reason or another, those of anger rather than grief. Even his weeping seems to have been associated with the thought of Mary's overwhelming sorrow at the merely physical loss, great though it was (v. 33). Christ's love saw further and would bring sure comfort.

Thus, Christ's love was different from all three. To Lazarus he was the mighty Lord. To Martha the eternal life. To Mary the Incarnate love. Thus he dealt with each according to temperament, in his kind, wise, sufficient, discriminating and satisfying affection.

4. *Perpetual Love.* Here and elsewhere it is clearly seen that Christ loves for all time. His love is at once persevering (John 13:1), powerful (Rom. 8:37), and permanent (Rom. 8:35).

5. *Practical Love.* In this and in all other passages there is an entire absence of rhapsody, nothing sensuous or glowing, but everything calm and balanced. Christ's love was ardent, and yet reverent, because it was a matter of action rather than emotion.

It is for us to receive that love (1 John 4:16), to abide in it as our home (John 15:10), to respond to it by letting God love us (John 13:35; 1 John 4:19), and then to reflect it by a life of definite, practical, unselfish, self-sacrificing love (Eph. 5:2).

CHAPTER 11:1–44

In order to look at the entire story of the raising of Lazarus, it is necessary to consider the earlier verses again. After the Feast of Dedication (10:22), in December, A. D. 29, Christ retired to Perea on the East of Jordan (10:40), where he rested in seclusion, in view of Jewish hostility, until the message came from Mary and Martha (11:3). It was this that brought him again to Bethany of Judæa.

1. *The Great Problem. Jesus and Suffering* (vs. 1–16).

 (1) The announcement (vs. 1–3).
 (2) The attitude (vs. 4–6).
 (3) The appeal (vs. 7–10).
 (4) The action (vs. 11–16).

2. *The Great Revelation. Jesus and Martha* (vs. 17–27).
 (1) The sorrow (vs. 19–21).
 (2) The conviction (vs. 22, 24).
 (3) The revelation (vs. 23–26).
 (4) The confession (v. 27).

3. *The Great Sorrow. Jesus and Mary* (vs. 28–37).
 (1) The grief (vs. 28–32).
 (2) The concern (vs. 33, 34).
 (3) The sympathy (vs. 35, 36).
 (4) The surprise (v. 37).

4. *The Great Victory. Jesus and Death* (vs. 38–44).
 (1) The command (v. 39).
 (2) The reminder (v. 40).
 (3) The prayer (vs. 41, 42).
 (4) The power (vs. 43, 44).

Resurrection is one of the great words of the New Testament, and is associated with some of the most important facts of the Gospel. Its prominence in the early Church teaching (Acts 2:24; 3:15; 4:10; 5:31; 10:40; 22:8; 23:6, etc.) suggests that in some respects it is the very center of Christianity. There are four resurrections in the New Testament, and each calls for special attention.

1. *The Resurrection of Christ.* This was according to his own promise (John 2:19), and it is this that makes Easter Day so vital and important. Resurrection was the proof of Christ's personal character (Acts 2:24), the testimony to his power (Rom. 1:4) and the assurance of his authority (Acts 17:31). It is also the means of our resurrection (Rom. 4:25), the pledge of it (1 Cor. 15) and the pattern of it (Rom. 6). It was the Divine assurance of the acceptance of the Atonement and is the foundation of the Christian Church, which could not be organized round a dead body.

2. *The Resurrection of Believers.* This will take place at Christ's coming (1 Cor. 15:51; 1 Thess. 4:16) and is the culminating point of redemption, which includes spirit, soul, and body in its Divine completeness. Only those who are Christ's will be raised at this time.

3. *The Resurrection of the Wicked.* The fact is clear from Christ's own teaching (John 5:28, 29) and it will take place at the close of the thousand years (Rev. 20:11–14). This will be for judgment, not for redemption (Rev. 20:4–6).

4. *The Spiritual Resurrection of the Sinner.* This means the spiritual resurrection of those who are dead in sins and therefore raised in Christ to newness of life (John 11:25, 26; Eph. 2:1; John 5:25). Their death in sins refers to moral inability, not moral insensibility, and they shall hear the voice of the Son of God and live. The words of verses 25 and 27, though very familiar through constant use at funerals, include very much more than the thought of physical death, for they apply to life as a whole. Resurrection from the death of sin is a necessity, and this is followed by spiritual life. The two are always experienced in this order and must be kept united. The

provision for this spiritual resurrection and life is in the personal presence of Christ: "I am the Resurrection and the Life." But in order that it may be realized in personal experience, it is essential that we believe it and receive him. "Believest thou this?" Faith in the personal, present, and powerful Christ is thus the secret of life here and of life hereafter. This resurrection is clearly stated to be at the present time, "and now is" (John 5:25), and is therefore a present possibility and opportunity. By faith we are united to Christ and obtain eternal life here and now (John 17:3).

So that Christ's resurrection is past; there are two resurrections still future; and one may be, and should be, in the present. The supreme question is whether we, in our deadness of sin, are ready and willing to receive into our souls the life of Christ, or, rather, Christ as our life. Faith guarantees our present resurrection. Hope anticipates our future, while love will enable us to declare the good tidings of Christ's resurrection and victory and thereby to win others to him.

CHAPTER 11:45–57

After the raising of Lazarus, Christ did no more signs publicly before the world. But a twofold attitude is seen, hatred on the one side and love on the other, showing the impression made by our Lord. The effect of the miracle was so great that the Jewish authorities felt compelled to take action. The results were immediate. Observe the wonderful picture of human life in relation to Christ.

1. *The people.*
   (1) Some believed (v. 45).
   (2) Others were untouched (v. 46).
2. *The Council.*
   Hostility combined with irresoluteness (vs. 47, 48).
3. *The High Priest.*

Cynicism (vs. 49–53). He suggested that it would be better to kill Jesus than to lose their position. Caiaphas was a creature of Rome and a Sadducee, and his counsel was good policy, because the continued popularity of Jesus would clash with their interests. Yet the cynicism was transformed into prophecy. The words had a deeper meaning than Caiaphas saw, something he had never contemplated. And so the Lord walked no more openly (v. 54), but went into a secluded place with his disciples. Meanwhile, as the Passover approached, the people were seeking for him in Jerusalem, and the rulers had given instructions for his apprehension (vs. 55–57).

The entire episode is a striking and sad example of human callousness.

1. *The fact of callousness.* Mark its extent, even to using religion. (1) In the people (vs. 46, 56). Christ evidently made no real impression on them. (2) In the Priest (v. 50). Self was his sole thought. (3) In the Council (vs. 53, 57). They had no regard for fairness, to say nothing of the deeper questions of righteousness and their duty to God.

2. *The results of callousness.* This decision of the Council really hastened the end of the Jewish nation, and the ultimate ruin of A. D. 70 was largely brought about by this attitude to Christ. But we can see God's love as well as his justice, for the deeper meaning of the words of Caiaphas show how different God's thoughts and ways are from those of man. What the hard-hearted high priest had unwittingly said was an exact statement of what Christ was about to do "for" the nation and for all the scattered ones of the family of God (vs. 51, 52). Calvary was the true explanation.

CHAPTER 12:1–11

The effect of the raising of Lazarus was immediate and important, and on account of the definite hostility of the Jewish leaders, Jesus withdrew again to the wilderness country northeast of Jerusalem (11:54–57). But the nearness of the Passover led people to seek for him, and the rulers took steps to make sure of his apprehension if he appeared. It is thus seen that the restoration of Lazarus was the immediate occasion of the Sadducean chief priests determining to take action, because their beliefs were thereby threatened. Then six days before the Passover, Jesus left Ephraim for Jerusalem (Mark 10:32), taking the road through Perea by Jericho, where he called Zaccheus (Luke 19:1–11) and healed Bartimæus. The anointing by Mary is recorded also by Matthew and Mark, but is given in another connection for a special purpose. But John gives the event in its order.

1. Simon entertaining (Mark 14:3; Luke 7:36–43).
2. Lazarus feasting (John 12:2; Isa. 55:1, 2).
3. Martha serving (v. 2; Luke 10:38–42).
4. Mary anointing (v. 3; Luke 7:44–50).
5. Judas murmuring (vs. 4–6; John 6:70, 71).
6. Jesus vindicating (vs. 7, 8; John 12:44–48).
7. People seeing (v. 9; John 6:25–27).
8. Priests plotting (vs. 10, 11; Matt. 16:1–4).

The story is particularly remarkable for its record of different attitudes to Christ, and as these are pondered we may discover what our own is and also what it should be.

1. *Contact with Christ.* As we think of Simon, Lazarus, Martha and Mary, we cannot help seeing four kinds of personal, spiritual contact with Christ. (1) Simon stands for *salvation*, as symbolized by his deliverance from leprosy. (2) Lazarus reminds us of *life*, as we think of his recent resurrection. (3) Martha, in her service and activity, suggests *work* for the Master. (4) Mary, in her attitude and action, reveals what we understand by *consecration*. These four together give us the true meaning of the Christian life.

2. *Criticism of Christ.* This is seen in Judas, whose remarks were altogether unworthy of the occasion and did not express his real sentiment. It is often the case that men criticize from wrong motives, revealing one thing and concealing another.

3. *Curiosity about Christ.* This is seen in the common people (v. 9). Love to Christ was apparently not the supreme motive, but only curiosity to see Lazarus after his resurrection. Curiosity of this sort usually does not lead to anything deeper, but often tends to become dissipated in mere interest that never

reaches spiritual blessing. And yet we know that, in some cases at least, the sight of Lazarus led to the acceptance of Christ (v. 11).

4. *Craftiness against Christ.* This is seen in the chief priests (vs. 10, 11), who were determined to take action not only against Christ himself as already decided (11:53), but also against Lazarus, through whom many of the Jews were actually believing on Jesus. This shows the awful extent to which sin will go when it is determined at all costs to oppose what it knows to be right.

As we consider these attitudes we notice the significant words: "There they made him a supper." Have we one for him? Have we a feast to give to him? If we have only a crust, no gifts, no position, little influence, few opportunities, he will as gladly accept and make use of that little as if we had great position, power, influence, and capacity. But, before we can make him a supper, we must accept the one he has made for us, the supper of salvation (Luke 14), to which he invites us and says, "Come, for all things are now ready."

CHAPTER 12:12–26

This public entry into Jerusalem took place the day after the Feast at Bethany (vs. 1–12). This would correspond either with our Sunday or more probably Monday. John's account of the entry is shorter than those of the other three, but its distinctive feature is the strong feeling aroused for Jesus by the restoration of Lazarus (vs. 10, 11, 12, 17). This action of a public entry is significantly in contrast with almost all Christ's previous action. Before this he had counseled privacy, but now he courted and even excited publicity at the Passover, when crowds were present. This change was doubtless due to his intention to offer himself deliberately to the nation at the close of his ministry as he had at the opening (John 2:12–25). It was a clear claim to Messiahship, and therefore would constitute a cause for accusing him and putting him to death. The episode of the Greeks (vs. 20–26) probably occurred on the Tuesday (Mark).

1. *The King's Preparation* (Matt. 21:1–3; Zech. 9:9).
    (1) Deliberate.
    (2) Purposeful.
2. *The King's Coming* (John 12:12, 14, 15; Micah 5:2).
    (1) The Claim.
    (2) The Character.
3. *The King's Welcome* (John 12:13; Luke 8:40).
    (1) Symbolized.
    (2) Typified.
4. *The King's Followers* (v. 16; Matt. 15:16).
    (1) Puzzled.
    (2) Enlightened.
5. *The King's Enemies* (v. 19; John 11:47, 48).
    (1) Dismayed.
    (2) Humiliated.
6. *The King's Recognition* (vs. 20–22; Mark 1:37).
    (1) The Desire.

(2) The Approach.
7. *The King's Response* (vs. 23–26; Isa. 53:12).
    (1) Self-sacrifice for the Master.
    (2) Self-sacrifice for the servant.

1. *The Revelation.* There was a fivefold manifestation of himself at this time. (1) As the Seer. We notice this in the way in which he knew beforehand where the ass was to be found which was to carry him into the city (Matt. 21:1–3). (2) As the Owner. Not only did he know where the ass was, but he claimed it for his own use by calling himself "the Lord," and he knew that the owners would recognize his authority (Mark 11:3–6). (3) As the King. Twice in John's account is this thought of Kingship suggested, and the whole bearing of Christ at the entry indicates the same truth. (4) As the Prophet. The people recognized Jesus as the Prophet, the Divine Spokesman (Exod. 7:1), when he entered into Jerusalem (see John 6:14). (5) As the Saviour. This is seen in the reference to his death, when the Greeks came (v. 24). This revelation of Christ is equally applicable today, and he desires to be all this to each one of us. He is at once our Prophet, Priest, and King. As Prophet he reveals; as Priest he redeems; as King he rules.

2. *The Response.* The question at once arises how we are to meet this revelation and what answer we are to give to him as he makes his claim to our lives. As we look over this lesson, we see a fivefold response to the fivefold revelation. (1) Trust. This is clear not only here, but throughout John's Gospel. Christ's disciples exercised faith in him. (2) Obedience. Arising out of the trust comes the conduct of the life which carries out what he commands. (3) Consecration. This is suggested by the solemn statement that, if we would really live, we must be prepared to surrender our life wholly to Christ (vs. 24, 25). (4) Service. The trust, obedience and consecration are to be expressed in actual work or service for our Master, for all true following will necessarily be proved in this way (v. 26). (5) Praise. The joy of the multitude as Christ entered Jerusalem should be the true and constant attitude of the believer, as he praises God for all that Christ is and does (v. 13). Then, when this fivefold response is assured, we know that where Christ is his servant will be, and there will come honor from the Father (v. 26).

CHAPTER 12:27–36

Although the death of our Lord brings such blessing to us, it was no light thing for Christ himself, as this episode plainly shows.

1. *The Saviour's Trouble* (v. 27). There was no shrinking. He did not pray to be saved from that dread hour, because he had come forth for the very purpose of dying. He prayed that God might be glorified thereby.

2. *The Father's Voice* (v. 28). The Divine assurance of glory.

3. *The People's Opinion* (v. 29). Two illustrations of a lack of discernment.

4. *The Lord's Explanation* (vs. 30–33). (1) Divine Testimony (v. 30); (2) The world's judgment (v. 31); (3) The Devil's overthrow (v. 31); (4) The Redeemer's power (vs. 32, 33). Note the "any man" of verse 26, and the "all men" of verse 32. "All" is used in the New Testament to apply either to all "without exception" or, as here, all "without distinction," that is, Jews and Gentiles.

The reference to Christ's death is very important, and may be illustrated by three quotations. Denney has said that it is Calvary, not Bethlehem, which is the "center of gravity" in the New Testament. "Christ could have been Teacher, Example and even Revealer of God without the Cross" (H. W. Clark, "The Christ from Without and Within," p. 193). Forsyth remarked that the Incarnation has no religious value but as the background of the Atonement. "The real Incarnation lay not in Christ being made flesh, but in his being made sin."

5. *The Multitude's Enquiry* (v. 34). Inability to see that the Messiah must die.

6. *The Master's Answer* (vs. 35, 36). Apparently the last words of our Lord's public ministry.

These closing messages are at once a farewell to the world and an earnest appeal. Under the metaphor of light, there is a fulness of spiritual meaning.

1. *A Great Opportunity:* "The light with you."
2. *A Clear Duty:* "Believe"; "walk."
3. *A Solemn Warning:* "While."
4. *A Terrible Possibility:* "Lest."
5. *A Glorious Prospect:* "Children of light."

CHAPTER 12:37–50

These verses give a recapitulation of the history recorded in chapters 1 to 12. The last words of the public ministry of Christ have been spoken, and all that remained was to indicate the general results.

1. *The Evangelist's Summary.* Testimony of Christ's works.
    (1) Failure (v. 37). Unbelief in spite of so much.
    (2) Anticipation (vs. 38–41). All foreseen and foretold.
    (3) Explanation (vs. 42, 43). The fear of man.

Note the three special testimonies: John the Baptist, chapters 1 to 3; Christ himself, chapters 4 to 10; the Father, chapters 11 and 12. Mark the references to Christ as the Light: 1:4; 8:12; 9:5, and the two classes of people in relation to it.

2. *The Lord's Summary.* Testimony of Christ's words.
    (1) The claim (vs. 44, 45).
    (2) The purpose (vs. 45, 46).
    (3) The alternative (vs. 47–50).

We see here, what has been evident all through these twelve chapters, the two attitudes of Rejection and Reception.

1. *Rejection.*
    (1) Not believing (v. 37).
    (2) Not confessing (v. 42).
    (3) Not keeping (v. 47).
    (4) Not receiving (v. 48).
2. *Reception.*
    (1) Believing (v. 44).
    (2) Beholding (v. 45).
    (3) Abiding (v. 48).

THE SIXTH CHAPTER AND THE LORD'S SUPPER

The instituting of the Lord's Supper is not recorded in John's Gospel. Yet it is sometimes urged that the sixth chapter is John's equivalent for that sacred feast. It is in that chapter that our Lord calls himself the true bread out of heaven, the bread of God, the bread of life, the living bread, and declares, "The bread which I will give is my flesh, for the life of the world." Then he goes on to make these tremendous statements: "Except ye eat the flesh of the Son of man, and drink his blood, ye have not life in yourselves. He that eateth my flesh and drinketh my blood hath eternal life; and I will raise him up at the last day. For my flesh is meat indeed, and my blood is drink indeed. He that eateth my flesh and drinketh my blood abideth in me, and I in him."

Let us, then, make a careful inquiry as to the relation of this wonderful chapter to the Supper of the Lord. For this purpose it is essential to look at what is here found from the standpoint of those who first heard what our Lord said.

1. The discourses recorded in this chapter took place at least a year before the Lord's Supper was instituted, and on this account the hearers could not possibly know, or even imagine, what Christ was going to do twelve months afterwards.

2. The messages found here are addressed to Jews, outsiders, men who for the most part were in deadly opposition to Christ. The Lord's Supper was instituted in the presence of disciples alone and apparently was intended only for them.

3. The succession of present tenses in this chapter indicate spiritual blessings that were intended to be immediate to those who heard the words.

4. Eating and drinking are said to give life ("except ye eat the flesh of the Son of man and drink his blood, ye have not life in yourselves," verse 53), and this is stated in so universal and unqualified a way that it does not admit of any exception.

5. Our Lord said that those who ate his flesh and drank his blood would be absolutely certain of resurrection at the last day (v. 54). This again is wholly unqualified and stated in most sweeping terms.

6. Christ gives his own explanation of "eating" and "drinking," for he says that they are represented by "come" and "believe" (v. 35), while another equivalent phrase is "behold" and "believe" (v. 40).

7. The Jews, who were forbidden by their law to eat flesh with blood in it, were naturally horrified at these very plain sayings, and yet Christ did not mitigate their intensity when he found how the Jews felt, though he clearly indicated that the mere physical eating of flesh would be of no spiritual profit,

that the words were "spirit and life" (v. 63) and were intended to be understood as spiritual and yet with all the intense reality that came from so clear a use of definite physical actions like eating and drinking.

What conclusions, then, can we draw from these facts?

1. Our Lord refers to the spiritual reality symbolized in the Lord's Supper, namely, himself as the object and food of our faith. As a thoughtful writer has said, Christ witnesses in John six to the same truths which were associated with the Passover Feast and the Lord's Supper; the blood of sacrifice and the food of strength. Godet helpfully says that the sixth of John and the Lord's Supper refer to one and the same fact; in the chapter by metaphor, and in the ordinance by emblems. Thus the true idea is that of union with Christ, expressed in words in John six and in action in the Lord's Supper. Our life comes from his death and through the faith which feeds on that death. It is only the acceptance of Christ that avails for life; not even his holy character, or his beautiful teaching, or his perfect example will suffice, but it is only his death (his "flesh and blood") that must be fed on. For his death accomplished what all else could not possibly do.

It is also significant that our Lord commands us here to eat blood, though under the law blood was forbidden. That was probably intended as a confession that the life, as symbolized by the blood, had reverted to God and was no longer in man's power, so that to eat "blood under the law would have been an attempt to regain life in our own strength—an attempt by man to reach that which he had forfeited." But now, under the glorious Gospel, everything is changed, and blood may and must be eaten. For the life, which had reverted to God, God himself has given to make atonement, and now we are commanded to take life from him. This is the Gospel of Divine grace, for under the old covenant the ordinance forbade the eating of blood, showing that there was no recovery of forfeited life by any human effort. But under the new covenant that ordinance is canceled, and now to believe in Christ is to receive life as the gift of God through his Son. It is this spiritual reality, not any outward rite that embodies it, which is to be understood in this chapter.

2. This view is in harmony with the best commentators in almost every age. Thus John Ferus, an eminent Roman Catholic preacher and writer in the sixteenth century, says that "To eat his body spiritually is from thy heart to believe … he speaketh not here (John 6:53) of the Sacrament, for not all are condemned who take the sacrament. He speaketh of spiritual eating, that is of faith in Christ." To the same effect is the modern and great authority of Bishop Westcott, who points out that the discourses spring naturally out of the position in which the Lord stood at that time. "That which is outward is made the figure of the inward." Then Westcott says: "It follows that what is spoken of eating (vs. 51, 53, 54, 56, 57, 58)—the succession of phrases is most remarkable—cannot refer primarily to the Holy Communion; nor again can it be simply prophetic of that sacrament. The teaching has a full and consistent meaning in connection with the actual circumstances, and it treats essentially of spiritual realities with which any external act as such can be co-extensive. The well-known words of Augustine, 'Believe and thou hast eaten,' give the sum of the thoughts in luminous and pregnant sentence." Westcott adds that any attempt to transfer the words to the sacrament is not only to involve the history in utter confusion, but to introduce insuperable difficulties into the interpretation of the discourses which can only be removed by arbitrary qualifications at various points.

3. All this shows the importance of distinguishing between the primary meaning and any secondary use made of it. The sixth chapter of John really refers to the atonement; and the Lord's Supper is only one out of several ways of appropriating by faith the efficacy of our Lord's sacrifice. Besides, it is clear that in this chapter Christ refers solely to spiritual eating, while in the Lord's Supper everything he said had reference to bodily acts.

4. We must, therefore, take the greatest possible care not to urge the Lord's Supper from this chapter, but to insist in every way in our power that men participate by faith in the sacrifice of Christ, without which it is impossible for them to have eternal life now or a blessed resurrection hereafter.

VIII

OUTLINE STUDIES (2)

CHAPTER 13:1–17

The record of Christ's public ministry closes with chapter 12, and with chapter 13 the second division of the Gospel opens. In the first five chapters (13–17) we have the record of the last conversations of our Lord with his disciples, in which he revealed himself more fully to them and elicited their deepening faith (16:30). In chapter 13 he shows his love in action, and then, after the departure of Judas, he manifested his love in words (chapters 14–17). This occurred on the eve of his death, and the various events between the visit of the Greeks on the Tuesday (12:20) will be gathered from the other Gospels.

1. *The Supreme Knowledge* (vs. 1–3; Matt. 11:25–27).
    (1) The time (v. 1).
    (2) The feeling (v. 1).
    (3) The authority (v. 3).
    (4) The origin (v. 3).
    (5) The destination (v. 3).
2. *The Lowly Action* (vs. 4–11; Luke 12:35–38).
    (1) The service (vs. 4, 5).
    (2) The expostulation (v. 6).
    (3) The assurance (v. 7).
    (4) The rebuke (v. 8).
    (5) The revelation (vs. 9–11).
3. *The Definite Example* (vs. 12–17; 1 Pet. 2:21–25).
    (1) The enquiry (v. 12).
    (2) The reminder (vs. 13, 14).
    (3) The purpose (v. 15).

(4) The illustration (v. 16).

(5) The proof (v. 17).

Let us see some of the features of true Christian service.

1. *Based on Knowledge.* We see this in verses 1, 3, 17. Notwithstanding the greatness of the Master, he was ready to stoop to serve. The motto of the Prince of Wales is "I serve," and there is nothing nobler or more royal than service.

2. *Actuated by Love.* We see the intensity of Christ's love for "his own," as he was about to leave them unprotected in the world (v. 1). Love is best proved by service.

3. *Marked by Humility.* James and John had just been striving for the highest places in the kingdom of God, and they were taught by Christ wherein true ambition and real greatness consisted (Matt. 20:20–28). So also when the Greeks came the lesson was taught of self-sacrificing, lowly service (John 12:24–26). In the same way Paul speaks of the restoration of the brother who had been overtaken in a fault, "in a spirit of meekness" (Gal. 6:1). There is scarcely anything so true to the Christlike spirit as humility. The Greek word for "humble" shows what the pagans thought of this grace, for they used for it a term expressive of the groveling of a reptile. Christ takes humility and glorifies it, so that now it is the highest, noblest, and truest expression of life. Augustine was once asked, "What is the first step to heaven?" and replied, "Humility." "And the second step?" "Humility." "And the third step?" "Humility." It has been quaintly said that when we attempt to wash the saints' feet, we must be particularly careful along three lines: (1) The water must not be too hot; (2) our own hands must be clean; (3) we must be willing for them to wash our feet.

4. *Expressed in Helpfulness.* There must be doing, not merely feeling (v. 17). Christianity is more than creed and includes deed, and our efforts on behalf of others will be shown in every circle of life.

Chapter 13:18–38

The conversation of Christ on this solemn and momentous occasion could not ignore the presence of Judas, and we now see how this fact affected our Lord's words and attitude. A last attempt was made to win the traitor.

1. *The Unutterable Shame* (vs. 18–30).
   (1) Warning (vs. 18–20). The clear reminder.
   (2) Sorrow (v. 21). "Troubled," perhaps because of the effect on the disciples. The word expresses great agitation.
   (3) Enquiry (vs. 22–26). The request and the sign.
   (4) Appeal (vs. 27–30). No effect. The failure of infinite Love.

2. *The Unrestrained Fellowship* (vs. 31–38).
   (1) The Son and the Father (vs. 31, 32). The "now" of relief and conscious triumph. "Glory" was the dominant thought, and this "glory" was to come through the Cross.

   (2) The Master and the followers (vs. 33–35). They are "little children," and their life was to be marked by reciprocal love.
   (3) The impulsiveness and the reminder (vs. 36–38). Peter's characteristic enquiry and rashness, with Christ's revelation of the denial.

As we review this scene, the following points stand out with definiteness:

1. *The Solemn Possibility.* The very presence of Jesus had no power to change Judas, or even to check his downward course. All the circumstances were conducive to holiness, and yet with everything to help him he went in the opposite direction. He was lost even after all this. Evil has the awful power to defeat good.

2. *The Splendid Prospect.* "Glory" (vs. 31, 32). See also chapter 17:5. This was the supreme end of all Christ came to be and do.

3. *The Surprising Power.* This was threefold: Christ on the Cross; the Father in the Son, and the Son in the Father (vs. 31, 32).

4. *The Simple Principle.* Love. This was the bond of discipleship (vs. 34, 35).

5. *The Searching Proof.* "Know" (v. 35). Love is the real test.

Chapter 14:1–27

This section (chapters 14–17) has been called "The Holy of Holies" because it contains some of the deepest and most spiritual of our Lord's teaching. It has been described in general thus: Chapter 14, Consolation, an exhortation to Faith; chapter 15, Instruction, an appeal to Love; chapter 16, Prediction, an incentive to Hope; chapter 17, Intercession, an anticipation of Glory.

The keynote of chapter 14 is seen in the repetition of the phrase, "Let not your heart be troubled" (vs. 1, 27), and there seem to be seven reasons given why they were not to be troubled. Notice how each reason follows naturally from the one before.

1. *The Future Home* (vs. 1–3).
   (1) The Place; (2) the preparation; (3) the reception.
2. *The Perfect Way* (vs. 4–11).
   (1) The destination; (2) the way; (3) the condition.
3. *The Guaranteed Life* (vs. 12–14).
   (1) Continued work; (2) increased work; (3) powerful work.
4. *The Coming Helper* (vs. 15–17).
   (1) Substituting; (2) abiding; (3) indwelling.
5. *The Present Lord* (vs. 18–24).
   (1) Returning; (2) manifesting; (3) abiding.
6. *The Divine Teacher* (vs. 25, 26).
   (1) Illuminating; (2) reminding; (3) revealing.

7. *The Abiding Peace* (v. 27).
    (1) The legacy; (2) the gift; (3) the comparison.

The chapter may be summed up as follows:
1. *The Substance of the Consolation.*

 (1) Christ is still living and working.
 (2) He reaches his people by the Holy Spirit.
 (3) They reach him through faith and prayer.
 (4) They manifest him by love and obedience.
 (5) And so they are assured of present grace and future glory.

2. *The Call to Consolation.* "Let not your heart be troubled"; this is our part; we are not to *allow* ourselves to be troubled. But how is this possible?

3. *The Secret of Consolation.* "Believe." If God is real, there will be no heartbreak, but if we forget him all will go wrong. "Only believe," and there will be peace (v. 27; see also Isa. 26:3).

CHAPTER 15:1–27

After the discourses in chapters 13 and 14, it is probable that this one was spoken on the way to Gethsemane (14:31). It was intended to encourage the disciples by the assurance of their Master's presence, notwithstanding his approaching departure (14:18, 20, 27). This thought of Christ's presence is illustrated by the allegory of the vine, which would be familiar to the disciples as Jews. Three trees in the New Testament illustrate Scripture teaching; the olive (Rom. 11:17–24), showing the relation to Abraham the root, and the Gentiles the branches; the fig (Mark 11:13), illustrating religious profession; and the vine, expressive of fruitfulness (Psa. 80:8–11; Isa. 5:1–7; Jer. 2:21).

It seems important to get a general view of the whole chapter in order to see the fulness of Christ's teaching.

1. *Our Relation to Christ*—Union and Fruitfulness (vs. 1–11; Col. 1:20–22).
    (1) The Vine (vs. 1, 5).
    (2) The Husbandman (vs. 1, 2).
    (3) The Branches (vs. 4, 5, 6).
    (4) The Fruit (vs. 2, 4, 7, 8, 16).
2. *Our Relation to Christians*—Love and Fellowship (vs. 12–17; Eph. 4:25–32).
    (1) Love commanded (vs. 12, 17).
    (2) Love illustrated (v. 13).
    (3) Love proved (vs. 14, 15).
    (4) Love inspired (v. 16).
3. *Our Relation to the World*—Hostility and Faithfulness (vs. 18–27; John 17:6–18).
    (1) Expectation (v. 18).
    (2) Inspiration (vs. 18, 19).
    (3) Explanation (vs. 20–25).
    (4) Vindication (vs. 26, 27).

Christ said four things: Come unto Me (as Saviour); Learn of Me (as Teacher); Follow Me (as Master); Abide in Me (as Life). So that to "abide" is the highest requirement of Christ, and therefore applies to his faithful disciples.

1. *Its Nature.* It includes union and communion. We are "in Christ" for life; including pardon, righteousness, rest, liberty, and purity. Christ is "in us" for life; including protection, power, testimony, and victory. From this union will come reciprocal communion. We are to abide in him and to allow him to abide in us. This does not mean seeking a new position, but remaining in one already attained, recognizing and living in the strength and satisfaction of our existing union.

2. *Its Secret.* It comes first from faith (John 6:56), and then it is maintained in fellowship; obeying (1 John 3:24); confessing (1 John 4:15); and loving (1 John 4:16).

3. *Its Power.* We find this in prayer (15:7) and in service (v. 5).

And thus we realize our position by the Holy Spirit (John 14:20; 1 John 4:13), and maintain it by the Word of God (1 John 2:14, 24, 28; 2 John 2, 9; John 5:38; 8:31). It is a real encouragement to remember that we abide even when we are unconscious of Christ. For just as when our body is asleep, natural food is in us and is being assimilated for our health and strength, so we rest upon the blessed fact of Christ's presence in us, whether conscious of it or not; and whenever there is an opportunity we realize it consciously and respond to it in surrender, trust, and obedience.

CHAPTER 15:26 to 16:14

Another part of Christ's farewell discourses on the eve of his crucifixion (13 to 16). In chapter 15 he indicates a threefold relation of his disciples: to himself (vs. 1–11), consisting of union and communion; to one another (vs. 12–17), consisting of love and service; to the world (vs. 18–27), consisting of enmity and persecution. In connection with the last point a promise is made of the Holy Spirit to vindicate Christ through his disciples after his departure. So that we have in marked contrast the enmity of the world and the power of the Spirit, the latter being the topic of the present lesson.

1. *The New Helper* (15:26; Acts 1:4, 5).
    (1) The Divine Advocate.
    (2) The Personal Witness.
2. *The Clear Destination* (15:26; 16:7; Gal. 4:4–6).
    (1) To believers.
    (2) To believers only.
3. *The Divine Source* (15:26; Acts 2:30–33).
    (1) Sent from the Father.
    (2) Sent by Christ.
4. *The Specific Character* (15:26; 1 Cor. 2:7–13).
    (1) The Spirit of Truth.
    (2) The world's hate.
5. *The Strong Assurance* (15:27; 16:8–11; Acts 5:29–32).
    (1) Testimony about Christ.

(2) Vindication of Christ.
6. *The Important Work* (16:7–11; Rom. 8:9–11).
   (1) Indwelling.
   (2) Outworking.
7. *The Great Results* (16:12–15; Eph. 3:14–19).
   (1) Guidance.
   (2) Utterance.
   (3) Revelation.
   (4) Glorification.

This section provides an opportunity of concentrating attention on the doctrine of the Holy Spirit as recorded in John's Gospel. There is a striking progress of doctrine which ought to find its counterpart in personal experience.

1. *The Incoming Spirit* (3:5). This is the commencement of the Christian life by the new birth of the Spirit.

2. *The Indwelling Spirit* (4:14). Under the same figure of water, the abiding presence of the Spirit in the believer is indicated.

3. *The Outflowing Spirit* (7:38, 39). Water again is used to suggest the Holy Spirit. The believer first drinks and then becomes a channel of blessing, rivers of living water flowing from him to others.

4. *The Witnessing Spirit* (14–16). This is the specific work of the believer through the Holy Spirit in testifying to the character of Christ, and thereby convicting the world of sin, righteousness, and judgment. This is vital, because no one has heard of a conversion to God apart from some human agency, direct or indirect, personal or written. Our Lord said that the world could not receive the Holy Spirit (14:17), and no one has ever been led to Christ in any part of the world without some testimony to the Lord by life or word. This shows the solemnity and importance of our being filled with the Spirit, in order that the world may know of Christ, because it is only in proportion to our reception and experience of the Spirit that our witness to Christ will be effectual. The consciousness that if the world is not convicted through Christians it will not be convicted at all is one of the most solemn incentives to holiness, earnestness, and world-wide evangelization.

Thus we see that the Holy Spirit is a unique and distinctive feature of Christianity. Other religions have their founders, their sacred books, their philosophy and their ethics, but only Christianity has the Holy Spirit, and as the "Spirit of Christ," the "Spirit of truth," and the "Spirit of grace" he unites the Jesus of history with the Christ of experience. It is this that makes the essential message of Christianity not "Back to Christ," but "Up to Christ."

CHAPTER 16:16–33

The farewell counsels have been given, concerning the Lord's own departure and the coming of the Holy Spirit. Now we notice the immediate results of what had been said.

1. *The Perplexity* (vs. 16–19).
   (1) The Statement (v. 16). Two different "little whiles," referring to Christ's absence prior to Gethsemane, through death and to his return afterwards.
   (2) The Difficulty (vs. 17, 18). The discussion showed their bewilderment and inability to grasp the meaning.
   (3) The Sympathy (v. 19). They had talked the matter over among themselves without consulting or asking him, and now he shows that he understands them. It is a comfort to know that he knows, and also is aware that we are "desirous of asking him."

2. *The Promise* (vs. 20–22).
   (1) The sorrow (v. 20). Because of their forthcoming loss.
   (2) The joy (vs. 20, 21). A glorious transformation.
   (3) The explanation (v. 22). The presence of their Master. Their grief would end but not their joy.

3. *The Power* (vs. 23, 24).
   (1) Fuller light (v. 23). No questions (Greek) would need to be asked "in that day" of the Holy Spirit.
   (2) Richer prayer (vs. 23, 24). Asking "in thy name" meant a new and deeper lesson on prayer, because it was asking in union and communion with the revealed character ("name") of Christ, and this was an advance on everything they had done hitherto.
   (3) Deeper joy (v. 24). Fuller enjoyment because of fuller knowledge.

4. *The Prospect* (vs. 25–33).
   (1) Knowledge (vs. 25, 26).
   (2) Love (v. 27).
   (3) Revelation (v. 28).
   (4) Confession (vs. 29, 30).
   (5) Warning (vs. 31, 32).
   (6) Assurance (v. 33).

These closing words (v. 33) may almost be said to sum up the great truths of these four chapters.

1. *The Believer's twofold Life.*
   "In" Christ. "In the world."
2. *The Believer's twofold Experience.*
   In Christ, "peace." In the world, "tribulation."
3. *The Believer's twofold Secret.*
   The Fact, "I have overcome." The Feeling, "Be of good cheer."

CHAPTER 17

The most deeply taught believer pauses before this wonderful combination of simplicity and depth. Coming just prior to Gethsemane, it affords a most remarkable index to our

Lord's attitude of mind and heart as he faced the great event of the Cross. Two ideas are seen to run through the entire prayer; the personal outpouring of the Son to his Father, and the intercession of the priest for his people. The lofty calm and victorious joyfulness in the very presence of death have often been noted. There seems to be a threefold petition.

1. *For Himself* (vs. 1–5).
   (1) The Petition (vs. 1, 5) "Glorify." The willing acceptance of the Cross (v. 1, "the hour"). The conscious position of the Son (vs. 1, 5).
   (2) The Purpose (v. 1, "that"). God, not himself, the only thought, "The self-abnegation of the Son."
   (3) The Plea (vs. 2–4). The completed work.
2. *For His Apostles* (vs. 6–19).
   (1) The Petition (vs. 11, 15, "keep").
   (2) The Purpose, unity (v. 11); joy (v. 13).
   (3) The Plea, relationship to God (vs. 6–8, 10); and to the world (v. 11).
3. *For His Church* (vs. 20–25).
   (1) The Petition, "one," in character (v. 21); in abode (v. 24). *Like* Christ and *with* Christ.
   (2) The Purpose, in the present (vs. 21, 23), and future (v. 24).
   (3) The Plea, Christ's union with the Father (vs. 21–23), and his authority from the Father (vs. 24, 25).

And so the prayer is for the Glorification of Christ; the Preservation of the Apostles and the Unification of Believers.

Perhaps the entire prayer may be regarded as summarized in verse 18, where there are four references: "Thou"; "Me"; "the world"; "them." What Christ was to the Father then, we are to be to Christ now. "As … so."

1. *Our Lord:*
   (1) Revealed God (vs. 3, 6).
   (2) Conveyed God's Will (vs. 3, 6, 8 ff.).
   (3) Fulfilled God's Work (vs. 4, 12 ff.).
2. *Ourselves:*
   (1) Similar Authority (v. 18).
   (2) Similar Object (vs. 20, 21).
   (3) Similar Consecration (v. 19).

CHAPTER 18:1–18

The change from chapters 13 to 17 to chapter 18 is like going from warmth to cold, from light to darkness. After the farewell discourses (13–16) and our Lord's prayer (17) for himself (vs. 1–5); for his disciples (vs. 9–19); and for his Church (vs. 20–26), came the incidents of the betrayal and trial. As in 13 to 17, we have the development of faith, so in 18 and 19 we have the culmination of unbelief. The picture of Christ in these chapters is one of calm dignity and real majesty, showing that the last and supreme test was met victoriously, and that his closing hours were in entire consistency with his beautiful life and ministry.

Although John was one of the three taken apart from the rest in Gethsemane, and was thus fitted to write of that solemn time, he omits all reference to it, not only because what others had written was sufficient, but also and chiefly because the special line of his Gospel was the presentation of the Lord as the object of faith rather than as the suffering Son of Man. Thus we learn from John alone how the Lord's personal presence at first overawed the company who came to apprehend him.

1. *The Betrayer* (vs. 1–3; Psa. 41:5–8).
   (1) The journey.
   (2) The place.
   (3) The meeting.
2. *The Lord* (vs. 4–9; Heb. 12:1–11).
   (1) Calm majesty.
   (2) Willing surrender.
   (3) Self-forgetful care.
3. *The Disciple* (vs. 10–18; Isa. 50:4–7).
   (1) Impetuous devotion.
   (2) Loving admonition.
   (3) Great danger.

1. *The Wickedness of the Fallen Heart.* This is exemplified in Judas. Notwithstanding the wonderful privileges of three years, he was ready to betray his Master. He does not seem to have been a monster of evil, but simply of selfishness, which led to insincerity as a disciple, falseness as an apostle, theft as a man, and at length perdition as a traitor. The cause of the crime may have been originally avarice, which perhaps developed into revenge. The sin had been growing for some time (6:64). All this shows the solemn truth that intellectual capacity is not everything and that formal adhesion to Jesus Christ, even to the extent of being numbered among his apostles, is not enough. We also see the awful possibilities of evil when the heart is separated from Divine grace. John Bradford, one of the martyrs in England at the time of the Reformation, once saw a criminal on his way to execution, and said, "There, but for the grace of God, goes John Bradford."

2. *The Love of the Divine Heart.* This is pictured in Jesus Christ. We see his willingness towards his Father (v. 11); we notice his effort, even at the last, to win Judas (Luke 22:48); we mark his thought for the safety of his disciples (v. 8); we note his attitude towards his captors; and we observe his reminder to Peter (v. 11). As we think of all this, we remember and rejoice in the love that gave Jesus to suffer and die.

3. *The Imperfection of the Renewed Heart.* This is illustrated in Peter. We naturally feel interested in the blessedness of enthusiasm (v. 10), and yet we must not fail to see the danger of mere impulse (v. 11). Looking at the whole story of the denial (vs. 15–18, 25–27), we notice beyond all else the weakness which comes from loss of faith (Luke 22:32).

As we contemplate these three aspects of character, we cannot help realizing the solemn lesson, based upon two contrasted texts: "Apart from me ye can do nothing" (John 15:5); "I can do all things in him that strengthened me" (Phil. 4:13).

CHAPTER 18:19–40

The particular purpose of each Gospel is not easily seen in the selections made of the events of the Passion. It has been suggested that John's account is marked by the proofs of consistency with what precedes, that the tests in all severity were triumphantly passed. "The end matches the beginning. The last scenes fit perfectly upon those that have gone before" (H. W. Clark, "The Christ from Without and Within," p. 217).

1. *Christ and the High Priest* (vs. 19–24).
   (1) The Enquiry (v. 19).
   (2) The Answer (v. 20).
   (3) The First Challenge (v. 21).
   (4) The Injustice (v. 22).
   (5) The Second Challenge (v. 23).
   (6) The Result (v. 24).
2. *Christ and Peter* (vs. 25–27).
   (1) The Peril (v. 25). There was danger in the company he kept. John was in no such peril because he was known to be a disciple (v. 15), and was fearless.
   (2) The Denial (v. 25).
   (3) The Persistence (vs. 26, 27). "Having once committed himself, the two other denials followed as a matter of course. Yet the third denial is more guilty than the first. Many persons are conscious that they have sometimes acted under what seems an infatuation. They do not plead this in excuse for the wrong they have done. They are quite aware that what has come out of them must have been in them, and that their acts, unaccountable as they seem, have definite roots in their character. Peter's first denial was the result of surprise and infatuation. But an hour seems to have elapsed between the first and the third. He had time to think, time to remember his Lord's warning, time to leave the place if he could do no better…. The remarkable feature of this sin of Peter's is that at first sight it seems so alien to his character. It was a lie; and he was unusually straightforward. It was a heartless and cruel lie, and he was a man full of emotion and affection. It was a cowardly lie, even more cowardly than common lies, and yet he was exceptionally bold." (Dods, "The Gospel of St. John").

(4) The Reminder (v. 27).
3. *Christ and Pilate* (vs. 28–40).
   (1) The Charge. Pilate and the Jews (vs. 28–32); insincerity (v. 28); evasion (v. 30); cruelty (v. 31).
   (2) The Conversation. Pilate and the Lord (vs. 33–38a); the first question and answer (vs. 33, 34); the second (vs. 35, 36); the third (v. 37); the fourth question (v. 38).
   (3) The Compromise. Pilate and the Jews again (vs. 38b–40); the confession (v. 38); the cowardice (v. 39); the compromise (v. 40). Pilate evidently saw that nothing short of Christ's death would satisfy the Jews, and yet, although he had declared the Lord innocent, he treated him as an evildoer.

In this episode we see four attitudes which tell their own story:

1. *The Jews.* Callousness. The degradation caused by wrongdoing.
2. *Simon Peter.* Carelessness. The duty of watchfulness—"resist beginnings."
3. *Pilate.* Cynicism. The danger of weakness.
4. *Christ Jesus.* Courage. The dignity of righteousness (see 1 Tim. 6:13).

CHAPTER 19:1–16

The Fourth Gospel gives a remarkable fulness of narrative in connection with the trial before Pilate, and very little of the proceeding before Annas and Caiaphas. The latter were powerless to accomplish what they wanted. Prudence also suggested that all possible consideration should be given to the Roman Governor, who is said to have been jealous of his own power.

The story is a wonderful study in human nature. It records a conflict between right and wrong and of the oscillations in Pilate's mind as he desired to do the former and yet succumbed to the latter. It is an illustration of what Simeon had long ago said, that in contact with Christ the thoughts of the heart would be revealed (Luke 2:35).

The passage seems to be naturally divided into four sections; verses 1–3; 4–8; 9–11; 12–16; and the recurrence of the word "therefore" is impressive.

1. The Injustice (v. 1). Although bent on saving Christ, Pilate compromises with the right.
2. The Admission (v. 4). We pity Pilate even though we deplore and denounce his weakness.
3. The Offer (v. 6). Pilate must have known that this proposal was impossible.
4. The Fear (v. 8). A new element enters into the situation and Pilate is awed.
5. The Anger (v. 10). The man's dignity was hurt and might asserts itself against right.

6. The Effort (v. 12). An evident impression was made and so Pilate tries again to release him.

7. The Mockery (v. 15). The fluctuations of the man's nature are sadly significant.

8. The Decision (v. 16). The evil prevailed, and to save his own position Pilate yielded to clamor and injustice.

The record shows the struggle between vacillation and malignity:

1. *The Wickedness of Weakness*. Pilate missed a splendid chance.
   (1) Vacillation. Loss through weakness of will.
   (2) Compromise shows the peril of expediency.
   (3) Love of position. Danger of proud selfishness.
   (4) One action determining the whole life.
2. *The Weakness of Wickedness*. The Jews made an awful choice.
   (1) Decision is necessary, but they made it on the wrong side.
   (2) Decision is important, and reveals what we really are.
   (3) Decision is fraught with immense possibilities for good, or, as here, for evil.
   (4) Wickedness is futile, if only men would see it.

CHAPTER 19:16–42

After the ecclesiastical trial (twofold) came the trial before Pilate, which is marked in John by seven aspects, the circumstances "shifting alternately from the outside to the inside of the palace" (Whitelaw). Note also the solemn repetition of "therefore" all through the scenes. The result of Pilate's weakness in yielding was the delivering of Christ to be crucified. John's account is in some respects supplementary to, and in others independent of, the other Gospels, and seems to proceed along two lines, illustrating at once man's sin and God's purpose. The picture of Christ is also strikingly majestic, and his life is seen to culminate in the sacrifice.

1. *Under the Cross* (v. 17; 2 Cor. 5:14–21).
   (1) The Weary Pilgrim.
   (2) The Varied Attendants.
   (3) The Sorrowful Way.
2. *On the Cross* (v. 18; Rom. 5:1–11).
   (1) Prepared.
   (2) Upraised.
   (3) Placed.
3. *Over the Cross* (vs. 19–22; Heb. 9:19–28).
   (1) Position.
   (2) Language.
   (3) Providence.
4. *At the Cross* (vs. 23, 24; Luke 23:32–43).
   (1) Inhumanity.
   (2) Insensibility.
   (3) Instrumentality.
5. *Near the Cross* (v. 25; Heb. 12:1–11).
   (1) The Names.
   (2) The Position.
   (3) The Privilege.
6. *From the Cross* (vs. 26–30; Psa. 22:1–8).
   (1) The Church's Head.
   (2) The Human Sufferer.
   (3) The Father's Servant.
7. *After the Cross* (vs. 31–42; Isa. 53:1–12).
   (1) The Sights Beheld.
   (2) The Reflections Made.
   (3) The Actions Performed.

1. *The Cross is Central*. We see this by a simple comparison of the passages in our Bible dealing with the events of the last week of Christ's earthly life, as contrasted with the lack of detail for the remainder of the three years. John gives nearly one-half of his Gospel to these few days. This alone shows the centrality of the crucifixion, but we may also look at it along these four lines: (1) Predicted in the Old Testament; (2) Foreseen by Christ; (3) Emphasized by Christ; (4) Proclaimed by the Apostles.

2. *The Need is Absolute*. Why should the death of Jesus Christ be made so prominent? The answer is "to save sinners" (1 Tim. 1:15). And we may think of the various aspects of sin, as they are dealt with by the Cross: (1) Sin as guilt; (2) Sin as bondage; (3) Sin as defilement; (4) Sin as enmity.

3. *The Value is Vital*. In every way the Cross is of supreme importance: (1) Against Rationalism, which tends to emphasize the life and forget the death, though Christ came into the world to die; (2) against Formalism, which tends to accept intellectually the fact without spiritually and personally trusting the One who died; (3) against Romanism, which, with all its emphasis on Calvary, tends to think only of the act and fact of the death of Christ rather than of the Christ who died and now lives forever (Rev. 1:18); (4) against Skepticism, which tends to deny the power of the Cross for human needs.

CHAPTER 20:1–29

This chapter is the second part of the section 18–20, and as 18 and 19 record the climax of unbelief, so 20 tells of the culmination of belief, and gives the crowning joy of the entire section beginning with chapter 13. After the burial of Christ (19:38–42) and the Jewish precautions for security (Matt. 27:62–66) came the resurrection. John's account, while in some respects supplementary, is yet selected on the principle of 20:31, to elicit faith. The various appearances are not easily arranged in order, but this constitutes a proof of their accuracy in the absence of any effort to fit them in. Certain features are common to all four Gospels, including the omission of any description of the actual resurrection and the limitation of the appearances to believers (Acts 10:40, 41). If only we knew all the circumstances, the arrangement of the appearances would be doubtless quite simple.

1. *The Fact of the Resurrection* (vs. 1–10; Luke 24:25–35).
   (1) First impression—Sorrow (vs. 1–3).

    (2) Second impression—Perplexity (vs. 4–7).

    (3) Third impression—Trust (vs. 8–10).

2. *The Power of the Resurrection* (vs. 11–29; Luke 24:25–35).

    (1) First impression—Sorrow dispelled (vs. 11–18).

    (2) Second impression—Perplexity removed (vs. 19–23).

    (3) Third impression—Trust assured (vs. 24–29).

1. *The Necessity of the Resurrection.* Why "must" Jesus rise? (1) As a proof of the truth of his own words, for he had foretold it so clearly that his veracity was at stake, unless he rose; (2) as a testimony to the truth of the Old Testament, which had foretold it (Psalms 2 and 16; Isa. 53); (3) as a vindication of Christ's character, for a perfect life could not close in a cruel and shameful death; (4) as a vindication of God, for all through his life Christ had appealed to God, and, as Paul said afterwards, it would have proved God to be false if Christ had not been raised (1 Cor. 15:15).

2. *The Proofs of the Resurrection.* How may we be assured that Christ did rise? (1) The fact of the empty grave and the disappearance of the body. It must have been removed by human or superhuman power. (2) The remarkable transformation in the disciples from gloom to gladness, from despair to hope, and from sorrow to joy. Only three days and this change took place. (3) The existence of the primitive Church, for every one believes that the Church of Christ came into existence as a result of accepting the resurrection of the Master. (4) The influence of Christ upon men and communities from the time of Paul onwards. Only One who is living and Divine could affect men's lives in this way.

3. *The Value of the Resurrection.* For what reasons do we make it prominent? (1) Evidential (Rom. 1:4); (2) Evangelistic (Rom. 4:25; 1 Pet. 1:21); (3) Spiritual (Rom. 6:4); (4) Eschatological (1 Cor. 15:20, 21).

CHAPTER 21

After 20:31 the addition of this chapter seems strange at first sight, but further consideration shows that it is an integral and essential part of the Gospel, and as an Epilogue answers to the Prologue and so completes the record of the glory of Christ as the Revealer of God and the Redeemer of man. There are three main parts: The Pre-Incarnate Life of Christ, 1:1–18; the Incarnate Life, 1:19 to 20:29; the Post-Incarnate Life, 21:1–22. This chapter forms a sort of parable of Christ's present life above in relation to his people. The keynote is Service.

1. *Christ and the Christian Community* (vs. 1–14). The seven men mentioned here may be regarded as representative of the Church as a whole (seven the perfect number).

(1) The Church's Failure (vs. 1–3). They had been told to wait for their Master, but apparently they had become somewhat impatient and had returned to their old work. But they were unsuccessful, as all work must be that is done apart from Christ and his command.

(2) The Church's Lesson (vs. 4–6). But the Master was watching and his enquiry was followed by his commission and promise of blessing.

(3) The Church's Faithfulness (vs. 6b–8). Obedience was honored by immediate results, and the disciples recognized who was the source of this success.

(4) The Church's Reward (vs. 9–14). On reaching the shore they found that their Master had prepared them a meal, and bringing their fish to land, they were welcomed and fed. See in this a symbol and foretaste of the future (Luke 12:37; Rev. 19:9).

2. *Christ and the Christian Individual* (vs. 15–22).

The disciple is now commissioned for his work.

(1) The Disciple Tested. The one requirement for service is "love."

(2) The Disciple Commissioned. Three classes of believers are committed to his charge (see Greek and Westcott).

(3) The Disciple Taught (vs. 18, 19). His past is described, his future disclosed, and his present declared.

(4) The Disciple Rebuked (vs. 20–22). Curiosity is met by the assertion of Christ's sovereignty, by the reminder of varied service (working or waiting), and by the call to implicit obedience.

Looking on this chapter as typifying or symbolizing the entire period of the history of the Church, we may note how it is marked by service which is to be crowned with glory.

1. *Power for Service.* The Lord's Will. Without Christ the disciples were unsuccessful, but in his presence and at his word came blessing.

2. *Peace in Service.* The Lord's Word. Amid weariness, depression, and discouragement, his instruction and promise, "ye shall find," brings rest and contentment.

3. *Prospect after Service.* The Lord's Welcome. When the night is past, we shall see him on the shore and shall hear his welcome.

III

THE THREE EPISTLES

I

THE FIRST EPISTLE

INTRODUCTION

While the Christian life is prominent in every part of the New Testament Epistles, there are perhaps four where detailed instruction is specially noteworthy. In Romans we are told how we come out of the house of bondage. In Ephesians we see how we enter into the banqueting house. In Hebrews we note how we are led up to the throne. In 1 John we perceive how we approach the Divine Presence. Perhaps these four Epistles are also capable of being considered in two separate pairs, Romans and Ephesians forming one, and Hebrews and 1 John the other. It is also possible to connect Ephesians and 1 John as giving respectively the corporate and individual aspects of the Christian life.

Westcott suggests that John's First Epistle was the last book of the New Testament in chronological order of writing, and if this is so, there is a striking contrast between the opening words of the Bible and the closing statement. "In the beginning, God" (Gen. 1:1); "Little children, keep yourselves from idols" (1 John 5:21).

There seems no doubt that this Epistle is to be closely associated with the Fourth Gospel. The purpose of the Gospel is that by believing men might have life (John 20:31). The purpose of the Epistle is that those who have life may know that they possess it (1 John 5:13). Thus the latter is written as the complement of the former, and is intended for believers.

The dominant note of the Epistle is that of fellowship with God, and in him fellowship with one another (1:3). The Christian life may thus be summed up in seven words. It commences with Sonship; it is marked by Discipleship; it goes on to Stewardship; it expresses itself in Worship; it responds to Lordship; it is realized in Fellowship; and it culminates in Heirship.

I. THE PURPOSE

It is difficult but not impossible to discover why the Epistle was written. There are three statements which at once describe the purpose of the Apostle in writing, and at the same time the object of the Christian life.

1. *Fulness of Joy.*—"These things we write that your joy may be full" (1:4). Joy is God's purpose for man, for sorrow originally came from sin. Our Lord's first miracle was wrought at a wedding; his second in a home; thus we have, first, Christ and life's gladness; and only afterwards Christ and life's sadness. Joy is necessary for all true life (Neh. 8:10). Even in education the influence of joy is undoubted, for young children are particularly responsive to a bright, buoyant, joyous teacher. Sorrow, while often made the instrument of discipline, may and sometimes does harden, but joy never hardens. We should, therefore, settle it in our minds that God intends us to have the fulness of joy.

2. *Freedom from Sinning.*—"These things write I unto you, that ye sin not" (2:1). This is another part of the Apostle's purpose. He wished and intended his readers not to sin. There is, as we shall see, a clear distinction between sin and sins, between root and fruit, principle and practise, and the Apostle, while carefully teaching that the principle of sin remains (1:8), is equally careful to teach that this root need not and should not produce fruit (2:1). But if there should be any sinning God has made provision in the Divine righteous Advocate (2:1, 2).

3. *Spiritual Assurance.*—"These things have I written unto you, that ye may know that ye have eternal life" (5:13). Assurance means the consciousness of our position and relation to God. Faith possesses; assurance knows that it possesses. This idea associated with the word "know" is in some respects the most prominent feature of the Epistle. "We know" is found fifteen times; "ye know" six times; "we have known" once; "ye have known" three times; "he that knoweth" once. The English word "know" stands for two separate and distinct Greek words, and when careful attention is paid to their usage the result is much spiritual illumination. One implies intuitive knowledge, that which comes from fact, the evidence of our senses, that which is independent of ourselves (1:2; 2:29. See John 1:33; 13:7; 8:55). The other indicates experimental knowledge, that which comes to us as the result of our personal testing and experience. Sometimes the present tense is used indicating the process of acquiring this experimental knowledge (2:3, 29; 3:24; 4:2; 5:2). At other times the perfect tense is found, indicating that which has been permanently acquired by experience (2:3; 3:16).

These three passages, when put together, give the purpose both of the Epistle and of the Christian life. There is a close and intimate connection between them. We are to have the fulness of joy because of our freedom from sinning, and this, in turn, comes from spiritual assurance. Thus, assurance is the secret of freedom from sinning and of the fulness of joy.

II. THE PLAN

The Epistle is confessedly difficult to analyze. Professor Law, in his fine book, "The Tests of Life," thinks the key to the interpretation is that the Epistle gives certain *tests* by which the question of the Christian life may be settled. These are three—doing righteousness, loving one another, and believing in Christ. They are dealt with respectively in 1:5; 2:28; 2:29; 4:6; 4:7; 5:21. Dr. Law suggests that there are three cycles of thought running through the Epistle. First, we have the idea of walking in the light as tested in three ways—by Righteousness, Love, Belief. Then comes the thought of Sonship, tested in the same threefold way. And last of all come the inter-relations of Righteousness, Love, and Belief. This suggestive statement of Law is not very much unlike those of Hort, Haering, and Brooke, all of which will be found discussed fully in the last-named author's volume on 1 John, in the "International Critical Commentary." It is suggested that the sections as given above by Dr. Law reveal an ethical and a doctrinal test in each case. Thus, from 1:5 to 2:27 we have the ethical test of walking in the light (1:5 to 2:17) and the doctrinal test of faith in Christ (2:18–27). In the second section we have the ethical test of doing righteousness (2:28 to 3:24) and the doctrinal test of the Spirit confessing Christ (4:1–6). In the third section we have both the ethical and the doctrinal tests combined. Love is shown to be based on life (4:7–21), and life is proved to be based on faith (5:1–12).

The essential feature of the Epistle is that it affords three proofs or tests of assurance, and in this respect it is particularly valuable as guarding against that purely emotional variableness that tends to seek the ground of assurance within. The old introspective verse was sadly at fault in the light of this Epistle:

'Tis a point I long to know.
Often causes anxious thought,
Do I love the Lord or no?
Am I his or am I not?

There is nothing like a thorough study of this Epistle to enable the soul to answer this question with confidence and certainty without once looking within or giving itself "anxious thought." The following is a brief outline suitable for this purpose:

1. *Introduction* (1:1–4).
2. *First proof of the Christian life.* Obedience (1:5 to 2:6).
(1) Negative. Sin must be out.
(2) Positive. Righteousness must be in (2:3, 5).
3. *Second proof of the Christian life.* Love. (2:7 to 3:24.)
(1) Negative. Love not the world.
(2) Positive. Love the brethren (3:14, 19).
4. *Third Proof of the Christian life.* The Holy Spirit. (3:24 to 5:12.)
(1) Negative. The false spirit.
(2) Positive. The true Spirit (3:24; 4:13).
5. *Conclusion.* (5:13–21).

It will be seen that these three proofs refer in turn to God, to others, to ourselves, and this is the proper order of the spiritual life. Obedience is the first result of faith. Love comes next. Then the possession of the Holy Spirit is the third, last, and in some respects the deepest.

But now comes the important question as to how we may know that we have the Spirit. Is this reference to the Spirit abiding in us—after all, leading us back to that introspection which tends to make us think of our assurance as coming from within?

The Epistle guards against this in a very significant way, as we shall see when considering the next point.

III. THE PROOF

The entire Epistle is concerned with the Person and Work of Jesus Christ, and in particular there are six occurrences of the phrase "as he," or "even as he," expressive of Christ as the definite standard of our life. It will be seen, too, that Christ is the basis with which the Epistle opens (1:1, 4), and he is the theme of its closing message (5:20).

And so the supreme inquiry is: What is Christ to me? For only in proportion as he is real and true, can we be sure of possessing the Holy Spirit. We must, therefore, pay special attention to these six occurrences of "as he," and we notice that they are found in three pairs:

1. *Christ our standard in relation to God.*
(1) 1:7, the inward life.
(2) 2:6, the outward life.
2. *Christ our standard in relation to self.*
(1) 2:3, the inward life.

(2) 3:7, the outward life.
3. *Christ our standard in relation to others.*
(1) 3:23, the inward life.
(2) 4:17, the outward life.

Thus, the purpose, plan, and proof of the Epistle constitute at the same time the purpose, plan and proof of the Christian life.

CHAPTER 1:4

Like the Prologue to the Gospel, this Epistle lays a good foundation in the Person and Work of our Divine Lord as a preparation for and vindication of the teaching that is to follow. It forms an interesting comparison to look at the opening verses of the Gospel and those of this Epistle, and when they are put together their oneness, and yet difference, are easily seen.

The Gospel may be considered thus:
(1) Verses 1–5: Christ's relation to God.
(2) Verses 6–13: Christ's historical manifestation.
(3) Verses 14–18: The personal appropriation of Christ.

The opening verses of the Epistle suggest the following ideas:
(1) Verse 1: Christ's relation to eternity and time.
(2) Verse 2: Christ's historical manifestation.
(3) Verse 3: The personal results.

Thus, although the two portions are quite evidently parallel, they are not strictly identical, but only complementary. As we have already seen, the Gospel is concerned with faith, while the Epistle emphasizes assurance. These complementary ideas are implied even in these opening verses.

But now it is important to look at the introduction, and consider its strong, satisfying basis for Christian life.

I. THE SUBSTANCE OF THE GOSPEL

This may be said to be summed up in the Person and Work of our Lord himself.

1. *He is Divine and Eternal.* As in the opening of the Gospel, and in the first words of Genesis, Christ was "from the beginning."

2. *He is human and historical.* He who was from the beginning, was manifested on the earth, and was seen in human form.

3. *He is life-giving and unique.* He is first described as "the Word of Life," revealing and bestowing life. Then comes the aspect which specially refers to our experience in "eternal life," involving fellowship with God (John 17:3).

Thus the Gospel starts with the Person of Christ at once Divine and human (Mark 1:1; John 1:1; Rom. 1:4). In the Gospel he is simply described as "the Word," while in the Epistle we have the additional thought of "the Word of life." And so we may say that "Christianity is Christ," and the foundation of our religion is the absolute fact of our Lord's Divine Person and Work. Christianity is the only religion that is based on reality, and is also inextricably bound up with the Person of the Founder.

II. THE GUARANTEE OF THE GOSPEL

We have now to consider how this Divine Christ, who is the substance of the Gospel, is brought near to us, and the Apostle clearly indicates this along three lines:

1. *Apostolic experience.* This is the first stage (v. 1). Christ had been heard and seen, contemplated and handled. There had been immediate perception, and deliberate attainment. They had heard and seen him in his earthly life, and they had beheld and handled him after his resurrection.

2. *Apostolic testimony.* Then the Apostles began to witness to the truth of what they had experienced (v. 2). The life was not only manifested and seen, but they themselves were bearing witness to its fact and preciousness.

3. *Apostolic communication.* The testimony took the form of actual communication of the truth to others (v. 3), and with all the force and authority of an Apostle of Christ these blessed truths concerning the Master were announced and actually told.

III. THE PURPOSE OF THE GOSPEL

Why was all this done? The answer is a very simple, but all-embracing, one: it was for fellowship both Divine and human (v. 3).

1. *What is fellowship?* It means here and always in the New Testament "partnership" in something common to a large number, the joy of possession of and participation in that which belongs to all. Thus fellowship or partnership is in some respects the highest possibility of the Christian life at the present time, for there is nothing beyond it in our privileges. The beautiful picture of fellowship which we see in Eden before the Fall is thus restored, and more than restored, in Christ. Every part of his redemptive work had in view this purpose of bringing man back from enmity to friendship, from loneliness to fellowship, with all that this implied, between him and God.

2. *With whom is the fellowship?* It is first with the Father, and includes access to his presence, the assurance of his favor, the consciousness of his love, the enjoyment of his truth, and the possession of his love. Then it also is "with his Son," and means the sympathy, knowledge, grace, and satisfaction that come from him who is at once Divine, "His Son," and human, "Jesus Christ."

3. *With whom is this fellowship from the human standpoint?* The Apostle, in writing "with us," means with himself and all fellow-Christians, and fellowship or partnership means joint participation in all that grace brings, in life, in light, in love, in labor, and in hope. This thought of fellowship between Christians is very important at all stages of the Christian life, but perhaps especially at its commencement. Converts need to be told that their life is not a solitary one, but is to be lived in union and communion with others who belong to Christ. There is, perhaps, nothing to compare with Christian fellowship to keep a soul from backsliding, and to incite it to progress in holiness.

IV. THE RESULT OF THE GOSPEL

The Apostle shows that the practical outcome in personal life of what he had written is "that your joy may be full." Joy is thus the supreme result of the Gospel.

1. *The fact of joy.* Joy is threefold: the joy of retrospect, of aspect, of prospect; the joy which is concerned with the past, the present, the future; the joy of faith, of love, of hope; the joy of appropriation, appreciation, anticipation.

2. *The source of joy.* This comes, and can only come, from fellowship (v. 3). Fellowship is the source and guarantee of joyousness. This at once shows the distinction between happiness and joy. Happiness depends upon what "happens," upon circumstances, while joy is independent of circumstances, and is based upon the reality of Divine relationship, which is untouched by any surroundings. The Apostle Paul was not always happy, because we are told of his sorrows, and yet he could say, "sorrowful, yet alway rejoicing" (2 Cor. 6:10), because his joy was not in circumstances, but in the Lord (Phil. 4:4).

3. *The nature of joy.* As this joy comes from fellowship, we must consider a little more in detail the elements of the joy it brings—(1) fellowship with the Father is associated with his pardon, his teaching, his love, his provision, his protection, his power, and so gives joy; (2) fellowship with his Son arises from the consciousness of his Divine Person, his redemptive work, his resurrection life, his blessed Spirit, and his glorious coming, and these produce joy; (3) fellowship with believers provides joy, because of the unity, encouragement, truth, and grace which are experienced in oneness with those who belong to Christ.

4. *The extent of joy.* The Apostle is not only concerned that his readers may have joy, but far more than this—the fulness of joy; not only the fact, but the fulness, "good measure, pressed down and running over." This phrase, "your joy may be full," is found six times in John's writings, four times in the Gospel, and twice in the Epistle. When they are all put together they show beyond all question the secrets of the fulness of joy. Thus, this full measure of joy is associated with consecration (John 3:29), with obedience (John 15:10), with prayer (John 16:24), with protection (John 17:13), with fellowship (1 John 1:3, 4), with brother-love (2 John 12).

Thus we see something of the splendid and solid foundation laid for us in Christ. "How firm a foundation, ye saints of the Lord." And if only we follow the Divine order, we shall see in turn that Christianity involves Fact, Faith, Feeling, Fellowship, and Fulness.

CHAPTER 1:5–10

In 1:1–4, the introduction giving the scope of the Epistle, we have seen that the Divine purpose for the believer is fellowship with God, fellowship with man, and, in this fellowship, perfected joy. Then from 1:5 to 2:17 the Apostle proceeds to show that "walking in the light" is the first real proof or test of fellowship with God. The earliest part of this long section now calls for notice. In 1:5–10 we are told of God's nature and of our relation to it. The section really extends from 1:5 to 2:2, and deals especially with three views of life which are false. So that in limiting our present attention to 1:5–10, we must keep in mind the full extent of the treatment ending at 2:2.

I. The Revelation (v. 5)

First of all, the Apostle has to tell of God's nature and attitude as the basis of all that follows. Revelation naturally proceeds any responsibility.

1. *The fact of a message.*—"This is the message." This shows that what he says is a Divine revelation, not a human discovery; it is news.

2. *The source of the message.*—"From him." The meaning of this is pretty certainly the Lord Jesus Christ.

3. *The reception of the message.*—"Which we have heard." The tense in the Greek seems to imply that in some way the Apostle was still hearing from Christ.

4. *The declaration of the message.* "And announce unto you." It was something that must not, and could not, be kept to himself.

5. *The substance of the message.* "God is light, and in him is no darkness at all." "God is light"—that is, God in his own nature is the perfect idea of what we understand by light. It is interesting to notice the three things in John's writings about God: "God is Spirit" (John 4:24), "God is light" (1 John 1:5), "God is love" (1 John 4:8). It is also to be observed that he does not describe God as "a light," or "the light," or "the light of man," or "the light of the world," or "the true light." It seems to suggest God's own nature in itself (1 Tim. 6:16). Light in Scripture stands for at least four different, yet connected, ideas. Sometimes it means glory, expressive of the Divine majesty. Sometimes it means purity, emphasizing morality. Sometimes it means truth, referring to intelligence. Sometimes it means fellowship, suggesting communion. Professor Law, however, maintains that this thought of God as "light" does not refer to his essential being or nature, but to his revelation of himself; that as it is of the very nature of light to be and make visible, so God is not self-contained, but has revealed himself in Christ. Dr. Law suggests that the Gospel supports this view in the order in which it speaks of Christ as the Word, the life, and the light (John 1:1, 4, 5). But perhaps, after all, the two ideas are included as cause and effect, for assuredly it is owing to God's essential nature as light that he necessarily reveals himself as light to others.

II. The Responsibility

Because of God as light, certain effects follow in human life.

This revelation of God is thus intensely practical and theoretical. "Light is a social power" (Findlay). The practical outcome is seen in three parallel pairs of opposed positions: 1:6, 7; 1:8, 9; 1:10; 2:1. Each of these calls for careful study as we contemplate our solemn responsibility to the Divine revelation of God as light.

1. *The reality of sin is sometimes denied* (v. 6). It is possible to make the assertion that we have fellowship with God, fellowship being, as we have seen, the highest possibility of life. This assertion, however, is sometimes connected with action which shows that we are still walking in darkness (2:11). The "walk" indicates the outward life of conduct in its activity and progress. But if we should claim fellowship while our conduct is still evil, the Apostle says in the plainest possible terms that "we lie and do not the truth," thus affirming what is false and neglecting what is true. Light reveals; darkness conceals; and, therefore, fellowship with God is impossible unless we are in the light. Truth means beyond all else moral and spiritual reality, and it is absolutely impossible for us to have fellowship with God if we are walking in darkness, however much we may claim it. Moral conduct *does* matter, and has a definite bearing on spiritual communion.

2. *The reality of life should he experienced* (v. 7). Here is the contrast with the former verse. Our spiritual condition is described as "walking in the light as he is in the light." God, who is light, is thus seen to be in union with the believer and the believer with him, and the outward conduct of the soul is in harmony with the character of God. The result is fellowship one with another—that is, with Christians as based on fellowship with God. When we know God, we get to know man. And another result experienced side by side with fellowship is the full assurance of mercy and forgiveness through "the blood of Jesus, his Son." It is significant that our Lord is described by his human and Divine titles, showing that the Atoning Sacrifice is at once possible because he is man, and powerful because he is God. It would seem best to understand the word "cleanseth" as judicial, not experimental, and in this respect it harmonizes with the Greek of the Old Testament, where the same word is used for the effect of atonement. It may be questioned whether "blood" is ever associated with anything else than an atoning sacrifice, for, apparently, it is never found in the New Testament as expressive of that which is applied experimentally to the believer for the purpose of purification. This atoning Blood thus cleanses "from every kind of sin."

3. *The reality of sinfulness is also denied* (v. 8). Another contrast is set up. The assertion is now made that "we have no sin," probably meaning no sinfulness, no sinful condition from which the actual sinning proceeds. This seems to be the denial of the continuous and permanent presence of sin as a principle in one who has committed sins. The Apostle had already used the phrase "to have sin" in his earlier writing (John 15:22, 24; 19:11). This assertion, however, is a proof of self-deception, for not only, as in verse 6, do "we lie," but, still worse, we are self-persuaded in evil and no reality exists in us. To such a one sin is only a mere incident without effects.

4. *The reality of sins is admitted* (v. 9). Again another contrast is seen, and sins are to be confessed. The existence of sin in Christians is a simple fact, but there is no need for sins to interfere with fellowship if God's conditions are fulfilled. Confession, which he requires, will not only lighten the burden, but will keep open the spiritual life and preserve the soul in loving, healing sensitiveness. With this consciousness of full responsibility and this outpouring of the heart in confession will come the assurance that "he is faithful and righteous to forgive us and to cleanse us." God is faithful in being true to his own nature, and the thought of faithfulness clearly indicates an attitude to believers, since to the unconverted it is a question of mercy, not of faithfulness. He is not only faithful, but "righteous," which means true to his character in relation to us. The outcome is twofold, forgiveness and cleansing. God releases the guilt and remits the penalty, removes the debt and takes away the defilement. Here, again, as in verse 7, it would seem that we are in the region of the judicial rather than the experimental. It is not that our nature is purified and all sin removed, but that our position in the sight of God is dealt with through the perennial efficacy of the sacrifice of Christ.

5. *The reality of sinning is denied* (v. 10). Once again we have the words "if we say," and the assertion this time is the denial of the fact of committing sin. Even though it be possible to admit the truths suggested in verses 6–8, there may still be the refusal to allow that sinful deeds have been performed. But if we have actually committed sin and deny this, the outcome is inevitably worse than anything that has preceded, for "we make him a liar, and his word is not in us." Thus we disregard God's revelation, and ignore its reality and claim upon us.

At this point we pause for a while, though the section is continued, as we shall see, in the next two verses. But let us ponder afresh the solemn threefold "if we say" (vs. 6, 8, 10), and see that no such impossible assertions ever pass our lips or affect our lives.

CHAPTER 2:1, 2

We have already seen that the subject of 1:5 to 2:2 is God's nature as light (1:5), and our responsibility to him with special reference to three false views of life. By means of some striking contrasts, the Apostle has taught how the reality of sin is sometimes denied (1:6); that the reality of life is to be experienced (1:7); that the reality of sinfulness is denied by others (1:8); that the reality of sins should be admitted (1:9); and then, that the reality of sinning is also denied in certain quarters (1:10). But now the sixth principle of this series is emphasized, and *the reality of sinning is met*. The question at once arose in some minds that if sin was universal, as was implied in the earlier verses (1:6–10), it was, therefore, inevitable. He hastens to show that this is not the case, by pointing out the true aim of Christian living, and also the Divine provision, if needed, in case of sinning.

The soul has two dangers. Sometimes it is the peril of presumption, and then comes carelessness; at other times there is the equally serious danger of despair, when the heart loses hope, and sin is regarded as certain to be victorious. In 1:6–10 the danger of presumption is frankly dealt with. And now with equal clearness the peril of despair is faced and met by showing the definite remedy for sin and sinning.

I. THE APPEAL

With beautiful and tender affection the Apostle addresses his readers as "my little children," and tells them in the plainest possible terms that there is no need for them to sin: "These things write I unto you that ye may not sin." Nothing could be clearer, franker, or more definite than this teaching. Christian people are not expected to sin, for the plan of the Gospel is intended to meet such a contingency. As we have already seen, there is a real distinction between sin and sins, between root and fruit, between character and conduct, between principle and practise. The root exists and abides in us (1:8), but it need not, and should not, bear fruit. This is the message of the Apostle.

II. THE ASSURANCE

On the other hand, if any one should fall, God has made ample provision. There is no need to sin, but, assuming the actuality of it, its results can be met. The various elements of this Divine provision are carefully brought before our notice by the Apostle.

1. *This provision is a personal and conscious possession, "we have."* It is interesting to notice that the word "have" in John's writings always means personal possession, together with the consciousness of it, including the ideas of obtaining and retaining. So that this assurance is intended for constant use and encouragement.

2. *An Advocate.* The word is *Paracletos*, and is exactly the same as that rendered "Comforter," referring to the Holy Spirit, in the Fourth Gospel (John 14:20; 15:26; 16:14). No one English word seems to be sufficient to express all the ideas included in this word. It means some one called in to help, and it is interesting and most truly helpful to realize the reality of our Lord's advocacy and the relation of the one Advocate to the Other. Our Lord is our Advocate "with the Father," directed towards him, in his presence, thereby assuring us of constant access and appeal. The Holy Spirit is our Advocate within, and is the "other Comforter" sent to take the place of Christ, who has ascended. Thus, by the Holy Spirit, we are linked to the Lord Jesus, and by the Lord Jesus we are linked to the Father.

3. *This Advocate is "Jesus Christ the Righteous."* The two names "Jesus" and "Christ" indicate respectively the true manhood and the Divine position of the One who is engaged on our behalf. And when he is described as "the righteous," we are reminded of his personal character, that he has power to deal with sin, and will treat it impartially, righteously, without leaning to the one extreme of undue severity, or to the other of

undue softness. God has no favorites, and even his children when they sin are dealt with by "Jesus Christ the righteous."

4. "*He is the propitiation for our sins.*" This is the basis of his advocacy. Some one has said that our Advocate pleads our cause with propitiation as his brief. It is because he is our propitiation that he can be our Advocate. Thus the One whose character is righteous is shown to be competent by reason of what he has done. And it is interesting to notice that the Apostle does not say, "His death was the propitiation," but that "He himself is the propitiation." It is the person of Christ who gives efficacy to his work, which means, as Hooker says, "the infinite worth of the Son of God." It is important to bear in mind that propitiation (a word in the original found only in this Epistle) means the removal of God's righteous judgment against sin by means of sacrifice, and it is obvious that man, as represented by Christ, is the subject and God the object of propitiation. It would be impossible to think of God as the subject and man as the object, since it was not man, but God, who needed to be propitiated. And yet, of course, we must take every possible care to avoid anything like severance between the Father and the Son, because the Son is the Father's gift, so that, to use the bold paradox of a modern writer, the death of Christ was really God propitiating God. We recall the publican's prayer, "God be propitious to me a sinner" (Luke 18:13). It is interesting to notice that in the papyri recently found in Egypt the word "propitiation" in heathenism means the appeasing of an angry God, and when the purely pagan element concerning God is removed from this, we see at once the true idea of our Lord's propitiation. As Professor Law points out, it is impossible to interpret it as merely the supreme expedient of God's love intended to remove man's fear. This would "empty the word of all that it distinctively contains," and, as Dr. Law goes on to say, "one may or may not accept the teaching of the New Testament, but it is, at any rate, due to intellectual honesty to recognize what that teaching is." Thus, propitiation can mean but one thing, the expiation of the guilt of sin, which restores the sinner to God by removing every barrier to fellowship (Law, "The Tests of Life," pp. 160–163). And so we rejoice to think that the work of Christ has made fellowship possible. As Dr. Brooke truly says: "His advocacy is valid, because he can himself bear witness that the only condition on which fellowship between God and man can be restored has actually been fulfilled, *i. e.*, the removal of the sin by which the intercourse was interrupted" ("Internat. Crit. Com.").

5. *This propitiation is intended for the whole world.* This means that the sacrifice is really inexhaustible. And yet it is important to remember the distinction between redemption and salvation. All have been redeemed, but all will not be saved. Christ's sacrifice is *sufficient* for the whole world, but only *efficient* for those who are spiritually united to him.

Thus the Apostle emphasizes the way in which the reality of sinfulness and sinning can be met and has been met by the Divine, glorious provision of Christ. We are responsible for sin; sin is universal, and affects our fellowship with God. And yet there is abundant grace in Christ through his sacrifice on the cross and his presence above with the Father.

Before passing on to the next section of the Epistle it will be useful to compare and contrast some of the expressions and see the progress of the thought:

"If we say" (1:6); "If we walk" (1:7).

"If we say" (1:8); "If we confess" (1:9).

"If we say" (1:10); "If any man sin" (2:1).

Another line of development can be seen as follows:

"We lie" (1:6), *i. e.*, we are false to knowledge.

"We deceive ourselves" (1:8); *i. e.*, we persuade ourselves that falsehood is truth.

"We make him a liar" (1:10); *i. e.*, we set ourselves above God.

Again, we may observe the following sequences:

"We do not the truth" (1:6); *i. e.*, we do not carry principle into action.

"The truth is not in us" (1:8); *i. e.*, there is no recognition of the principle of truth.

"His Word is not in us" (1:10); *i. e.*, we do not possess the fundamental revelation.

Once more, it is deeply interesting to observe the following:

In 1:7, "*We have* fellowship."

In 1:9, "*He is faithful and just.*"

In 2:1, 2, there are both expressions, "We have" and "He is."

CHAPTER 2:3–6

It is generally recognized that a new section commences at this point, though it is, as usual, difficult to follow in order the Apostle's thoughts. But from 2:3–11 there seems to be a section in which there are two views or tests of walking in the light. The first test (vs. 3–6) is obedience, and the second test (vs. 7–11) is love. The former will now occupy our attention. It is interesting to notice the remarkable parallelisms between 1:6 to 2:2, and 2:3–11. In the former there are negative tests, and in the latter positive. Thus, God's light not only reveals sin (1:7 to 2:2), but also his requirement for us (2:3–11). The particular parallelisms are clearly observable in a comparison between "if we say" (1:6, 8, 10) and "He that saith" (2:4, 6, 9). A careful study will show the striking parallels and also complementary ideas between the following texts: 1:6 and 2:4; 1:7 and 2:5; 1:8 and 2:6; 1:10 and 2:9. In each of these there are three definite statements showing the parallels and the additions to the thoughts.

It should be said that a few writers connect verse 3 quite closely with the verses immediately preceding, and if this is so, these verses now to be considered will afford the proofs that we have duly used the provision given by God, involving three proofs of the efficacy of the Divine Advocacy and propitiation (2:1, 2). But the former connection seems in every way better and clearer.

I. THE PROGRESS

The Apostle shows that "walking in the light" has three results.

1. *Knowledge* (v. 3). "Hereby we know that we know him." The original is very striking, and may perhaps be rendered something like this: "Hereby we are continually getting to know by experience that we have experienced and still do experience him." The Apostle is, as usual, very practical, for knowledge is always far more than anything merely intellectual. It involves spiritual perception through personal experience. It is also noteworthy that he never uses the word "knowledge" as a substantive, though the verb to know is found in one way or another nearly two hundred times. So, also, he rarely uses the noun "faith," but almost always employs the verb. Perhaps this is a suggestion that doctrine with him was not intellectual knowledge only, but a real experience. We may perhaps include in his thought of knowledge the three ideas of intellectual observation, personal experience, and spiritual certainty.

2. *Union* (v. 5). "Hereby we know that we are in him." This is more than knowledge, for it involves the actual oneness of the soul with Christ. "In him" is both judicial and experimental, for we are "in him" for justification and also for sanctification. Perhaps both are included here, especially because the Epistle is so concerned with the definite practical life of the Christian.

3. *Abiding* (v. 6). "He abideth in him." This, again, is a further step in the progress of the soul. Not only do we know and are united to Christ, but we are to abide in him. This thought of abiding is very characteristic of John's Gospel (chap. 15), and may be said to include mind, heart, and will. It means that the soul is not only "in Christ," but also stays there, makes its permanent abode in union and communion with the Lord.

Thus, as we consider this threefold progress, we see at once the soul's perception, position, and persistence. Bengel, in his characteristic way, has described these three aspects as *cognitio, communio, constantia.*

II. THE PROOF

But it is now necessary to concentrate attention on the twofold statement "hereby we know." The similarity and yet the difference are very characteristic of the Apostle's mode of thought. Thus we have first, "Hereby we know that we know him" (v. 3). Then "Hereby we know that we are in him" (v. 5). What is the force of "hereby"? The answer is, Obedience, and it is put in a threefold way.

1. *Obedience in Practice* (v. 3). "If we keep his commandments." The thought is that of the watchful observance and faithful obedience of the separate commandments of God. The word "keep" is said to suggest "sympathetic obedience to the spirit of a command rather than the rigid carrying out of its letter" (Brooke). But perhaps even this contrast between spirit and letter is hardly accurate, since there is no incongruity between them, for the soul in carrying out the letter will necessarily obey the spirit. But in every respect the obedience here suggested is spiritual and not merely intellectual. (John 15:10; 17:12; Eph. 4:3). This practical obedience is at once contrasted with the statement of the man who claims to have an experience of Christ (v. 4), and yet is not heeding the duty of obedience. Such an one is an utter counterfeit, "whatever he may think" (Law), and his attitude is absolutely inexcusable, for he does not possess any reality. Thus plainly does the Apostle speak.

2. *Obedience in Principle* (v. 5). "Whoso keepeth his word." From the practice of separate commandments the Apostle leads up to the one expression of God's will in his Word as summing up everything. And the man who does this realizes completely what is meant by "the love of God." From knowledge he proceeds to love, because of "the emptiness of a loveless knowledge" (Findlay). The words "love of God" may include his love to us and ours to him, because our love is always inspired and prompted by his, and the perfection of love means its consummation in life: it has reached its goal in the one who is thus obedient to the Word of God. Findlay calls attention to the somewhat parallel idea of faith perfected by works (James 2:22), just as here we have love perfected by obedience.

3. *Obedience in Obligation* (v. 6). "Ought himself also to walk even as he walked." "Walking" as usual means the outward expression in conduct of the life we possess in Christ, and the idea implied by "ought" indicates our duty and moral obligation. The standard of our conduct is "even as he" (John 6:38; 17:4), and it is interesting to notice the use, and also the rarity of the use, of the example of Christ in the New Testament. Why should it be so infrequently found? Perhaps because Christ is so much more than our example. We need a model, but, more than this, we need a power to enable us to approximate towards and realize the standard that we have to imitate. This thought of the example of Christ is very frequently noted by writers, and in some very familiar words John Stuart Mill spoke of Christ as "the ideal representative and guide of humanity," and then he goes on to say, "nor even now would it be easy, even for an unbeliever, to find a better translation of the rule of virtue from the abstract into the concrete than to endeavor so to live that Christ would approve of our life." And yet we must never forget that Christ is first our Redeemer before he is or can be our Example. This is the virtue and value of that fine little book by Caroline Fry, "Christ our Example." It is one thing to have an ideal; it is another to realize it. Emerson once said, "Hitch your wagon to a star," but there above is the star, and here down below is my wagon. How are the two to be united? Only by means of the redemption in Christ Jesus, and when the Apostle says, "Walk even as he walked," it is because the soul is already assumed to be "in him" and resting upon the great Divine foundation already stated in the introduction (1:1–4).

Thus walking in the light is proved by means of obedience, and anything else is seen to be impossible. Righteousness is absolutely essential, and all our profession will count for nothing unless our life is in accordance therewith. There is nothing in its way more striking than the plainness with which the Apostle here stigmatizes the attitude and action of the mere pretender. First he is said "to lie and do not the truth" (1:6). Then that "the truth is not in him" (1:8). Then, still more, that he "makes God a liar" (1:10). And, not least of all, he is himself a liar (2:4).

N. B.—Before we pass away from this section it may be useful to look at the seven "ifs" in these two chapters, three of them bad, four of them good. (1:6, 8, 10; and 1:7, 9; 2:1, 3).

CHAPTER 2:7–11

The first test of walking in the light is, as we have already seen, Obedience (2:3–6). The second test is now to be considered, Love, which is equally God's requirement. It is significant that this section opens with the word "beloved," which is used for the first time, and this special affectionate form of appeal seems to suggest the importance of what the Apostle has to say.

I. THE COMMANDMENT (vs. 7, 8)

1. The commandment which the Apostle has to give is first described as "old," the reason being that they had received it "from the beginning." This seems to mean that they had heard it from the first moment of their Christian life, and for this reason it had no novelty for the readers (cf. 2:24). It is impressive to realize that this commandment of love was an essential part of their earliest Christian teaching, for it shows how full and how practical were the primitive messages to converts.

2. The commandment is also described as "new," and for the reason that it is always vital and real in Christ and in Christians. Love is thus not only old, but ever fresh, and is, as our Lord himself described it, "a new commandment" (John 13:34; 15:12). The newness pretty certainly lay in the new object of love, fellow-Christians, because while other aspects of love had been known for ages, this was something entirely novel, because it represented the spiritual tie between one Christian and another.

3. The reason of the Apostle writing in this way was that "the darkness is passing away and the true light already shineth." This appears to refer to the Gospel revelation already announced as "light" (1:5). Love is thus seen to be necessitated by the light of Gospel truth. Selfishness is always associated with the condition of moral darkness, while love is the practical expression of "the true light."

II. THE CLAIM (v. 9)

1. Again we are called upon to notice the man who says "he is in the light." It is a marvelous claim to make, and should be carefully compared and contrasted with the other two assertions: "He that saith I know him" (v. 4); "he that saith he abideth in him" (v. 6). It is something, indeed it is a great deal, to be "in the light," and it is splendid if a man, being in the light, is able to say so.

2. But this is a case of saying and not doing, because, while he "says" he is in the light, he is all the while hating "his brother." Superior knowledge without deeds counts for nothing, and, indeed, if possible, worse than nothing, since it brings utter discredit upon the claim of the man to be in the light. The word "brother" here, as elsewhere in this Epistle, and, indeed, in the New Testament, refers to Christian relationship. As Westcott points out, it never means in the New Testament our modern idea of the universal brotherhood of man, but always and only the specific spiritual relationship of those who are united to and are in Christ.

3. The outcome of this saying without doing, this claim to be ia the light and yet expressing animosity, is that the man is "in the darkness even until now." Darkness is another word for evil, and already it has been seen in various connections. Thus, if we say that we have fellowship with God and "walk in darkness," we are untrue (1:6). Through the glorious Gospel, "the darkness is passing away" (2:8). Then in verse 11, as we shall see, there is a threefold statement of the darkness, which includes mental, moral, and spiritual blackness as expressive of the utter alienation of the soul from God, notwithstanding all its professions.

III. THE CONTRAST (vs. 10, 11)

1. First the Apostle speaks of the man who loves his brother. He abides in the light, for "light is love's home and love is light's offspring," and as a result "there is no occasion of stumbling in him." He does not upset himself and he does not upset others, because love means humility and unselfishness, the opposite of pride, jealousy, envy, or revenge.

It is interesting to observe the three stages associated with "light." The man first of all "walks in the light" (1:7), then he is "in the light" (2:9), and as the outcome "he abideth in the light" (2:10).

2. Then, in marked contrast, the man is described who hates his brother. Three things are said of him. He is "in the darkness," he "walks in the darkness," and does not know where he is going "because the darkness hath blinded his eyes." Nothing could be more sadly impressive than this description showing that the man's life is wholly in the darkness without any possibility of even a glimmer of light.

The stages of darkness are also significantly stated. The false professor "walks in the darkness" (1:6). The effect of this is that he is "in the darkness" (2:9), and then he is so absolutely associated with the darkness that his life is entirely untrue, for "the darkness hath blinded his eyes" (2:11).

3. It is important to observe this solemn twofold antithesis between light and darkness, between love and hate. There is nothing between, and we are thus reminded that in the realm of things spiritual there is no neutrality. In some countries there is a long twilight, which means "betwixt the lights," but in the spiritual world there is nothing of the sort; a man is either in the light or in the darkness. In the same way a man either loves or hates; it is impossible for him to possess and express any other attitude. The Apostle is just echoing the Saviour's

words which he had heard years before: "no man can serve two masters."

CHAPTER 2:12–14

Up to the present the thoughts have been mainly the amplification of 1:5, 6, intended to emphasize and show the way to complete Christianity. But at this point the teaching becomes more definite, and an appeal is made to the readers to recognize their position as Christians and to make it real. As it has been truly pointed out, the Apostle had no doubt of them, but, because of his confidence, he incites them by this special appeal. Hitherto he had been telling them about the character of God and the consequences arising out of it. Now he has to tell them, or rather remind them, what they themselves are and the consequences that arise out of this.

There are two difficulties connected with this section. The first is as to whether the Apostle has two or three classes in mind when he speaks of "little children," "young men," and "fathers." Most writers seem to think that there are only two classes, the term "little children" applying to all, with a division into "young men" and "fathers." This is based on the thought that in verse 1 all the readers are addressed as "little children." One writer suggests that all are intended by the term "little children," and that then there are three separate divisions— "fathers," "young men," and "little boys" (v. 14, Greek). But perhaps for our present purpose we may think of three classes of Christians, according to their experience, respectively as "little children," "young men," and "fathers."

Another point of some difficulty is as to why the Apostle should use the present tense in verses 12 and 13, and the past tense in verse 14—"I write," and "I wrote." Some suggest that there is a reference to the Gospel in the past tense, and to this Epistle itself in the present, and certainly there is a connection between the two (1:1; 5:13). This view has some weighty names, like Rothe, Ebrard, and Plummer. Others think that the repetition is intended for emphasis. One of the most recent and able writers, Brooke ("International Critical Commentary"), suggests that the present tense refers to the whole Epistle, and the past tense to that part of it which has already been finished (1:1 to 2:11). But, whether it is a difference of communication, or of emphasis, or of standpoint, there is no doubt that the appeal is made very definite, and even solemn, as it is addressed to the various classes.

I. CHRISTIANS AS LITTLE CHILDREN (vs. 12, 13)

1. *The description.* They are called "little children" (v. 12), expressive of the Divine life and kinship which they possess. They are described as "little boys" (v. 13) perhaps because of their feebleness and imperfectness as "little ones."

2. *The characteristics.* They are first described as forgiven, and the ground of this forgiveness is "His name's sake." The pardon is complete and permanent, and it is based upon the Divine revelation (Name). Then as "little ones" they are said to "know the Father." They had come to know him as the result

of forgiveness, and, like children with their father, they had a real experience of God as their Heavenly Father. This thought of fellowship as distinctive of Christian immaturity is very beautiful, and shows that from the very outset of the Christian life we have a definite experience of God.

II. CHRISTIANS AS YOUNG MEN (vs. 13, 14)

The statements here are much fuller, and deserve thorough attention.

1. *The character.* They are described as "strong," or, as the Greek might be rendered, "powerful," or "able." Perhaps this includes conviction of mind and purpose of will—two features that should always mark the young manhood, whether in things physical or things spiritual.

2. *The conflict.* Twice over they are said to have "overcome the evil one." It is well that the Apostle reminds them so definitely of "the evil one" who had opposed their Master, and was, therefore, necessarily opposing them. No Christian life is worthy of the name that does not face conflict and realize the fact and power of the enemy.

3. *The conquest.* But the original of the word "overcome" clearly indicates the completeness and permanence of their victory. These Christian young warriors had met and vanquished the adversary, and the result was abiding. This is full of encouragement for all those who are conscious, as we all more or less must be, of our "adversary the devil" (1 Pet. 5:8).

4. *The condition.* The secret of it all was that "the Word of God abideth in you." It was this that, like a sword, enabled them to fight and gain the victory (Eph. 6:17). There was power in the Word of Divine truth as against the falsity of the adversary's "wiles," and there was power in the Word of Divine grace as against the adversary's "works." The place of this Word was "in them," and it was permanently there—"abideth in you." This is always the secret of victory. God's Word is at once the food of the soul and the sword of the warrior. When the Word of God is in mind and heart and conscience and life, victory is inevitable. For this purpose there are three requirements in connection with our use of the Word of God—attention, intention, retention. The mind, the heart, and the life must be occupied with the Divine Word.

III. CHRISTIANS AS FATHERS (vs. 13, 14)

There seems to be no doubt that the reference is to those who had been long in the Christian life and had become, as it were, "fathers" of the community. "A hoary head is a crown of glory if it be found in the way of righteousness."

1. *The authority.* They are called "fathers" because they were, by their age and experience, leaders of the little flocks of Christians in various places.

2. *The experience.* They were thinkers, because the Apostle says "ye know," and the word implies a permanent, personal experience. The "little children" may be described as learners; the "young men" as soldiers; the "fathers" are Christians of deep, profound experience. It is also striking that in the

repetition of the appeal to the children something more is added, and this is also the case with the young men, but when the repetition of the appeal is made to the fathers there is nothing higher to be said, and so the exact words are given again: "Ye have come to know him who is from the beginning."

3. *The maturity.* It is said that they "know *him*," showing that their experience was of the person rather than the work. And the Person is described as "him who is from the beginning," clearly indicating his essential Being rather than his relationship to us. This is, therefore, a mark of very profound Christian life and their ripeness of fellowship. This knowledge of the Person of Christ in himself as distinct from, or, at least, additional to his work for and relationship to us is in some respects the supreme knowledge, for there is nothing beyond it (Phil. 3:7–11).

As we review this important passage, and dwell upon the three different sections of the Christian community thus described as children, young men and fathers, it will help us to look at them afresh as follows:

(1) They may be regarded as three *successive* stages of experience. They are strikingly like the three classes mentioned in the Gospel (21:15–17). Whether under the figure of lambs, sheep, and "growing sheep" (the best reading), we seem to see a parallel to these three descriptions in the Epistle. Then, too, we cannot help noticing how the Apostle Paul apparently had similar distinctions in mind when he spoke of "the grace of God," "the kingdom of God," and "the whole counsel of God" (Acts 20:24–27). Once again we may see a somewhat similar suggestion in the three aspects of joy found in Psalm 5:11: the joy of trust, answering to the "little children"; the joy of protection, answering to the "young men"; and the joy of love, answering to the "fathers." At any rate, there is no doubt that the Christian life is intended to be one of constant growth, and as we start by being little children who rejoice in forgiveness and fellowship with the Father, so we go on increasingly conscious of strength and victory until at length we reach the culminating point of a personal, rich, deep, full experience of God himself (2 Pet. 3:18). It is particularly noteworthy that in the later Epistles of Paul, the last Epistle of Peter, and this Epistle of John, the emphasis laid upon "knowledge" shows that it is the mark of a ripening, growing, maturing Christian. The young believer knows very little, because he has had so short an experience of God. And as such he is often the prey of error, as we shall see later on in this Epistle. But the fathers who "know" are thereby enabled to perceive and appreciate the truth as in Jesus and to rejoice in personal fellowship with God.

(2) And yet, while these experiences may, from one point of view, be regarded as successive, they must also be emphasized as *simultaneous.* There is a sense in which we are to be always children, always strong, and always experienced, because our Christian life will necessarily take up and include these elements in its wide, deep, strong, and ever-growing position.

CHAPTER 2:15–17

The special appeal in these verses is pretty certainly addressed to all those to whom the Apostle had been writing (12–14), although one or two writers think the application is to the "young men" only. But it seems in every way simpler and better to regard this as definitely addressed to all Christians. God's light shows the world as it really is, and on this account the Apostle solemnly states certain truths as he urges his readers to take every possible precaution.

I. THE DANGER STATED

1. What are we to understand by this reference to "the world"? We have already seen that Christ died for "the whole world" (2:2), and it is also said that the Father sent the Son to be the Saviour "of the world" (4:14). It cannot, therefore, mean the material world or the world of man, but rather the world regarded as apart from God (v. 19). It is equivalent to what the Apostle Paul calls "this present evil world" (Gal. 1:4), even though a different word is used in the latter passage. The world is thus not so much a sphere as an atmosphere, and includes everything which is sinful or is likely to be so.

2. But what, more definitely, is "the world"? The line cannot be drawn with absolute clearness. There are certain things in the world about which there is no question. But there are others which may be described as on the border lines, and each one must decide for himself in fellowship with God whether or not a thing is "worldly" for him. The great principle of Paul applies here, "whatsoever is not of faith is sin."

II. THE DANGER DESCRIBED

The Apostle speaks of what has been termed the trinity of evil, "the lust of the flesh, and the lust of the eyes, and the vainglory of life." Each of these needs the most careful consideration in regard to the spiritual life.

1. The desire of having; "the lust of the flesh."
2. The desire of seeing; "the lust of the eyes."
3. The desire of being; "the vainglory of life."

This is the usual way of describing these three aspects of evil, and it is important to distinguish between desires that are true and desires that are sinful. There are many things which are not wrong in themselves, but become wrong when they are abused. Some writers endeavor to form a parallel between these words and the temptation of Eve (Gen. 3) and the temptation of our Lord (Matt. 4), in their threefold form, but in neither case does it seem quite satisfactory, especially because in our Lord there was nothing sinful connected with his human nature. Some authorities consider that in these three statements we have two forms of desire and one of boasting, the latter being a love of display, with special reference to outward and external elements of life. It is certainly significant, as already noted, that the Greek uses two words for "life," one referring to that which is inward and real ($\zeta\omega\acute{\eta}$), and the other to that which is outward and temporal ($\beta\acute{\iota}o\varsigma$). Perhaps a similar distinction may be seen in the use of our words, also taken from the Greek, *zoology* and *biology*. All this emphasizes the importance of taking heed to our desires lest that which is right in itself may become wrong either by being centered on an unworthy object or extended beyond its proper limit.

III. The Danger Contrasted

1. In opposition to the love of the world is the love of the Father, and it is important to realize that this "love of the Father," including his to us and ours to him, is at once real and satisfying. Scripture contrasts and opposes the Divine Trinity to the trinity of evil. Thus the world is opposed to the Father, the devil to the Son, and the flesh to the Spirit.

2. The world is contrasted with the Father. The two are mutually exclusive, for everything that is "of the world" cannot possibly be "of the Father." As our Lord said: "No man can serve two masters" (Matt. 6:24).

IV. The Danger Faced

1. The call comes, "love not the world, neither the things that are in the world." This appeal is necessary, because of the danger of loving self and sin rather than God.

2. This will mean true separation from the world. Christians are in the world but not "of the world" (John 17:14, 16), and yet we are told "God so loved the world" (John 3:16). Why, then, may we not "love the world"? We may freely do so if our motive and purpose is the same as that which actuates God. We are to love the world back to God, and in this sense we cannot love the world too much. Indeed, our attitude to those around us should be actuated by what the Apostle Paul so beautifully calls "the philanthropy of God" (Tit. 3:4, Greek), but any love that has not for its object the winning of the world to God is certain to bring evil in its train.

V. The Danger Averted

1. The transience of the world is one reason why we are not to love it in this wrong sense. "The world passeth away, and the lust thereof." All its sin, pleasure, satisfaction will end in nothing. Like a mirage, it will prove an illusion. When Mark Twain was seventy-one he met a well-known American commercial magnate, who was a little younger. Mark Twain, as is well known, was utterly opposed to Christianity, and speaking to the other man he said: "Well, I don't know what you think of it, but I think I have had enough of this world, and I wish I were out of it." The other replied: "I don't say much about it, but that expresses my view." This is how Twain's biographer comments on the conversation:

"This from the foremost man of letters and one of the foremost financiers of the time was impressive. Each at the mountain-top of his career, they agreed that the journey was not worth while, that what the world had still to give was not attractive enough to tempt them, to prevent a desire to experiment with the next stage.

"One could remember a thousand poor and obscure men who were perfectly willing to go on struggling and starving, postponing the day of settlement as long as possible; but perhaps, when one has had all the world has to give, when there are no new worlds in sight to conquer, one has a different feeling."

2. The permanence of the Divine will is shown in marked contrast to the temporal character of the world. "He that doeth the will of God abideth forever." This is the true life, pleasing him, not ourselves, and this alone gives satisfaction because it lasts through time and extends into eternity.

CHAPTER 2:18–20

The Christian life is full of perils. Already the Apostle has dealt with some of these (vs. 15–17), and now he takes up others. After the contrast between God and the world comes this second important contrast of the true and the false. But life is not only encompassed with peril; it needs protection, and John is clear in regard to both. While he will not minimize the danger, he is equally certain that there is no real need to trouble, if only we are careful to observe the Divine conditions.

There are many dangers in the Christian life, but perhaps the very worst is that of false teaching. It has such an inoffensive look, and as such is unlike anything immoral. It often deceives, because it seems to suggest new ideas. The soul would quickly reject anything openly and avowedly sinful, and yet may easily succumb to the fascination of novel thoughts and ways. But God's light reveals at once the peril and the protection.

I. The Solemn Warning (v. 18)

1. *Needed.*—The Apostle addresses them as "little children," just as in verse 14 he had spoken of them as "little ones," or "little boys." Their position as spiritual children necessitated what he had to say.

2. *Introduced.*—He points out his first warning by saying that "it is a last hour," referring to the period just before the close of the dispensation. For comparison, we may think of the "last days" of the Old Testament; the "last day" in our Lord's teaching (John 6:39), and the "last days" of the Apostle Paul (2 Tim. 3:1). To the Apostle the world seemed transitory (v. 17), and would soon come to an end. This was in harmony with what Paul had said many years before, that "now is salvation nearer to us than when we first believed" (Rom. 13:11). To the same effect is his other phrase, "in the latter times" (1 Tim. 4:1), while Peter also remarks, "the end of all things is at hand" (1 Pet. 4:7). It was the thought of the imminence of this great crisis that served to give special force to the warning.

3. *Given.*—The substance of the warning is "that antichrist cometh," and not only so, but "even now have there arisen many antichrists." This was the proof that it was "the last hour." John's teaching about the antichrists is found here and in three other places (v. 22; 4:3; 2 John 7). Antichrist is associated with the denial of Jesus as the Messiah, and thereby the denial of the Divine Fatherhood and Sonship. The fact that there were in John's day "many antichrists" shows that there was real danger of false teaching leading to false practice. When

Paul was at Miletus he warned the elders of Ephesus against the entrance of "grievous wolves" (Acts 20:29), and in writing to the Thessalonians he gives his own special teaching about the "man of sin," who is also "the lawless one" (2 Thess. 2:3–8). It would seem as though the numerous antichrists are to head up gradually into one who will be the supreme opponent of our Lord. But it is interesting to notice the twofold thought suggested by the preposition "anti." The first idea is indicated by the thought of "instead of," meaning a spurious Christ, and then arising out of this comes the additional idea of "in opposition to," which shows that the ultimate outcome will be opposition and hostility to Christ. This has always been the history of error in the past, and so it will continue to the end.

Perversions of Christianity become opposing forces, the spurious develops into the hostile. Antichrist hereafter, if we understand the New Testament aright, will not at first be ranged against Christ, but will endeavor to suggest himself as in the place of Christ, and only afterwards will be seen in his true color. Man may be said to be "incurably religious," and the devil well knows that there must be some sort of religion to occupy human attention. Then, when a false conception of religion is in possession, it soon degenerates into undisguised hostility to the true faith. We see this today in such movements as Russellism, Christian Science, Theosophy, and Spiritism. They are all intended as substitutes for the true religion, but they soon prove themselves to be absolutely opposed to it.

II. THE SAD REMINDER (v. 19)

In connection with his earnest and urgent appeal, the Apostle has to speak of those who had formerly professed the Christian faith, and everything he says has a sad but searching interest for us today.

1. *Apostasy Shown.*—"They went out from us." This was the fact within the experience of the Apostle and his fellow Christians, and the fivefold use of the term "us" is a hint of the beautiful fellowship that marked the earlier believers.

2. *Apostasy Explained.*—"They were not of us." This shows the true character of those who had gone out, and proves that they were not really Christians, because if they had been they would certainly have remained. Those who have really experienced the preciousness of Christ and the fellowship of his people are not likely to surrender these inestimable privileges.

3. *Apostasy Proved.*—"They went out that they might be made manifest that they all are not of us." When these mere professors separated themselves from the body of Christ's people it was obvious to all what they were in reality. Thus all their profession went for nothing. They might have had a genuine experience of Christ with all the blessedness, power, peace, and protection resulting from it; but, instead, they determined to leave the community of Christ's followers, though, in so doing, they both revealed and condemned themselves. There is scarcely anything sadder in life than deliberate apostasy after Christian profession.

III. THE SAVIOUR'S PROTECTION (v. 20)

Then in contrast the Apostle turns from the unreal to the real people, and shows them the way in which they would be guarded against any such terrible experience.

1. *The Fact.*—"Ye have an anointing." The original is very striking in its contrast with the term "antichrist." It is as though the Apostle said: "You have the real anointing, the chrism, while the others have the counterfeits, the antichrisms." This anointing, or "unction," is, of course, the gift of the Holy Spirit who is bestowed upon us at the moment of our acceptance of Christ (2 Cor. 1:21; Eph. 1:13).

2. *The Explanation.*—This anointing came "from the Holy One"—that is, the Lord Jesus Christ himself—and the fact that he is thus described as "Holy" shows the effect of the anointing, and provides one of the greatest proofs of the reality of the true life in opposition to everything that is false and counterfeit, because unholy.

3. *The Result.*—"Ye know all things." The word "know" here, as often elsewhere, means immediate, direct perception, as the outcome of the gift of the Holy Spirit in Christ. Just as there is sagacity in animals and natural insight and taste in man, so in the Christian there is spiritual knowledge as the outcome of a personal experience of Christ. The Holy Ghost possesses mind, heart, and will, and enables us to understand and know (1 Cor. 10:15). This does not mean any reflection on teachers (Eph. 4:11), because these are the gift of God. Nor does it involve any independence of the truth of God recorded in his Word; on the contrary, the knowledge comes through the truth applied by the Spirit, and both Spirit and Word come from Christ himself (John 15:26). It is this combination of the Word of God and the Spirit of God that will preserve us from all danger of what is sometimes called the "inner light," considered apart from the Bible or God's truth. The Holy Spirit speaks of Christ through the Word, and never in any sense in opposition to it.

"Here is the exterior test of the inner light. The witness of the Spirit in the living Church, and in the abiding apostolic word, authenticate and guard each other. This must be so, if one and the self-same Spirit testifies in both. Experience and Scripture coincide. Neither will suffice for us apart from the other. Without experience, Scripture becomes a dead letter; without the norm of Scripture, experience becomes a speculation, a fanaticism, or a conceit." (Findlay, "Fellowship in the Life Eternal," p. 224.)

Thus we see that to be forewarned is forearmed, and we may perhaps sum up this solemn message by emphasizing three requirements for the spiritual life which are particularly applicable today in the face of all forms of erroneous teaching.

(1) We ought to distrust our own intellectual powers and our reasoning in things spiritual. The deepest truths are often not to be grasped by the intellect, but are a matter of spiritual apprehension and discernment. It is true that the Lord says that we are to love him "with all the mind," and yet the mind is only one faculty, and needs to be tested and balanced by other elements of our nature, equally important, and in some respects more important, for spiritual understanding.

(2) We ought also to be very specially on our guard against the counsel of other people in reference to spiritual truths, if those who give the counsel are not converted to God. There is a sense in which it is as true as ever, notwithstanding all modern education, that "the natural man receiveth not the things of the Spirit of God, for they are foolishness unto him, and he cannot know them, because they are spiritually judged" (1 Cor. 2:14). While listening carefully to all opinions, the final decision must be made by the spiritually illuminated soul.

(3) Meanwhile, as we distrust our own reason, and hesitate to put too much confidence in the advice and reason of the unconverted, we must take the greatest care to become constantly and fully exercised by the Word through the Spirit, in order that we may know by experience what God would have us do. This is what Paul meant when he said, "Be not foolish, but understand what the will of the Lord is" (Eph. 5:17). To the man who is in constant fellowship with Christ by the Spirit, through the Word, will come "a spirit of wisdom and revelation in the knowledge of him," and then, "having the eyes of the heart enlightened, we shall know" (Eph. 1:17, 18).

CHAPTER 2:21–28

From 2:18 to 4:6 great stress is laid upon the peril of error and the consequent need of protection. It is at once significant and sad that the greatest dangers in all ages have been due to a perverted Christianity rather than to open and gross violations of the moral law. All the more reason, therefore, to give attention both to the aspects of error and to the secrets of safety.

I. THE BELIEVER'S POSITION (vs. 21, 26)

1. *Assurance.*—"I have not written unto you, because ye know not the truth." This is an encouraging word, telling them that he was not writing to them because of their ignorance, but only to show the true and direct bearing of their knowledge on conduct.

2. *Intelligence.*—"But because ye know it, and because no lie is of the truth." It is worth while remembering that truth is fact. It is not something which a man "trows," as though it varied with individual opinion, but it is something unchanging and unchangeable, always the same to everyone. And this reference to the knowledge of the truth is shown by the word used to imply a direct instinctive understanding of the objective reality of the Gospel. They knew this truth, because it was not something novel, but that which had been their portion since the beginning of their Christian life.

3. *Danger* (v. 26).—"These things have I written unto you concerning them which would lead you astray." This shows the peril of these believers. Wrong ideas inevitably lead to wrong conduct, and it is clear that this was no mere question of erroneous opinions, but of the definite danger of erroneous living (3:7; 4:6). It may be said, without much question, that one of the greatest needs, if not the very greatest, is an ever-new experience of old truths rather than the possession of anything new, however true. The original word found here, and in the other passages, includes the two ideas of wrong thoughts tending inevitably to wrong action. So that the peril was not merely one of intellectual but of moral declension.

II. THE BELIEVER'S POWER (vs. 22, 23)

How, then, was this position to be maintained? The Apostle at once shows that it was only by means of a close connection with the Lord Jesus Christ.

1. *The Work of Christ* (v. 22).—It is clear that this was no mere Jewish unbelief, but something practical and aggressive in its opposition to our Lord. Christ in the fulness of his work is our Prophet, Priest, and King, and these three are included in the term Messiah, or "the Christ." It follows, therefore, that the denial of our Lord's Messiahship carries with it the solemn fact that there is no salvation, because it is only possible to be saved by means of the work of Christ (Acts 4:12).

2. *The Person of Christ* (vs. 22, 23).—The Work is seen here, as elsewhere, to depend upon the Person, so that he who denies Christ denies the Father as well, and does not possess any part or lot in the Father; while, on the other hand, he who continually confesses the Son possesses the Father. This relation between the Father and the Son, and between the Son and the Father, shows quite plainly the value of the Person of Christ as intimately associated with God.

3. *The Connection of the Work and the Person.*—This is clearly implied in the statements about Christ, his Person, his Work, and his relation to the Father. If there be no Godhead there can be no Atonement, and without Atonement there is no Redemption. If Christ were only an Example, he would be nothing more than man, but because he is Redeemer and Messiah as well, he must be both God and Man. Here, as in the Gospel, the title "the Son," carries its own profound significance, implying a unique relation to the Father that involves his Deity, and thereby his redemptive work. This connection of the Work and the Person is vital and essential.

III. THE BELIEVER'S PROTECTION (vs. 24, 25)

But it is necessary to consider more definitely how this Divine Person and Work are to be related to the individual life of God's children.

1. *The Command.*—"As for you, let that abide in you which ye heard from the beginning." From the outset of their Christian life they had been taught the Christian truth (2:7) and they were simply to allow it to remain in and with them. Christ had been revealed and declared to them as a Divine Saviour, and all that they had to do was to allow that blessed and powerful truth to remain part and parcel of their life (1:1). There was no possibility of moral and spiritual development except from this germ, for everything else that might come into their life would be merely accretion.

2. *The Consequence.*—"If that which ye heard … abide in you, ye also shall abide in … Father." The result of their permitting the truth concerning the Divine and human Messiah to remain in them would be that they in turn would

be enabled to abide both in the Son and also in the Father. Thus the Incarnation is seen to be eminently worthy of God, and from the Son we naturally proceed to the Father.

3. *The Explanation.*—"And this is the promise which he promised us, even the life eternal." Eternal life is the final outcome of our union with Christ (John 17:3), and those who possess him possess God's own life in that fellowship (v. 12).

IV. The Believer's Provision (v. 27)

But there is something still more for the believer to realize, for not only is he in union and communion with the Father and the Son, there is in addition to, or rather in connection with, these blessings, the glorious privilege of the Holy Spirit, and it is this which constitutes the provision set out in such detail in this verse. Each point calls for careful attention in order that we may see the fulness of God's grace on our behalf.

1. *A Divine Gift.* "The anointing which ye received." The contrast between the Christian and their deceivers is very striking. "As for you," that is, in opposition to those who would lead you astray (v. 26). This anointing has already been mentioned (v. 20), and here it is spoken of as a Divine gift received by the Christian.

2. *An Indwelling Gift.* "In you." This is one of the many instances where the force of the preposition "in" has to be noticed as expressing the actual abiding *in* the soul as distinct from any mere accompaniment. The believer is "in Christ" and Christ is in him (John 14:20). In like manner we are in the Spirit and the Spirit is in us.

3. *A Permanent Gift.* "Abideth." This blessing of the Holy Spirit lasts because God does not take it away.

4. *A Sufficient Gift.* "Ye need not that anyone teach you." This means that they had spiritual resources in the presence and power of the indwelling Divine Spirit, and it is well that from time to time we should recall these resources instead of unduly depending upon outside assistance.

5. *A Complete Gift.* "Teacheth you concerning all things." This shows that there is nothing outside the power of this wonderful gift that God has bestowed upon us.

6. *A Reliable Gift.* "Is truth, and is no lie." This statement is at once guaranteed by Scripture, and proved again and again in personal experience.

7. *A Practical Gift.* "Even as it taught you, ye shall abide in him." Thus, as it has been in the past, so in the present and in the future, the indwelling Spirit will be our teacher, and will enable us to abide in Christ. This reciprocal abiding of the Spirit in us and of our abiding in the Spirit is one of the most blessed features of the Christian life.

At this point it may be asked why there should be differences, disagreements, and divisions among Christians if the Holy Spirit is all this to the soul? Perhaps the answer may be found along such lines as these, which have been often pointed out.

(1) Differences among Christians are not usually and mainly on the chief facts of the Gospel, but on secondary, even though important, aspects. There is a far greater and deeper fundamental unity than is sometimes imagined. (2) It is possible, too, that some of these differences may be due to the sad fact that all Christians are not wholly surrendered to this indwelling Spirit. Very often the trouble is not that we should seek for more of the Spirit, but that we should allow the Spirit to have more of us. (3) Then it must never be forgotten that individual temperament and personal ecclesiastical environment count for very much. The Holy Spirit works through individualities and through circumstances, and if he is not allowed his proper place and complete sway, it is not surprising that differences emerge.

V. The Believer's Prospect (v. 28)

This verse is apparently transitional, looking backwards and forwards. Some writers connect it with the preceding (Law), others with the following (Haupt and Findlay). Probably, as elsewhere in this Epistle, it includes the earlier and the subsequent sections, but, on the whole, it seems better to regard it as closing the section, because the next verse will be seen to introduce an entirely new thought.

1. *The Fact.* "If he shall be manifested." This is a definite expectation of what we call the Second Coming of Christ, and the "if" does not imply any doubt, but simply assumes the fact. This is, indeed, the prospect of God's children, "that blessed hope."

2. *The Result.* "We may have boldness." The word "boldness" means "freedom of speech," and refers to that feature of true friendship which implies absence of all reserve and the presence of perfect frankness. It shows what ought to be true of the believer in that great day. "That we may tell him everything."

3. *The Possibility.* "And not be ashamed before him at his coming." This is the only place where the word *Parousia* (coming) is found in the writings of John, and the thought of possible shame shows that believers may not be able to meet that day with the joy which God expects and intends from us. It is not a question of salvation, but of sorrow at unfaithfulness; it does not mean that we are afraid, but it certainly does indicate the possibility of our feeling utterly ashamed of ourselves, because we have not been true to his wonderful love and grace since our conversion. This is one of several passages in the New Testament which clearly show the solemn possibility of the Lord's coming finding us not as faithful, as ready, as true, as earnest as we might and ought to be.

4. *The Call.* "Abide in him." This shows how we may prevent all such sorrow and shame, and be able to lift up our faces without spot, and have perfect confidence when he appears. Abiding is a familiar word, and it means nothing less, as it can mean nothing more, than staying where we are. We are to abide in Christ, in his love, in his Word, in his grace, and allow him to be the Master and Lord of our life. Then we shall have boldness here and boldness hereafter.

Looking over the entire passage, we may consider, with Findlay (p. 226), the three safeguards provided for the Christian. (1) The Spirit within; (2) the Word without; (3) the

Lord above. When these three have their proper place and power in the soul, the result is protection in spite of every peril, power over every weakness, peace in all perplexity, and permanence amidst everything that fluctuates in the world around us.

CHAPTER 2:29 to 3:3

At this point we may review the Epistle, especially because some writers consider that a new part opens here. Thus it is suggested that from 1:5 to 2:27 (or 28) we have as the main thought God is Light. Then from 2:28 (or 29) to 4:6, God is Righteous. And from 4:7 to 5:21, God is Love. Dr. Law suggests that these are the three divisions of the Epistle, and represent three tests of the Christian life: doing righteousness, loving one another, and believing in Christ. This agrees practically with the view of three other modern writers: Hort, Haering, and Brooke, though with a somewhat different analysis of the entire Epistle.

The new thought that starts with 2:29 is that of our being "begotten of God," and this idea of Sonship runs through the whole passage, and gives it its unity.

I. THE FACT OF SONSHIP (2:29; 3:1, 2)

1. *What?* We are regarded as children of God, and it is important to distinguish this from mere natural birth (John 1:12). Our Lord institutes a solemn and even awful contrast between children of God and children of the devil (John 8:44).

2. *How?* We become children of God by regeneration, the gift of God's own life by his Spirit (John 3:5). This possession of the Divine nature is in striking contrast with and also a spiritual complement to Paul's idea of adoption. This seems to be the distinction between "children" and "sons," for the latter are the grown-up children. Thus we are at once possessors of the Divine nature, and adopted into the Divine Family.

II. THE MARK OF SONSHIP (2:29)

1. *Knowledge.* "If ye know that he is righteous, ye know that." This knowledge is at once absolute and experienced, and those who are children of God possess this twofold understanding (see Greek).

2. *Life.* "Everyone that doeth righteousness is begotten of him." This is the supreme proof and evidence of a Divine life. There must be righteousness in thought, word, and deed. God himself is righteous, and those who receive his life necessarily manifest the same feature. Without this there is no possibility of anyone being born of God.

III. THE PRIVILEGE OF SONSHIP (3:1)

1. *Whence?* The Apostle bursts out with the call of "Behold, what manner of love the Father hath bestowed upon

us." This privilege is thus the direct gift of our Heavenly Father.

2. *Why?* It springs from his love, and is shown in the free gift which he has permanently bestowed on us. This love is thus not only shown, but given; not only exhibited, but imparted. It is the gift of himself, and thereby we become his children.

IV. THE CONSCIOUSNESS OF SONSHIP (3:1, R. V.)

This is a point which we owe to the Revised Version, for, after the outburst expressive of God's love, the Apostle adds, "and such we are." In this realization we have two separate, though connected, thoughts.

1. *Experience.* "Such we are." The soul rejoices in the consciousness of a new life which comes from the love of God. There is nothing to compare with this personal realization.

2. *Expression.* But the soul cannot keep this blessing to itself. There must be testimony to others, and so the words "such we are" are the witness to those around us of what God has done to us.

V. THE MYSTERY OF SONSHIP (3:1)

This relationship between God and the believer is not understood by all, and so the Apostle says, "for this cause the world knoweth us not, because it knew him not."

1. *The Enigma in Our Case.* The world does not know the Christian as the child of God because spiritual things are only spiritually discerned (1 Cor. 2:14). To the man of the world the believer does not differ essentially from other people, and the possession of a Divine life is altogether hidden from the one who does not possess this experience.

2. *The Enigma in His Case.* The world did not know Christ, for during his earthly life his claim to be the Son of God was rejected and opposed. They thought they knew his mother and earthly father and human sisters and brothers, but they did not realize the essential Divine relationship that existed between him and his Heavenly Father. It is always so, for people of the world are as incapable as ever of appreciating the Divine reality of Jesus Christ. It, too, needs a spiritual experience.

VI. THE CROWN OF SONSHIP (3:2)

Notwithstanding the inestimable privilege and joy of being children of God, even this is not all, for there is something yet to come.

1. *Unknown Glory.* "It is not yet made manifest what we shall be." It is almost beyond our conception to think of anything higher than our present privilege of being children of God, and it is pretty certain that the difference between the present and future is one of degree rather than of kind, and will consist in our future condition rather than in any change of position.

2. *Known Glory.* "We know that, if he shall be manifested, we shall be like him; for we shall see him even as he is." This is

something that, at any rate, we already know, whatever the future may bring. We shall see Christ, and be like him, and the sight will transform us into his image and likeness. Bishop Westcott relates an incident that may help us to understand these wonderful words. A missionary was occupied with the assistance of a native teacher in translating this Epistle into the language of the people among whom he was working. When he came to these words, "we shall be like him," the scribe laid down his pen, and said, "No, I cannot write these words; it is too much; let us write, 'we shall kiss his feet.'" But, as Dr. Barrett says in narrating this incident, "It is not 'too much' for the love of God."

VII. THE DEMAND OF SONSHIP (3:3)

The paragraph appropriately ends by showing that sonship must of necessity have a practical result.

1. *The Incentive to Purity.* Everyone that possesses this hope fixed on seeing and being like Christ hereafter will necessarily purify himself here and now. Purity is one of the requirements of sonship.

2. *The Standard of Purity.* This purity is to be realized by means of nothing less than the purity of Christ himself, "even as he is pure." The thought that he is to be manifested, and that we are to be like him hereafter, is to be our constant consideration day by day, and everything in thought, word, and deed is to be related to him.

Thus we see some of the main aspects of New Testament Sonship. It starts from life. It is expressed in love. It is marked by loyalty. And it will culminate in likeness.

CHAPTER 3:4–10a

God's life (3:3) is now to be seen as in constant and inevitable antagonism to sin, showing once again that sin is absolutely inadmissible (2:1). This solemn truth is proved in four different ways.

I. THE ESSENCE OF SIN (v. 4)

1. The practice of sin here described as "doeth sin" proves the possession of the principle from which the practice springs, and this, in turn, seems to imply that the man who does wrong holds that the moral law is not binding on him.

2. The principle is "lawlessness," meaning opposition to all legal requirement, and in this, the denial of all moral obligation. The man who takes this view shows that he refuses to accept the fundamental difference between right and wrong. The reference to sin as "lawlessness" should be compared with the similar statement that sin is "unrighteousness" (v. 17), for the absence of law carries with it the absence and denial of what is right (1:9).

II. THE MANIFESTATION OF CHRIST (vs. 5, 8)

This is another reason why sin cannot be admitted into the Christian life.

1. Christ was manifested to "take away sins" (v. 5), and the Apostle reminds his readers that this simple but significant fact was instinctively known by them. It is interesting to notice that in John 1:29 our Lord is said to take away "sin" (the root), while here he is said to take away "sins" (the fruit).

2. Christ was also manifested that he might "destroy the works of the devil" (v. 8). This is one of the aspects of sin that needs constant attention, and to commit wrong is not merely to break a Divine law, but to deny the entire purpose of Christ's coming. In the face of these two solemn statements, it ought to be clear to all that sinning is wholly incompatible with any revelation of Christ as the Son of God.

III. THE LIFE OF THE BELIEVER (vs. 6, 7, 9)

A third reason is now given to show the inadmissibility of sin.

1. *Experience* (v. 6). There seems to have been a real danger in the lifetime of the Apostle by people teaching that conduct did not matter. It was along this line that unwary believers were liable to be led astray (2:26). For this reason the teaching is clear that whoever continues to abide in Christ does not practice sin—sin is no part of his normal experience; and if anyone indulges this practice, it is a clear proof that he has not seen Christ nor had a personal or permanent experience of him.

2. *Expression* (v. 7). The Apostle is particularly anxious that his "little children" should not be led into error of thought and conduct, and so he speaks in the most definite terms that the man who practices righteousness is righteous even as Christ himself is righteous. Thus it is shown that unrighteousness is wholly inconsistent with the idea of the Christian life.

3. *Principle* (v. 9). Then the Apostle lays down the absolute and unqualified principle that the man who is possessed of God's life does not continue to practice sin because the Divine seed remains in him, and he is unable to go on sinning "because he is begotten of God." All this is rightly said to indicate that the matter was practical, not theoretical, and that the Apostle's solemn statement is in direct opposition to some false claim of an adversary of Christ and Christians. To assert that a man who is truly "begotten of God" can at the same time live in sin is thus definitely and, even indignantly, denied, for "to assert the contrary is to assert a blasphemy, a calumny upon God" (Law, "The Tests of Life," p. 228). Thus the passage, so far, when read in the light of the familiar statements (1:8–10) shows that there must be, there can be, no apology for sin, and no allowance for sin in the believer's life.

IV. THE ORIGIN OF SIN (vs. 8, 10a)

This is the fourth and final proof that sinning and the Christian life are absolutely opposite.

1. *The Devil* (v. 8). The man who practices sin is said to be "of the devil," and the devil is stated to have sinned "from

the beginning." This is one of the many proofs from Scripture that sin originally was external to man. The record of the Fall tells of the entrance of sin into human life, but not of its entrance into the universe, and the teaching of Scripture about the devil in relation to sin is as plain as it is solemn. The personality of Satan is clearly recognized here, although, as in other places, there is very little told in detail of his person or the account of his original fall. But no one can really doubt that the New Testament, following the Old, indicates the double truth that man fell through the temptation of Satan, and that Satan fell from a former high estate. At this point it may be usefully noted that, in the words of an able writer, "the New Testament conception of diabolic agency is one for which modern Christian thought has no moral difficulty in finding a place." And he goes on to refer to one of the most popular and best-known modern theological books in which "there is not a single reference to it." But, as the same writer proceeds to state, there are three thoughts in the Epistle of great value and permanent validity contained in this thought of the agency of the devil. The first is that sin in principle has a diabolic character, and is, therefore, infinitely more terrible than anything human can explain. The second is that the moral conflict in humanity is associated with personal agencies, and not mere ideas. "Of impersonal influences or of actual moral forces residing in impersonal laws the New Testament knows nothing." The third truth is the ultimate victory of Christ over the devil in regard to the possession of mankind (Law, pp. 144, 145). To this may be added by way of illustration the words of Disraeli in his novel, "Endymion": "Give me a single argument against his person which is not applicable to the personality of the Deity."

2. *His children* (v. 10). In solemn contrast, the Apostle speaks of "the children of God" and "the children of the devil." This latter phrase is evidently an echo of his Master's words, and as such calls for the most serious and thorough consideration (John 8:44). The Apostle Paul similarly spoke of Elymas as "thou son of the devil," and on another occasion our Lord referred to "the sons of the evil one" In these solemn statements we have the thought of that moral and spiritual affinity by which evildoers are described as the progeny of the devil. Nothing must be allowed to weaken this plain and definite truth in relation to human sin.

And so for all these reasons, as above stated, sin is impossible. (1) It is opposed to God. (2) It is opposed to Christ. (3) It is opposed to Christianity. (4) It comes from the devil. (5) It is the mark of the devil in human beings. Surely these are sufficient reasons why the Christian believer should not sin.

Chapter 3:10b–18

The distinction between the children of God and the children of the devil consists in two great facts, doing righteousness and loving the brother. The first test is towards God, and has been considered already (2:29 to 3:10a), and now it is necessary to think of the other test, towards man. The key thought, therefore, is brother-love.

I. The Proof (vs. 10, 11)

1. *Its character* (v. 10). One fact is so important that it calls for repetition. It has been pointed out by Westcott and others that the term "brother" here and elsewhere in the New Testament always refers to the specific relationship between Christians, and never to the modern idea of the "brotherhood of man." This is an important point, and the emphasis laid upon loving our Christian brother is very strong in the New Testament. It is the "new commandment" given by our Lord (John 13:34), and it is more than likely that the newness consisted in the object of our affection, the man who is united with us to Christ. It is particularly striking that the New Testament gives such prominence to the idea expressed by the Greek word *philadelphia* (Rom. 12:10; 1 Thes. 4:9; Heb. 13:1; 1 Pet. 1:22; 3:8; 2 Pet. 1:7), which should be rendered "brother-love," not brotherly love. To speak of "brotherly love" means brother-*like* love, which means love *as though we were* brethren. But the word means far more than this, indicating love *because we are* brethren, and so the true interpretation is brother-love.

2. *Its claim* (v. 10). This love of the Christian brother is clearly shown to be "of God," that is, it is a sign of life. Because we are begotten of God and possess Divine life, we are certain to love our brother. But if we love not, we may be equally certain that we are not possessors of God's love, and nature.

3. *Its call* (v. 11). This message of brother-love was part of the earliest Gospel. They had heard it "from the beginning" of their Christian life and profession. We see from this simple statement how much was included in the first proclamation of Christian truth.

II. The Precept (vs. 12–15)

1. *The example* (v. 12). Cain is used as the illustration of what has been rightly called the "loveless soul," and while the emphasis suggested by the word "slew" suggests the brutality of the act, the chief stress is undoubtedly laid on the motive. It was the absence of love in Cain's character and conduct that led to his action, which was originally "of the evil one" himself, who is the essence of lovelessness and hatefulness. And the cause of this action was the simple yet significant one that "his works were evil, and his brother's righteous." Everything showed the utter absence of love and with that the awful presence of hate.

2. *The experience* (vs. 13, 14). The Christians were not to be surprised if they had the hatred of the world (John 15:18, 19). On the contrary, they would know by their love of the Christian brethren that they had passed out of the sphere of death into that of life.

This blessed change would be within the realm of their consciousness. They knew it, and the evidence, sufficient and ample, would be the love of their brethren, and the equally obvious, though contrasted fact, that any one who did not love was really living in the old sphere of death. Once again we observe how the Apostle sharply contrasts the two realms, not allowing even the possibility of anything like a third or even a border line. It is either death or life, hate or love.

3. *The fact* (v. 15). But the absence of love and the presence of hate is even more than abiding in death; it is the positive presence of murder, which is hatred in expression, and there was the clear consciousness on the part of Christians that "no murderer hath eternal life abiding in him." This twofold appeal to their knowledge is particularly significant in the use of the word which means instinctive, direct, objective knowledge. Such a fact does not really need personal experience even though the practical result is an experience of the great change.

III. THE PATTERN (vs. 16–18)

Now we are to be shown the supreme revelation of love as seen in service.

1. *Sacrificing* (v. 16). In contrast to Cain, who took life, this is a reference to One who laid down his life. And as he thus expressed his love for us, we are under the great obligation of imitating that model and laying down our lives for the brethren. Our personal experience of Christ's love to us is intended to impel and compel us to show similar self-sacrifice.

2. *Simple* (v. 17). Small things are the best test of love, and it is shown that if we are unwilling to help our brother in his need, it is impossible that God's love is dwelling in us. There ought to be in every believer a reality of love in the threefold expression of it; in a capacity to help, a knowledge of needs, and a self-sacrificing attitude. It is not the utterance of some great or profound truth, or the accomplishment of some wonderful deed, but the quiet, simple help of a needy brother that beyond all else demonstrates our possession of the love of God. The two words, "hath" and "beholdeth," followed by "shutteth up," show with great clearness the danger of a terrible selfishness, for to possess life's good things and then to gaze at a needy one, and at the same time to shut up as with a key our compassion, is to disprove our possession of the first principle of love.

3. *Sincere* (v. 18). And so the Apostle urges us to love, not in word but in deed, not with the tongue but in truth. Whether we think of the family or of the Church, this must be the proof of our affection. It may take all kinds of forms, sometimes in hospitality, at other times in the help of the poor, at others in the furtherance of world-wide evangelization. But whatever may be the object of our affection, it is to be practical and not theoretical, in actual reality and not in mere profession.

Thus love is seen to be the manward evidence of our being children of God. Not what we think, however accurately; not what we feel, however strongly; not what we say, however eloquently; but what we do in genuine, practical, self-sacrificing activity, is the sole proof and test of our brother-love.

CHAPTER 3:19–24

Christianity is love, and love means action. This is a proof of spiritual reality, and the assurance of reality is one of the essential features of Christian experience. It is this thought of assurance, as based on practical action, that the Apostle now emphasizes.

I. ASSURANCE DESCRIBED

What are the features of the assurance which is here so prominently taught? The following points are included:

1. To be of the truth (v. 19). This seems to refer to our spiritual state rather than to our judicial standing, and means belonging to Christ (John 18:37). The Apostle had already referred to their knowledge of the truth (2:21), and here is the additional thought of being "of the truth."

2. To be confident in the presence of God (v. 19). The believer will not fear, but will be assured in heart as he lives before the face of God.

3. To be free from condemnation of heart (v. 20). There are some textual difficulties at this point, though the general meaning seems clear. The Apostle teaches that even though our own hearts condemn us, God is tenderer, and is ready to make every allowance because of his perfect knowledge (John 21:17).

4. To be frank with God (v. 21). The word "boldness" means, as in the other three places in this Epistle, "freedom of speech," the attitude of perfect candor in our personal relation to God.

5. To have answers to prayer (v. 22). There is no doubt in this respect, in view of the unqualified statement, "whatsoever we ask, we receive," and the explanation is "because we keep his commandments, and do the things that are pleasing in his sight." Thus, answers to prayer are associated with our obedience. A Jewish saying, quoted by Dr. Brooke (International Critical Commentary), says: "Do his will as if it were thine, that he may do thy will as if it were his."

6. To abide in him (v. 24). It is interesting to notice this and other instances of reciprocal abiding of the believer in God and God in the believer. Sometimes only the one side is mentioned, God abiding in us. At other times, our abiding in God is alone mentioned. But the full relationship is the reciprocal abiding which is found four times (3:24; 4:13; 4:15; 4:16). (Law, "The Tests of Life," p. 198.)

7. To know that he abides in us (v. 24). This is by no means the least important element of the reality of assurance, and the word used indicates a continuous experience of this abiding.

II. ASSURANCE DERIVED

As we review these aspects of assurance, it is inevitable to ask how they may become ours, and in the course of his statement the Apostle makes this clear. Assurance comes from the observance of the following conditions:

1. *Love* (v. 19). This is seen in the word "hereby," referring back to the former verse, and shows how practical love is, and how unselfish. It is no question of great knowledge, or

profound philosophy, for nothing so subtle or partial as these can give assurance. The one requirement is love, as our Lord himself pointed out when he remarked, "ye did it," and "ye did it not" (Matt. 25).

2. *Sincerity* (vs. 19, 20). As the believer lives in God's presence, and allows God to search and know the heart, he is able to have the experience of sincerity and thereby becomes persuaded that all is well.

3. *Obedience* (vs. 22, 23, 24). This emphasis on the Commandments and our observance of them, and doing what God tells us is another opportunity for obtaining assurance. There is nothing meritorious in this obedience (John 15:7), for it is only the condition of blessing. The word "keep" (vs. 22, 24) signifies watchfulness and carefulness in our daily response of obedience. It is also important to notice that doing righteousness is the proof of new life (2:29), while the possession of new life is in turn proved by doing righteousness (3:24). It is particularly impressive to remember this stress on simple obedience, and the precise "Commandment" has a twofold outlook, belief in Christ and love to one another. This is the first time that believing is mentioned in the Epistle.

Thus assurance is seen to be no mere matter of the inner consciousness, still less of emotional feeling, but something objective, ethical, and practical. Knowledge (v. 19), fearlessness (vs. 20, 21), power (v. 22), and permanence (v. 24) are seen to come through belief, love, and righteousness. There is perhaps nothing more important today than the realization of the objective and ethical grounds of assurance, because we are only too apt to associate it with the subjective and emotional elements of the Christian life. What is sometimes called "the witness of the Spirit" is due to no tide of feeling within, but to the definite attitude of the heart towards Christ and the equally definite action of the life in love and obedience

CHAPTER 4:1–6

In 3:23 two matters are mentioned, faith and love, and these are now taken up in turn, faith in 4:1–6, and love in 4:7–21. Another link of connection is that in 3:24 reference was made to our knowledge of God's abiding in us by the Holy Spirit. But the question may be asked how we know the Spirit, and the answer is now to be given in connection with the one definite requirement of the confession of Jesus Christ as having come in the flesh (4:2). It is important to compare this passage with 2:18–28, though here reference is made to false spirits as well as the true Spirit.

I. THE CALL (v. 1)

1. *The Appeal.* The Apostle starts with the endearing word "beloved," as in 2:27, showing the intensity of his attitude. He begs them not to believe every spirit, because they are not all true.

2. *The Duty.* "But prove the spirits whether they are of God." This appeal to test and prove the spirits is very important, and Paul refers to the power as one that was specially associated with the bestowal of the Divine grace (1 Cor. 12:10). There are several other things mentioned in the New Testament as needing "to be proved": thus we are to prove ourselves (1 Cor. 11:28; 2 Cor. 13:5), God's will (Rom. 12:2), others (2 Cor. 8:8), our time (Luke 12:56), our work (Gal. 6:4), and indeed "all things" (1 Thess. 5:21). This would require spiritual discernment, especially because of the presence of so much, that was counterfeit. The spirits would speak through prophets, and in this process of proving the Christians would be enabled to see that a thing might be supernatural without necessarily being Divine. "Enthusiasm is no guarantee of truth" (Law).

3. *The Reason.* "Because many false prophets are gone out." This reference calls attention to the remarkable feature found throughout the Bible, the presence of false prophets. In the Old Testament, in particular, they are quite prominent, and constitute an element that calls for the most careful and thorough consideration (Deut. 13:1–5). Even in the New Testament they are only too visible (Matt. 7:15; Acts 13:6). This contrast of false and true is very solemn, and shows how the right is counterfeited by the wrong. Almost everything connected with God and truth finds its counterpart in various forms of error. Thus, in contrast with the Divine Trinity of Father, Son, and Holy Spirit, we have the trinity of evil—the world, the devil, and the flesh. In contrast to the wheat, we have the counterfeit tares; in contrast with angels, we have demons.

"In every age the false has counterfeited the true. In Egypt the magicians imitated Moses, and in the Apostolic Church Simon Magus imitated Philip. Whenever the Church experiences a great revival there always spring up many spurious forms of enthusiasm that are counterfeits of the true. It is this that makes it so important for us to be able to prove the spirits. Half a truth is more dangerous than a lie. The form of godliness that lacks the power will deceive many who will be uninfluenced by blank atheism. Those who modify truth have always injured the truth more than those who have denied it openly" (First Epistle of John, by L. Palmer).

II. THE STANDARD (vs. 2, 3)

But how is this proof to be applied? What is the criterion by which the truth may be known and distinguished from the false?

1. *The Test.* The first mark of the Spirit of God is the confession of the Person of Christ, and this is closely bound up with the confession of Christ as Incarnate. "Every spirit that confesseth that Jesus Christ is come in the flesh is of God." This clearly refers, especially in the original language, to the permanence of the Incarnation. In opposition to any heresy which implied that the Divine element in Jesus was only temporary, the Apostle emphasizes in the strongest way the abiding truth of "Jesus Christ come in the flesh." This is equivalent to the words of the Apostle Paul that "no man can say that Jesus is Lord but in the Holy Spirit" (1 Cor. 12:3).

2. *The Value.* The reason why this point is made so impressive by the Apostle is that in the Incarnation there was, and still continues, a union between God and man. Without such an Incarnation there could be no contact between the Divine and the human, and, therefore, no redemption. Thus we see that the emphasis laid on the Incarnation is no mere matter of intellectual speculation, but touches the springs of life in the need of redemption from sin. There is a mediæval legend that Satan once appeared to a monk in his cell, and said that he was Jesus Christ. When the monk asked him to show the nail-prints, Satan disappeared. The death of Jesus Christ is the supreme proof that his life was at once human and Divine.

3. *The Issue.* In contrast with this confession of the Incarnation as a proof of the Divine Spirit, the Apostle adds that the opposite is the spirit of the antichrist (2:18). Men have always been tested as to their relation to Christ, and this is equally true of the spirit-world. It is well known that in spiritualistic séances today the simple, yet sufficient, test is invariably this: Has Jesus Christ come in the flesh? Is he God Incarnate? And those who know say that never once has an affirmative answer been given in connection with Spiritism. This is clear proof that Spiritism is not, and cannot be, from God.

III. THE OUTCOME (vs. 4–6)

Now the Apostle wishes to express his satisfaction that those to whom he was writing were not at all likely to be led astray. Indeed, he may be said to congratulate them on their faithfulness, for it is clear that they were so true to this confession of Christ that there was nothing to fear.

1. *The Victory* (v. 4). Without any qualification he emphasizes the fact that they are "of God," and had overcome the evil spirits around, and on this account "because greater is he that is in you than he that is in the world." This was no boasting, but a simple, quiet consciousness that, notwithstanding all the forces at work in the world against them and their Master, the victory was certain because of the greater power of the indwelling Christ.

2. *The Contrast* (vs. 5, 6). In striking words the Apostle refers to the false teachers and to himself and others, and does not hesitate to put one against the other by saying "they are of the world; we are of God." It was because the erroneous and evil teachers were of the world that they spoke and were listened to by those of the same mind.

3. *The Result* (v. 6). It was this that constituted the essential difference between truth and error, and the Apostle emphasized this as the mark of difference: "By this we know the spirit of truth and the spirit of error." The spiritual perception was twofold; they knew the true and they knew the false, and hence they accepted the one and rejected the other.

These simple, yet searching, truths show that not only for the Apostle's day, but for our own, the attitude we adopt to the Incarnation is absolutely and immediately decisive. For each and all, for every circumstance and time, the one supreme question is, "What think ye of Christ?"

CHAPTER 4:7–13

It is interesting to notice the almost exact repetition found in two texts (3:24 and 4:13): "Hereby we know that he abideth in us, by the Spirit which he gave us" (3:24); "Hereby we know that we abide in him and he in us, because he hath given us of his spirit" (4:13). This double reference to the proof of the indwelling of the Holy Spirit clearly suggests that in between the section come the two marks whereby we may know this. The first of these is the acceptance of true doctrine—namely, Jesus Christ as Incarnate (vs. 1–6), which we have already considered. And the second is the manifestation of true life in the fact of love (vs. 7–12), which we have now to study.

Love has already been mentioned as a sign of God's Kingdom (2:5–11), as a mark of Sonship (3:10–18), as a proof of obedience (3:23). Now it is to be considered as indicating likeness to God. Love is thus based on the revelation of the Divine nature, and we are to love on this account.

I. THE CALL TO LOVE (v. 7)

As before, the Apostle uses the special term "beloved" (4:1), indicative of his special and urgent appeal to them to manifest love. His desire is for Christians to "love one another," thereby carrying out their Lord's "new commandment" (John 13:34, 35; 15:12).

II. THE REASON OF LOVE (v. 7)

We are to love one another because love is of God, finding its source in the Divine nature.

III. THE TEST OF LOVE (vs. 7, 8a)

It is a striking statement that "every one that loveth is begotten of God and knoweth God." Love is thus the test of life and of knowledge. While the life is described in the original as having taken place in the past, though with permanent results, the knowledge is spoken of as continuous and indicative of personal experience. This association of life, knowledge, and love is important, especially because it shows that to love is to know, while the absence of love means the absence of knowledge, for "he that loveth not knoweth not God." The phrase is very searching as the Apostle uses it, for it seems to mean "he who does not want to love." Once again, therefore, emphasis is laid upon spiritual perception as arising out of love, and this is always opposed to any mere intellectual perception of truth which may easily stop short with itself and not become expressed in love. Someone has helpfully distinguished between faith and love by saying that "faith is the appropriation to self of what applies to all; love is the extension to all of what applies to self."

IV. THE NATURE OF LOVE (vs. 8b, 10)

At this point we are reminded that "God is love," and in this we see the true character of love.

1. *Love is self-communicating.* Since God is love, he must always have had an object of his affection, for love is obviously impossible without an object. Thus, we may say that anyone who does not love has no experience of God.

2. *Love is spontaneous.* It has its roots in God, and, as such, it comes unbidden. God has already been shown to be Light (1:5) and Spirit (John 4:24); but now, including and even surpassing these, he is Love.

V. THE PROOF OF LOVE (vs. 9, 10)

We proceed to notice that the eternal and essential character of God as love became manifest in history in the Person of Jesus Christ. Thus, the eternal fact becomes revealed as a constant factor in human life.

1. *God sending* (v. 9). This act and fact was the manifestation of God's love in our case.

2. *God sending his best.* When he sent "his only begotten Son into the world," he bestowed his supreme gift, for he had nothing higher or more valuable to send.

3. *God sacrificing.* God's love was seen not only in the gift of his Son, but in the gift of that Son as a sacrifice. We cannot ponder too often or too deeply this wonderful proof of the Divine heart of love (John 3:16).

VI. THE PURPOSE OF LOVE (vs. 9, 10)

But we must still further inquire as to the reasons why God thus manifested his love in the gift of his Son.

1. *Life* (v. 9). "That we might live through him." The supreme purpose of God for man is life, and this life is only possible through Jesus Christ, God's Son (John 10:10).

2. *Propitiation* (v. 10). Inasmuch as sin was a barrier to God's love, it was necessary for his Son to die on our behalf, and we know already that the scope of the propitiation is at once personal, "our sins," and universal, "the whole world" (2:2).

The connection of "propitiation" and "life" is evident. The former is the cause of the latter, for it is through the sacrifice of Christ that we obtain everlasting life.

VII. THE CLAIM OF LOVE (v. 11)

1. *The Character.* Once more the Apostle drives come his message by the term "beloved," and, as in the Gospel, he dwells upon the nature of God's love by the use of the little yet unfathomable word "so"—"if God so loved us" (compare John 3:16). How shall we explain what is included in this "so"? It is obviously beyond our full comprehension, but we may perhaps apprehend a little when we think of God's love as spontaneous in its source, universal in scope, long-suffering in intensity, self-sacrificing in character, aggressive in action, and constant in duration. Be it ours to ponder again and again the meaning of "so loved us."

2. *The Obligation.* "We also ought to love one another." Based upon what God has done for us comes the present, increasing and permanent obligation that arises from God's gift of his Son, the example he has himself set us, and the power of his love as it is realized in our experience. Thus, the pressure of "we also ought" should weigh heavily upon us day by day.

VIII. THE CONSUMMATION OF LOVE (v. 12)

1. *God as invisible.* Perhaps the reason why this point is mentioned here is in order to show that as God is unseen to mortal eyes we cannot help him directly, and also because he does not need our help. But we can help others who are visible, and if we do this, we, too, shall manifest the Godlike nature of love.

2. *God as indwelling.* "If we love one another, God abideth in us." Love thus brings God near and makes him real to the soul. Spiritual fellowship becomes actual as we exercise love towards those around us.

3. *God's love as perfected.* When we love one another, "His love is perfected in us." Fellowship with him is thus fully realized, and love attains to its culmination.

Thus, we see the second proof of the gift of the Holy Spirit in the exercise of love (4:13). God is shown first as the foundation of life (4:3), and then as the foundation of love (4:9, 10). It is for us first to receive him in his love, then to realize it, and then to reproduce it in love to others.

CHAPTER 4:14–19

The two ideas of belief (vs. 1–6) and love (vs. 7–12) are here blended, and shown to be connected by the Spirit. As the Spirit of Truth, he witnesses to Christ, and as the Spirit of Love he produces love. Some writers think that the "herein" of verse 13 looks forward, not backward, but probably it is a mark of transition, linking the two sections.

Dr. Law suggests that as love has been indicated as a test of life three times (2:7–11; 3:10–24; 4:7–12), so now belief is mentioned as a test for the third time (2:18–28; 3:24 to 4:6; 4:13–16).

I. LIFE (vs. 14, 15)

1. *The Root* (v. 14). The Apostle lays a strong foundation in four ways. He speaks of the Father who is the origin, the Son who is the agent, the "Saviour" as suggesting the purpose, and the world as indicating the destination.

2. *The Revelation.* "We have beheld and bear witness." Thus, once again the Apostle gives his personal testimony to these realities.

3. *The Requirement.* "Whosoever shall confess that Jesus is the Son of God." As elsewhere, so here, confession is no mere lip service or intellectual theory, but a personal, spiritual experience. Already reference has been made to confessing the Son (2:23), and the coming of Jesus Christ in the flesh (4:2).

Here, however, there is the further specific requirement of confession of the human Jesus as the Divine Son.

4. *The Result.* "God abideth in him and he in God." This reciprocal indwelling should be noted here, and in every other place (v. 13). The outcome of a personal confession of the Lord Jesus Christ in his redemptive character and purpose leads to this mutual indwelling.

II. LOVE (v. 16)

1. *As a Fact.* The Apostle speaks of the love "which God hath in us," thereby referring to the actuality of this love and its relation to us. Perhaps the word "in" means only "towards" or "in our case."

2. *As a Feeling.* "We know and we believe." The Apostle, speaking for himself and for his friends, is able to testify at once to their own experience and conviction of this love. The two verbs seem to imply the recognition and persuasion of love (Law).

3. *As a Foundation.* This is seen in the nature of God, which is once again described as love (v. 8). Beyond this no one can go, for love includes everything involved in the Divine nature.

4. *As a Force.* "He that abideth in love abideth in God, and God abideth in him." Once again we have this reciprocal abiding (v. 15). And it is said that when we abide in love, we experience this mutual indwelling. Since God is love, he who abides in love naturally and inevitably abides in God.

Thus we see that belief is a test of life and the outcome of our union with Christ.

III. LIBERTY (vs. 17–19)

1. *The Cause.* The reference to "herein" seems again to link the two verses looking backward and forward. It is because we are abiding in love that we are enabled to look forward with confidence. It is not quite clear whether the phrase "with us" is to be connected with "love" or "perfect." If the latter, the difference from verse 12 "in us" is noteworthy.

2. *The Character.* The idea of "love made perfect" seems to suggest that the mutual relation is entirely one of love, and that in the highest measure. Like Paul's phrase, "the fulness of God" (Eph. 3:19), the life of the believer may be said to have reached its end and culmination. As it has been suggestively remarked, "Faith is the flower that receives the dew and the sun, while love is that flower reflecting beauty and fragrance."

At this point it is important to recall the three proofs of "love made perfect" as found in this Epistle. The first is Obedience, our relation to God (2:5). The second is Love, our relation to others (4:12). The third is Boldness, our relation to ourselves (4:17, 18).

3. *The Consequence.* "That we may have boldness." The thought is that of present possession, "have," though it also looks forward to the "day of Judgment." Boldness is as before (2:28) that confidence which comes from perfect frankness between our souls and God. And the additional thought is

given that as Christ is one with the Father, so are we in Him, even though we are still in this world. The phrase "as he" is particularly significant, and should be noticed here and everywhere else (2:6; 3:3; 3:7).

4. *The Confidence.* On account of our love we do not experience any fear, especially because God first loved us. The fear mentioned here is, of course, slavish, not reverential (2 Cor. 7:1). There is nothing to cause us to feel afraid because of God's love, the consciousness of which inspires us with such confidence that all dread is necessarily and forever banished (3:18–21).

And so we may say of Love that it is (1) based on faith; (2) casts out fear; (3) unites us to God; (4) assures our future.

CHAPTER 4:20 TO 5:3a

The Apostle's subject is still that of "Love." In 4:17–19 he has shown that love to God is connected with belief in Christ, and is at once rooted in confession and perfected in confidence. Now he is to show that love to the brethren is connected with love to God, that the latter is realized in the former. So we look again at the thought of love, though this time with special reference to those around, our fellow Christians.

I. AS A SIMPLE NECESSITY (4:20)

1. *The Attitude.* "If a man say I love God." Once again the reference is to the man who talks without doing (1:6; 2:4, 6, 9). The Apostle naturally criticizes such an attitude of mere words without deeds.

2. *The Character.* "And hateth his brother." It is striking that here, as elsewhere, nothing is regarded as possible between "love" and "hate" (2:9; 2:22; 3:15). To John there was no middle pathway, a man either loved or hated. The heart is incapable of moral neutrality; it must be one thing or the other.

3. *The Accusation.* "He is a liar." This plain speaking is the definite charge made against a man who says one thing and shows another, the opposite, in his life. John uses this term "liar" in various connections, and all are associated with the attitude of moral and spiritual unreality (1:10; 2:4; 5:10).

4. *The Reason.* "For he that loveth not his brother whom he hath seen cannot love God whom he hath not seen." Love has already been shown to be action, not feeling, and as action needs an object, the only visible object is the child of God in whom God dwells. So that "his brother" means the visible presentation of the image of God as the sole opportunity of the bestowment of love.

II. AS A SPECIAL COMMAND (4:21)

1. *Its Unity.* "This commandment." As in 3:23, one commandment includes and involves all the rest. Thus the thought of love is concentrated and made more definite.

2. *Its Divinity.* "From whom." This shows that the word of command concerning love comes from none other than God himself.

3. *Its Spirituality.* "He who loveth God love his brother also." Once again the emphasis is laid on the necessity of expressing our love by bestowing it on some visible object, and there is none more fitting than our Christian brother, our affection for him being a genuine proof of our love to God.

III. As a Sure Consequence (v. 1)

We are now to see that love to the brethren is based on our affinity of nature with God as indicated by three steps.

1. *Life comes through faith.* "Whosoever believeth … is begotten of God." To deny that Jesus is the Messiah is a mark of the antichrist (2:22), while to believe in him is the means of receiving Divine life (John 1:12).

2. *Love comes through life.* When we, through believing, receive God's life we begin to love because our life is one with God who is love. The love of child for parent is the natural outcome of their living connection, and our love to God necessarily comes from the fact that we possess his life.

3. *Love comes through love.* When we love God because we are begotten of him, we necessarily proceed to love those who, like ourselves, possess his life. From the filial relationship comes the fraternal. Thus, by believing we are born, because we are born we love God, and because we love God we love the brethren.

IV. As a Spiritual Principle (vs. 2, 3a)

We are now to see how love to God's children is based on our relationship to God.

1. *The Fact.* "We love the children of God." This is what may be called spiritual nature, for there is such a thing as moral affinity, just as there are natural and chemical affinities.

2. *The Knowledge.* "We know that we love." The word indicates a continuous, personal experience, and shows again the importance of this as a personal possession of the soul.

3. *The Proof.* "Hereby we know." The test of loving God's children is loving God and doing what he tells us. There will be careful observance and a constant watchfulness of God's Commandments, and in this will be the best proof that we really possess the Divine life and enjoy the Divine love (John 14:15, 21).

So that Christianity and love are seen to be the same thing, and we say that love must be based on faith, for faith is a sign of the genuineness of love. We ought, therefore, to ask ourselves whether we love others in relation to God, whether we love spiritually, whether we are really concerned for the *souls* of men.

We also see that love is practical, not sentimental, for it overcomes dislikes and rises above prejudices. To love is one thing, to *like* is another, and while it is impossible to like everybody, because there are many people with whom we have nothing "alike," we must, and can, love all with the unselfish, self-sacrificing affection which is the essence of true Christian love.

If it should be asked why there is such emphasis on "brethren," perhaps the answer is that as love is a practical test of the Christian life, the best sphere and opportunity for exercising it is in relation to our Christian brethren. Thus, we are reminded that Christianity is no "loveless intellectualism" (Law).

And so we sum up by saying that love is (1) of God, (2) in Christ, (3) by the Spirit, (4) to the brethren (Rom. 5:5; 2 Cor. 13:12).

Chapter 5:3b–5

Love is to be shown by obedience (vs. 2, 3a), and the nature of God's Commandments is such that the freeness and spontaneity of love are not crushed by the endeavor to do God's will. Thus the Commandments are not a heavy burden, but are associated with a sense of moral and spiritual power. Three times over in these brief verses the word "overcometh" occurs, and this gives us the keynote of power.

I. Power Experienced (v. 3b)

"His Commandments are not grievous" or "burdensome." This is the definite statement, and the evident personal testimony of the writer.

1. When are God's Commandments "grievous"? Either when they are opposed by sin within, arising out of enmity, or when they are observed by law without, arising out of bondage. Our Lord charged the Pharisees with binding heavy burdens on men's shoulders so grievous that they could not be carried (Matt. 23:4; Luke 11:46). But in regard to his own claim on the soul, he said, "My yoke is easy and my burden is light" (Matt. 11:30). The sinner, so long as he is hostile to God, cannot possibly feel otherwise than that God's law is a heavy burden. And even the believer, when he is struggling to do the will of God in his own strength, is involved in bondage by reason of his present inability. Thus, it is impossible for man to justify himself by his own efforts (Rom. 3), and also to sanctify himself by his own efforts (Rom. 7). In each case the Commandments are assuredly "grievous."

2. When are the Commandments not "grievous"? First, when condemnation has been removed and thereby enmity has been abolished (Rom. 8:1). Then, when character has been renewed, with the result that there is no bondage (Rom. 8:2–4). Those who have thus been made free judicially and experimentally (Rom. 6:7, 18, 22; 8:2) are enabled to carry out God's requirements because they are no longer living in and by their own power, but in the presence and grace of the Holy Spirit (Rom. 8:14–16). In this spiritual condition the soul rejoices to say with the Apostle, "His Commandments are not grievous."

II. Power Exemplified (vs. 4, 5)

The idea running through these statements is associated with victory.

1. *The Foe.* Once again the "world" is seen to be the great and powerful enemy of the Christian. The word means everyone and everything around considered apart from God (2:15–17). As already observed, it is not always easy to decide definitely what is "the world," but it may be said that anyone who would have us believe that God's Commandments are a heavy burden, and anything in life that tends to make us accept this view, is assuredly of "the world" for us. It has also been said that one of the finest tests of "the world" is to inquire whether a thing leaves us less inclined for prayer and fellowship with God. If it does, we may be sure it is "of the earth, earthy."

2. *The Conquest.* With the Commandment comes the power, and the soul realizes continuous victory as it faces the vigilant and virulent foe.

III. Power Explained (vs. 4, 5)

It is now necessary to inquire more definitely how this victory is obtained, and the passage reveals a twofold secret of power.

1. *Commencement.* "Whatsoever is begotten of God overcometh." This shows that victory depends first of all on our new life. It is well known that virtues can often be cultivated and developed without regeneration, for many a man is honest, truthful, and exemplary who has never been born again. But for genuine and continuous victory over the world we must have spiritual life, because of the power of desires within and the bondage of custom without. We know how even ascetics have been able to curb, restrain, and even refine, their natures, but they certainly have not been able to obtain that victory over all things in the world which comes alone from the possession of Divine life.

2. *Continuance.* "This is the victory that overcometh the world, even our faith." Life begets trust, and from trust comes power. Faith unites us to Christ, and in union with him we have a deeper insight, a more sensitive conscience, a purer heart, and a more determined will. This faith appropriates Christ's victory (John 16:33), and so we are "more than conquerors through him that loved us" (Rom. 8:37).

As we look again at these verses revealing the elements of power in daily living, we may say that (1) faith makes all things possible, because it is the means of receiving the Divine life. (2) Life makes all things easy, because it is the condition of receiving Divine power. (3) Love makes all things delightful, because it rejoices in the Divine presence.

Chapter 5:6–10

The references to believing (vs. 1, 4, 5) are now shown to rest upon a solid basis by a fuller statement of what is implied in the Lord Jesus Christ as the Son of God (v. 5).

I. The Historical Foundation (v. 6)

Without going into elaborate discussion on this text, and giving various views, it will suffice to state what seems to be the best interpretation.

1. *The Life of Christ.* "This is he that came by water." The reference seems to be to John's baptism as marking the beginning of Christ's ministry (John 1:31; Acts 1:22). Thus the Apostle desires to emphasize the importance of the actual life and historical appearance of Jesus Christ.

2. *The Death of Christ.* "This is he that came by water and blood." Not only did Christ come to live, he came to die, and his death was an essential part of his historical revelation. Perhaps the Apostle has in mind the tendency (which certainly appeared very early) to suggest that the Divine Christ came on the human Jesus at his baptism, but left him before his passion. This, as we know, was a familiar Gnostic idea, and it may be the reason for John's emphasis both on the life and on the death of our Lord. It is a great satisfaction and a real comfort to know that our faith is thus based upon the reality of Christ's historical manifestation. "Christianity is Christ."

II. The Divine Attestation (vs. 7–9)

It is now necessary to show that this historical revelation of Christ Jesus in his life and death obtained a Divine testimony in support of it.

1. *The Spirit* (v. 7). "It is the Spirit that beareth witness." We have already seen the relation of the Holy Spirit to Christ (4:2), and we know from our Lord's own teaching that the Paraclete was to bear testimony to him, and thus show what God thought of his Son (John 15:26). This as a matter of simple fact has been done all through the ages, for the presence and power of the Holy Spirit in the Church from the first day until now have been concerned with one thing only, testimony to the Lord Jesus Christ. This is so "because the Spirit is truth." Thus we have "the Spirit of truth" recognizing and testifying to him who is "the truth," and we know that this would not take place unless Christ were truth. Everything that the Holy Spirit does in connection with Christian life, holiness, and power is really a testimony to the reality of Jesus Christ as the revelation of God.

2. *The water and the blood* (v. 8). This seems to imply the testimony of a real Incarnation. Some writers think that this is an allusion to the abiding use of the two Sacraments of Baptism and the Lord's Supper as evidences of Christianity (Law), and certainly their evidential value is great. Every time we administer Baptism and celebrate the Lord's Supper we are bearing witness to beliefs and facts which have been in the Christian Church from the start. But it seems much more natural to interpret the water and the blood here in exactly the same way as in verse 6, and to think of them as referring to the witness of Christ's life and death. If any reference is intended to the Sacraments, it can only be indirect, because of their being symbols of spiritual realities, and it is much simpler to think of "the water and the blood" as the spiritual realities themselves, constituting a real Incarnation as the basis of the witness of the Spirit which assures us of God's revelation (4:2).

3. *God* (v. 9). Behind the witness of Christ and the Spirit is the testimony of God himself, who is ever bearing witness to his Son. This Divine evidence is infinitely greater than anything human, and if we are ready to accept the witness of men we ought to be still more ready to accept the witness of God which he bears concerning his Son. In the Fourth Gospel we read more than once of the Father's testimony to Christ (John 5:36, 37). It is also interesting and deeply significant that a Divine voice was associated with the commencement of our Lord's ministry at his Baptism; with the middle of it. on the occasion of the Transfiguration; and with the close of it, when the Greeks sought an interview with Christ. At all times the Father was ready to testify to his Son, and that which was true of the Lord's earthly life is infinitely truer today, for everything that comes from Christ in Christianity is really the gift of the Father (John 3:16).

III. The Personal Confirmation (v. 10)

Now we are to observe how all these evidences are crowned in personal experience.

1. *Realisation.* "He that believeth on the Son of God hath the witness in himself." This means a personal possession of Christ dwelling in the soul. We trust, and then we credit what we trust, and the outcome is a blessed personal consciousness.

2. *Rejection.* "He that believeth not God hath made him a liar." This is an awful alternative, and the original really means "he that does not want to believe." He is said to ascribe falsehood to God because he does not and will not believe what God says concerning Christ. It is profoundly solemn and searching to realize that when we are thus denying Christ, we are actually ascribing falsehood to God (1:10).

Thus we see the sure foundation on which our spiritual life is based. (1) Faith rests on facts. (2) Faith is realized in experience. (3) Faith is reproduced in evidence.

Chapter 5:11–15

The keyword of verses 7–10 is "witness," and now the Apostle proceeds to define the substance of God's testimony in order to give a solid foundation for faith. Such a basis necessarily leads to assurance, and it is this that constitutes the essential feature of the Christian life as indicated in the entire Epistle; "that ye may know" (v. 13). We must now mark the various stages of the process whereby we become assured and may use this spiritual confidence.

I. Giving (v. 11)

As the Apostle has made reference to God's testimony concerning his Son, it is essential to understand what this witness is.

1. *The Gift.* "God gave unto us eternal life." The complete phrase "eternal life" calls for constant and careful attention in the twofold expression, "life" and "eternal." This is defined elsewhere (John 16:3) as continuing in the knowledge of God and of Christ, meaning thereby a spiritual experience resulting in blessed fellowship. Thus, "eternal" life does not mean mere existence, but union and communion with God, and it is concerned not so much with duration, or indeed with duration at all, so much as with quality, though, of course, duration is naturally involved. This present gift of union and communion with God in Christ embraces everything needed for the spiritual life here and hereafter, including remission of sin, reception into God's favor, renewal in the spirit, and reunion hereafter. This idea of life and life in its fullest possible degree, is the simple but all inclusive purpose of God for us (John 10:10). And it must never be forgotten that life is invariably a gift, not an attainment.

2. *The Giver.* "God gave." This emphasis on the Divine source of eternal life calls for special attention, because it goes to show still more clearly the reality of that witness to which reference has already been made (v. 10).

3. *The Means.* "This life is in his Son." The solemn addition to the thought indicates that only in Christ is this gift possible. We may "exist" in the ordinary sense apart from Christ, but it is only through participation in "his Son" that eternal life becomes ours. This is another way of saying what is so characteristic of the New Testament, that only in Christ can spiritual blessings be obtained (Acts 4:12).

4. *The Destination.* "Unto us." This, of course, refers to Christians and to them alone, thereby showing the limitation of this gift. God does not scatter his blessing of "eternal life" indiscriminately and everywhere; it is only for those who are willing to receive, those who accept through faith the new and divine life (v. 1). Once again the Apostle marks off the Christian from the man of the world and shows the vital and essential difference between them,

II. Having (v. 12)

This is an explanation of the latter part of verse 11, telling us in simple yet unmistakable language the essential features and conditions of this gift of God.

1. *What?* In the possession of the Son comes the enjoyment of the life, and when the Son dwells in us the life is sure to enrich us. The way in which the Apostle speaks both of "the Son" and "the life" indicates that he is appealing to the spiritual experience of his readers.

2. *How?* "He that hath." The present tense is particularly noteworthy, "hath," and is characteristic of the writings of John (John 3:36; 5:24). But, as is well known, the word "hath" in the New Testament means both to obtain and to retain, including not only possession but conscious possession. We may almost say that "to have" means "to have and to hold." The contrast is very solemn: "He that hath not the Son of God hath not the life." The Apostle seems to suggest in the language he uses that the description refers to one who does not wish to possess and enjoy this blessing. "He who does not want to have" might almost be used as the proper rendering, and it reminds us of our Lord's words: "Ye will not come to me, that ye may have life" (John 5:40).

III. KNOWING (v. 13)

Now the Apostle begins what has been called his postscript, and perhaps he looks back over the entire Epistle, though there seems no doubt that there is also a special reference to verses 6–12, and in particular to verses 11 and 12. Perhaps, too, he wishes to lead on directly to prayer as part of our spiritual knowledge, because such confidence concerning Christ is best seen in the exercise of confident prayer.

1. *Who?* The words are addressed definitely and solely to believers, "you that believe," for it is quite evident that only those who have faith can possibly have knowledge. In the Gospel the purpose was that they might "believe" (20:31), and here as a natural sequence the Apostle wishes them to "know."

2. *What?* The one thought is that they might "know that they have eternal life." He wishes them to realize what is involved in their faith in Christ, and it is probable that they lacked assurance (Brooke). If so, they were virtually powerless in regard to spiritual progress and blessing. The way in which the Apostle emphasizes assurance in this Epistle (3:19–24) seems to suggest this weakness in their life, and so he urges them to enter fully into their inheritance by instinctive, objective knowledge.

IV. BELIEVING (v. 13)

But it is necessary to look still more closely at what the Apostle has to say about faith.

1. *The Meaning.* When he addresses himself to those that "believe on the Name of the Son of God," he may be referring to a mature rather than an elementary faith, because the "name" invariably means the revealed character, what is known of a person, and to believe "on the name" implies a knowledge of Christ that can hardly be applicable to the beginner in Christianity. Thus we read of believing on the Son of God (v. 10), and also of believing "on the name of his Son, Jesus Christ" (3:23).

This emphasis on the "Son" is also very striking, for in these verses (5–13) the word occurs no fewer than eight times. It shows at once the definiteness of the object of our faith, and also at the same time his relation to God.

2. *The Power.* When the Apostle says "you that believe," he is revealing the secret of everything that is worth while in the Christian life, for if God gives we receive by faith; if God bestows we possess by faith; if we are to understand we know by faith. Faith is thus the key to receiving, possessing and knowing.

V. OBTAINING (vs. 14, 15)

Christian assurance leads on to prayer, and those of whom the earlier words are true will readily and gladly express their assurance in pouring out their hearts in prayer.

1. *The Confidence.* "This is the boldness which we have toward him." This is the fourth time the word is used in this Epistle, and it always means, as we have seen, freedom or frankness of speech, that absolute lack of reserve which characterizes true friendship. Twice it is found in connection with the spiritual life in the present (3:21; 5:14), and twice in regard to our attitude towards the future (2:28; 4:17). It thus marks one of the essential and most blessed features of the true Christian life. We ought to be able to tell God everything.

2. *The Condition.* "If we ask anything according to his will." This is the one requirement of prayer, so that, as it has been well pointed out, prayer does not reduce God to our level, but lifts us to his. The more we know of his will the more intelligent and the more confident will be our prayers.

3. *The Consequence.* "He heareth us." The word seems to imply both hearing and answering, and the natural way in which it is stated as the outcome of the former idea of confidence and condition marks the true life of prayer.

4. *The Consciousness* (v. 15). The Apostle adds that the knowledge that God hears carries with it the knowledge that we shall have that for which we ask. This expression "we know that we have" is another element of true Christian experience, for it indicates a present assurance of the answer even though the actual fulfilment has not yet arrived. Like his Master before him, the Apostle was absolutely confident that in asking, according to the will of God, the prayer would be answered, even though it took a long time for its full realization (Mark 11:24).

In all this we see two blessed truths. (1) The simplicity of the Christian life. It consists of giving by God and receiving by us; of asking on our part and granting on God's part. All this comes to us and is enjoyed by us through the simple medium of faith. (2) The satisfaction of the Christian life. These words indicate the blessed reality of our possession in Christ. The Lord is seen to be indwelling; God is shown to be real; and as a consequence the soul is free, blessed, joyous, restful, "satisfied with favor, full with the blessing of the Lord."

CHAPTER 5:16–21

Now the Apostle comes to his closing words. From verse 13 to the end he seems to be concerned with a summary of the essential features of the Christian life, especially assurance, and its expression in prayer. And yet there is one thing to be specially mentioned before he can reach the concluding testimony.

I. PRAYER LIMITED (vs. 16, 17)

1. *The Fact of Intercession.* The prayer to which he has referred (vs. 14, 15) will not be concerned only with ourselves, but as life is truly shown in love (4:12), one way of proving our love is by prayer for others. This blessed and yet seldom thought of prayer reveals one of the prime secrets of true Christian living, and it would be well for us if we realized more than we do the duty and the power of prayer for those around, and especially for the Christian brotherhood. Samuel felt that if he ceased to pray for the people of Israel he would be committing a sin against God (1 Sam. 12:23), and if there was

more of this prayer and less of complaint to others (Matt. 18:15), the result would be greater blessing to ourselves and those around (Gal. 6:1). "More things are wrought by prayer than this world dreams of," and it may well be that through prayer we may be the means of the greatest spiritual blessings. Forbes Robinson in one of those wonderful letters of his says that our influence finally depends upon our own experience of the unseen world and on our experience of prayer. "To influence you must love; to love you must pray."

2. *The Limitation of Intercession.* And yet prayer as one form of love is decidedly limited, and the Apostle here refers to one particular feature in which this limitation is seen. He speaks of a sin unto death, and in quiet yet significant language he clearly deprecates prayer in this connection. What is this, this "sin unto death"? Much has been written on it, and it is hardly likely that the problem can be solved with our present knowledge. Most writers think of it as expressing an attitude of wilful unbelief, that which, if persisted in, will inevitably lead to separation from God and eternal death. There are, perhaps, five considerations that call for attention in the study of this difficult subject. (1) There is no doubt that it should not be "a sin," but "sin," thereby indicating not any particular act as distinct from others, but an entire attitude. (2) The verb rendered "sin" means "continually sinning," thereby suggesting that whatever it is it is no mere isolated action. (3) It is also the sin of "a brother"; that is, a fellow Christian, the thought of brotherhood being as much limited here as elsewhere. (4) Then it must be some sin which was visible, and, therefore, known, for it says "if any man see," suggesting that it was possible to observe the precise form of wrongdoing. (5) But, of course, the great difficulty lies in the phrase "unto death," and, inasmuch as every sin in itself, apart from grace, involves the soul in spiritual death, it is very difficult to see what this means when applied to a Christian brother. For this reason it seems to many simpler and better to understand "death" of bodily or physical death; and, if so, the passage will be parallel with the circumstances at Corinth, where Paul pointed out that many were ill and even dead, because of their abuse of the Lord's Supper (1 Cor. 11:30). May it not be the same here, that there were Christians who had sinned in some way so as to involve themselves in physical death, and that as this was inevitable the Apostle, while not absolutely forbidding prayer, suggests that no request should be made concerning those?

Dr. Law strongly opposes this view and says that "death" in the Epistle and in the Gospel always refers to spiritual and not physical dissolution. But notwithstanding this emphatic objection, the difficulty of conceiving of a Christian brother so deliberately and constantly sinning as to involve himself in spiritual and eternal separation from God seems to constitute an insuperable difficulty. The reference to physical death is simpler, and certainly satisfies all the five conditions indicated above and also corresponds with the well-known reference to Lazarus (John 11:4).

II. PURITY ASSUMED (v. 18)

1. *The Fact.* In contrast with this thought of unrighteousness and sin (v. 17), the Apostle once more asserts in the most unqualified way that everyone who possesses God's love does not continually practice sin (3:9). But though he clearly implies the possibility of evil, he will make no allowance for it (2:1), showing that the Christian life is essentially incompatible with continued practice of wrongdoing.

2. *The Knowledge.* "We know." Thus the Apostle insists on the instinctive knowledge that no such idea of sinning is considered to be in harmony with true Christianity, notwithstanding what has been said about the brother sinning (v. 16). There is a principle within the believer which is in itself sinless, and overcomes the evil nature if it is only allowed to dominate the life.

III. PROTECTION ASSURED (v. 18)

1. *The Cause.* "He that was begotten of God keepeth himself." This is the rendering of the old version, and is still urged as the only true one by two modern and able writers (Law and Kelly). But as the original language has two distinct expressions for "begotten of God," the one in the perfect tense and the other in the past, or aorist, it is urged by other writers that we must distinguish between the two references, the former being applied to the Christian and the latter to Christ, as the One who is uniquely begotten of God (Westcott, Findlay, and Brooke). If the latter is the right view, then we must read "him" instead of "himself," and understand that the reason why the believer does not sin is that Christ, "the begotten of God," keeps him. But, in spite of this strong and able advocacy, it seems more natural to interpret the text in the old way, and think of the believer in two aspects, the one as not sinning, and the other as keeping himself, taking heed by watchful observance. There is no contradiction between the believer keeping himself and being kept, for both aspects are true (Jude 21).

2. *The Fact.* "The evil one toucheth him not." Whether the reference is to Christ or to the believer, this is the immediate and blessed result. The devil "does not lay hold" of the Christian, because he is "kept by the power of God" (1 Pet. 1:5).

IV. POSSESSION REALIZED (v. 19)

1. *The Place.* Once again reference is made to the contrast between the believer and those who are outside the sphere of the Gospel. "We are of God, and the whole world lieth in the evil one." This claim to be "of God" naturally follows from the gift of life in being "begotten of God" (v. 18), and the contrast between the Christian and those who are "in the evil one" is particularly striking. Christians are of God, but the rest of the world is in the power of the devil. It seems, on the whole, best to make this phrase personal, "evil one," rather than impersonal, "evil" or "wickedness." The world is thus again regarded as the entire universe of men and things considered as morally separated from God (2:15–17).

2. *The Experience*. "We know." What a magnificent assurance the Apostle expresses when he indicates at once the position of himself and his fellow-believers, and the contrasted place of those who are outside Christ. Nothing could be stronger or more definite than this conviction.

V. PROVISION MADE (v. 20)

1. *The Fact*. "But we know that the Son of God is come." In contrast to the world which lies in the evil one mention is made of the blessed reality of the incarnation of "the Son of God."

2. *The Gift*. "And hath given us an understanding." This is the only place where the word "understanding" is used by John. We might have thought he would employ a word like "experience," but instead, he emphasizes the intellectual perception as the permanent gift (Greek) of the coming of our Lord.

VI. PURPOSE ACCOMPLISHED (v. 20)

1. *Knowledge*. "That we may know him that is true." Here comes in the thought of experience. Our intellectual perception is intended to lead to this personal and continuous (Greek) consciousness of Jesus Christ as "the genuine one." There are two words in the New Testament rendered by "true," the one referring to the truth in opposition to the false, and the other to the real in opposition to the shadowy, the genuine and not the artificial. It is the latter that John uses here, referring as it has been well put, to the Lord in his verity, not veracity.

2. *The Experience*. "And we are in him that is true." Not merely do we know him, but we are in him, and the contrast between being in him and "in the evil one" (v. 19) is particularly significant. Once again the Apostle speaks out of a perfectly convinced mind and perfectly satisfied heart in saying "we are in him."

VII. PRACTICE EMPHASIZED (vs. 20, 21)

1. *The Contrast*. The Apostle closes by pointing out that the substance of his teaching concerns the "true God and eternal life" in opposition to idols. The former was real and genuine; the latter were unreal, hollow, impossible.

2. *The Call*. As a last appeal he addresses "his little children," and begs them to guard themselves from everything unreal. Thus, the paternal and the practical blend as he brings his earnest and urgent messages to a close. As already mentioned, Westcott suggests that these words represent in chronological order the last statement of the New Testament, and if this is so, the contrast between the opening words of the Bible is very significant, "in the beginning God" (Gen. 1:1); "guard yourselves from idols."

These closing words of the Epistle stand out with unmistakable clearness and force, and call for the most thorough study. We are accustomed to speak of a certain formula as the Apostles' Creed. Suppose we think of these verses as "the Apostle's Creed," or the Apostle's assurance. They have been called "triumphant certainties" because three times over he says "we know," not merely "hope" or "think" or "suppose" or "imagine," but "know." As we trace the teaching from stream to source, from effect to cause, from roof to foundation, let us pray to enter into the same "blessed assurance."

(1) "We know" (v. 18). This is the assurance of *holiness*, and marks the Apostle's conception of the true believer.

(2) "We know" (v. 19). This is the assurance of *life*, and tells us how the Apostle was able to speak as he did about holiness. It is only those who are of God who are able to live without the practice of sin.

(3) "We know" (v. 20). This is the assurance of *redemption*, and herein lies the secret both of life and holiness. It is because the Son of God is come that all this grace and power are ours, that life and holiness become possible, and that we are enabled to glorify God and keep ourselves from everything sinful and unworthy of "the true God and eternal life."

II

THE SECOND EPISTLE

A small yet very important part of the New Testament. It probably presupposes a knowledge of the First Epistle (v. 9). Whether it was addressed to a Church or to a family is uncertain. One writer (Brooke) very strongly favors the former, thinking that several indications, like verse 4 and the use of plurals, suggest a community. But to others it seems more natural to think of the destination as that of a lady and her family so far as they were believers. But whether the one or the other, this little writing is full of spiritual counsel, with special reference to the reception of strangers. The Christians were encouraged in every way to show hospitality, and yet there was constant need of care, because of the obvious dangers of abuse. The Epistle is naturally divided thus: (1) verses 1–3, salutation; (2) verses 4–11, counsels and warnings; (3) verses 12, 13, conclusion. But it will be best to look at it with special reference to the theme that runs through it in various ways.

I. THE PERIL (v. 7)

It is clear that those to whom the Apostle wrote were surrounded by danger, and it was necessary for him to warn them and guard them. When he says, "many deceivers," the same word is used as in the First Epistle (2:26), implying deception of both heart and life. It was no mere intellectual error, but one that inevitably led people astray in conduct. The trouble was a deception of heart which expressed itself in wandering in life. The original word is that from which we get our word "planet." The Apostle does not hesitate to speak, as in the former Epistle, of this danger as essentially anti-Christian (1 John 2:26).

II. THE PROOF

The precise peril which evidently troubled the Apostle more than anything else was in regard to those who were not prepared to accept, but, indeed, rejected the fact and reality of our Lord's incarnation; "they that confess not that Jesus Christ cometh in the flesh" (1 John 4:2). The precise word "coming" suggests at once the permanence and continuance of the Incarnation in relation to human life, and the expression, moreover, implies that these deceivers did not want (Greek) to acknowledge the Incarnation. It has been well said that it is possible to say at once what a person is by discovering where he is prepared to place Jesus Christ. The danger of this denial of the Incarnation was that people were apt to go forward beyond the proper limit, and not to remain constant to the teaching of Christ (v. 9). It would seem as though there were people in that day who considered that Christianity was not "up to date," and that it was necessary to "go beyond it." But as then, so now; the simple, sufficient, and supreme test is whether men are willing to "abide in the teaching of Christ." Here again the expression implies that these erroneous teachers, in their efforts to go forward, were unwilling to be limited in the way John emphasizes.

III. THE PLEA

The Apostle is naturally concerned that those to whom he was writing should not be led astray, and he urges two things in particular (v. 8). First, that they should take care not to lose what they already possessed. Second, that they should enjoy full satisfaction by receiving a complete reward. Thus, negatively and positively, Christians were to watch and give heed to themselves. John knew well that only as they were faithful to the Lord Jesus Christ and his teaching could they expect blessing and power.

IV. THE PROTECTION

But all through the Epistle one thing is emphasized that clearly indicates by this prominence how in the Apostle's judgment these Christians could be safeguarded against error. In almost every verse, in a variety of expressions he lays stress on "the truth," and it is in this connection that we see for ourselves today the adequate provision against every form of error.

1. *Truth as a sphere* (vs. 1, 3, 4, 9). The Apostle uses the phrase "in truth," or "in the teaching," thus showing that if we are only abiding in the teaching that we have obtained all will go well. Truth here and elsewhere in the New Testament is at once intellectual and moral, and is intended to affect with illuminating and inspiring force every part of our being.

2. *Truth as an experience* (v. 1). The Apostle speaks of "them that know the truth," thereby suggesting a personal experience—and that of a permanent character. As before, so now, he emphasizes something that is far beyond any intellectual conception of Christian teaching, and refers to a personal experience and possession of the truth of God.

3. *Truth as a motive* (v. 2). Then he speaks of "the truth's sake, which abideth in us, and it shall be with us forever." The possession of this truth is thus shown to be a reason, perhaps the chief reason, why we are to remain faithful and not to be led astray. This truth abides in us, and will remain with us permanently, and on this account we are to be true to it.

4. *Truth as a standard* (v. 4). The Apostle was able to rejoice exceedingly that some of those associated with the "elect lady" were walking in truth. Walking always indicates life and progress, and "walking in truth" implies that truth was the standard, rule, and guide of their life.

5. *Truth as a power* (vs. 5, 6, 8). The Apostle goes on to speak of a commandment with which they had been familiar from the earliest days of their Christian life, the commandment to "love one another." Then this was seen to involve conduct according to God's commandments (v. 6), and the outcome of everything was their definite work (v. 8). Thus, in regard to the three aspects of love, obedience, and service, the Apostle shows that truth was intended to be the power of their life.

6. *Truth as a home* (v. 9). He had already spoken of truth abiding in us, and now he is to speak of our abiding in the teaching of Christ. Thus truth is seen to be the home of the soul, and those who thus abide are the blessed and holy possessors of the Father and the Son.

7. *Truth as a test* (vs. 10, 11). This truth was not only to be a power in these respects in the individual life and experience, but it was also to be used as a criterion in relation to others. If anyone should come to these Christians, and was seen to be without this teaching, he was to be left severely alone. They were not to give him hospitality; indeed, they were not even to greet him, for a greeting might easily be misunderstood to indicate approval of his evil ways. The Apostle thus does not mind his converts being regarded as "narrow," or severe, because he knows that the truth is, after all, the supreme matter, and everything, however attractive and otherwise delightful, must be tested thereby.

Looking over the Epistle, we observe three things: (1) The personal concern. The Apostle is conscious of a real danger facing these Christians, and on this account he urged them to a specific duty in regard to it. (2) The pressing claim. Beyond all else, he insisted on the Incarnation of our Lord, and we know how in all ages this has been the very heart of Christianity. Without Incarnation there could be no fellowship with God, and, of course, no salvation. "A Saviour not quite God is a bridge broken at the farther end" (Bishop Moule). (3) The practical counsel. On all these accounts he urges his friends to keep close to Christ by keeping close to the truth. For us today the same message is appropriate and necessary. We can only abide in the Incarnate Word in proportion as we keep close to the written Word of God. Thus we shall keep close to God and to all that is good.

III

THE THIRD EPISTLE

VERSES 1–8

There is no doubt that this Epistle is addressed to an individual, although we do not know anything more of Gaius than is here found. The Epistle gives a vivid picture of some of the aspects, bright and dark, of those early days, and in his emphasis on the Christian, life we are enabled to see the features that he thought most important. He was anxious to obtain help for Christians as they traveled from place to place, but there had been a difficulty through the overbearing action of one member (v. 9), and it was this in particular that made it necessary for the Apostle to write with unusual plainness. It is suggested that here, too, a knowledge of the First Epistle is implied (v. 11).

I. THE CHARACTER (vs. 1–2)

1. *The Name.* Calling himself merely "a presbyter," he addresses himself to his "beloved Gaius." Ten times in the Epistles of John is this word "beloved" found, and it is significant and carries its own lesson to contrast the greeting to the lady in the Second Epistle with this to a man. We are reminded of the equally significant counsel of Paul to his young friend Timothy (1 Tim. 5:1, 2). This expression "beloved" shows the beautiful oneness in Christ between the Apostle and Gaius. Well might Tertullian, a century or so after, refer to the heathen astonishment as they said, "See how these Christians love one another."

2. *The Feeling.* "Whom I love in truth." Let us mark the two aspects here, the esteem and its limit. While the Apostle was tender he was also true. There was fellowship and faithfulness, love and truth in perfect balance and proportion.

3. *The Prayer.* He wishes for Gaius to be as well physically as he is spiritually, a striking contrast to what may be regarded as the usual experience. The Bible has not a little to say about "prosperity," though the words in the Hebrew and the Greek invariably indicate progress, "having a good journey" (Rom. 1:10; 1 Cor. 16:2). He actually prays that Gaius may have as much bodily strength as he has spiritual power. We are accustomed to think the very opposite, but here is the remarkable experience of a soul prosperous and a body weak, and the spiritual health is to be the standard of the bodily vigor. It would be well if we could pray in this way for our friends. We have only to think of the marks of bodily strength and health to see what is meant by spiritual prosperity. When we think of appetite we may ponder whether we enjoy our Bible. When we think of bodily rest we may inquire whether we know anything of the rest of faith. When we think of physical work we may inquire what we are doing for Christ.

II. THE CONDUCT (vs. 3–4)

1. *The Fact.* The Apostle speaks of Gaius as a man who possessed faith and proved it in his life. "The truth, even as thou walkest in truth." The man's conduct was genuine, strong, and constantly progressive. No wonder it could be described as prosperity of soul (v. 2).

2. *The Record.* This reality was seen by the brethren when they went to the home of Gaius, and on their return they testified to it. This is the real life, one that is not only enjoyed but expressed. Our Lord said that our light was to shine that others might see (Matt. 5:13–16).

3. *The Result.* All this gave the Apostle great joy, and he says that he had no higher joy than this, for when he heard that his spiritual children were "walking in the truth," enjoying and manifesting prosperity in the spiritual life, the faithful Apostle found his joy full.

There is still no greater satisfaction in the Christian life than the consciousness that those whom we have led to Christ are living consistently and earnestly for the Master's glory.

III. THE COMMUNION (vs. 5–6)

1. *The Action.* Now the Apostle reminds Gaius of the work that he was doing to Christian brethren from other places. Hospitality is clear in the New Testament as a duty incumbent on Christians, and in those days when brethren traveled from place to place it is easy to see its necessity and value as one of the marks of true fellowship (Rom. 12:13; 1 Tim. 5:10; Tit. 1:8; Heb. 13:2; 1 Pet. 4:9).

2. *The Character.* This work is described by the one and yet sufficient word "faithful." It was a work that sprang from faith and was in every way genuine and true, because of these brethren who came from other places and who would have had no satisfactory hospitality if it had not been provided by the Christians where they visited.

3. *The Recognition.* The work not only elicited the approval of the Apostle, but the people who enjoyed the hospitality bore witness before the whole Church to the love of Gaius. This testimony was a beautiful evidence of the Master's love and of the spirit of true fellowship that actuated him. Christ was, indeed, a reality to one who could show this love.

IV. THE COUNSEL (vs. 6–8)

1. *The Need.* The work that Gaius had been doing was necessary because of the circumstances, and the Apostle tells him that he will still do well if he continues this fellowship of hospitality. These traveling Christians were thus to be "set forward on their journey worthily of God." It is a striking thing to think of their traveling and the hospitality they were to receive as something "worthy of God." Nothing could be higher than this in the Apostle's eyes.

2. *The Cause.* He was able to speak in this way because these Christians went forth on their spiritual enterprise without receiving any help from people outside and were actuated only by devotion to our Lord Jesus Christ (v. 8).

3. *The Motive.* This constitutes the reason why Christians should welcome such and give them all possible sympathy, for in so doing they would become "fellow workers for the truth." Thus the Apostle strikes another high keynote. This work was to be done "worthily of God" and "for the truth."

As we review these verses we cannot help seeing the intensity of the Apostle's love and the strength of his devotion to Christ as he rejoices in the marks of true Christianity shown in "Gaius the beloved." Love, truth, joy, faithfulness, service, dominate his thought and reveal both in him and in Gaius the splendid reality of their Christian experience and love. If only we "love in truth" (v. 1) and "walk in truth" (v. 3), we cannot help becoming "fellow workers for the truth" (v. 8).

VERSES 9–14

Side by side with the delightful description of the faithful worker referred to in the earlier verses is this darker picture of one who did the exact opposite. Then follow two other pictures of the early Church, recording once more some of the best elements of Christian character. We must now look at these three aspects of Christian life.

I. FAITHLESSNESS (vs. 9–10)

This is seen in Diotrephes, of whom nothing is known beyond this brief reference, though his character is here set out very clearly in a few words.

1. *Faithlessness Described.* He is seen to be marked by exclusiveness, being unwilling to receive even an Apostle. Not only so, but his speech against John was marked by evil, and not content with saying wrong things, his actions were equally deplorable, for he would not welcome the brethren by showing hospitality, and also actually repelled and cast out of the Church those who were willing to show this kindness. It is almost incredible that any professing Christian man could have taken such a harsh attitude.

2. *Faithlessness Explained.* When we endeavor to discover why he acted in this way we see at once that it was due to pride, self-pleasing, and the consequent dethronement of Christ. He loved to have the preeminence, thus showing marked contrast to the true life in which Christ is to be first in everything (Col. 1:18). These two are the only places where the word "preeminence" occurs in the New Testament, and the contrast is deeply significant. It will always be either self or Christ.

Let us try to imagine this man, who evidently loved power, and, so far from endeavoring to show Christian kindness, was ready to cause other people to suffer if they would not do as he desired. He was particularly concerned about any lessening of his own authority. People might think it (and he might be self-deceived in considering it) loyalty, but in reality he was solely concerned about his own place and importance. As some one has said, "he is the father of a long line of sons." There are men today with an intense zeal for place and power, but it is difficult, if not impossible, for them to distinguish between love for the Church and love for their own place in it. When a man wants to hold office for the purpose of service, there is danger of degeneration into holding the office for its own sake, and this inevitably leads to the cause of the Church becoming identified with our own cause. Any church which has an officer of this kind, however effective he may be, and however much he may have done for the community, will undoubtedly find its spiritual life weakened, prevented from advancing, and perhaps involved in disaster. If anyone should tell him of this, his hyper-sensitiveness leads him to attribute to his informers animosity and malice, and if he should become displaced he either loses interest in the church or does his best to oppose those who have succeeded him. The explanation of it all, if men would only be honest with themselves, is pride of place, and this means the inability to put Christ and his Church in the foremost position.

II. FIDELITY (vs. 11–12)

This is seen in Demetrius, a striking contrast to Diotrephes.

1. *Fidelity Counseled* (v. 11). The Apostle, using his favorite term "beloved" for the fourth time in this brief Epistle, refers to the nature of that which every Christian man should be occupied with, "that which is good," as contrasted with "that which is evil." The method of fidelity is seen in the suggestion of imitation, and, inasmuch as all good comes from God, this advice to imitate means really to imitate none other than God himself because "he that doeth good is of God; he that doeth evil hath not seen God."

2. *Fidelity Exemplified* (v. 12). Demetrius is shown to have carried out this very counsel, and there are no fewer than three separate yet connected testimonies to this blessed reality. He had the testimony of all men, and it is worth while remembering that the New Testament gives great prominence to the impression made upon non-Christians by the life of believers. It is one of the best recommendations of the Gospel that a follower of Christ impresses and attracts those around by his reality of life. When the Seven were appointed, one recommendation was that they should be "men of honest report," that is, men of good reputation (Acts 6:3). This feature is often noted in the New Testament (Acts 10:22; 16:2; 22:12; Eph. 5:15; Col. 4:5; 1 Thess. 4:12; 1 Tim. 3:7). This is exactly what is said of our Lord himself as a youth, for he was in "favor with God and man" (Luke 2:52). Another testimony was that of the truth itself, for it was evident that the life of Demetrius exactly harmonized with the teaching of Christ. Not least of all, but in some respects greatest, the Apostle himself bore the same testimony, and he appeals to Gaius in support of the truth of his own witness. It is splendid when the life of any Christian can have this complete witness, for there is simply nothing beyond it.

III. FELLOWSHIP (vs. 13–14)

This is seen in the Apostle John himself, and in the closing words of this, as of the former Epistle, we have a new and beautiful picture of the "Apostle of love."

1. *Fellowship Realized.* The Apostle had many things to write out of the fulness of his heart towards Gaius, and perhaps they were too sacred to be put on paper, since he was for some reason unwilling to write them, but there was the satisfaction that he would shortly see his friend and they would enjoy "face-to-face" intercourse. It was this that the Apostle felt gave him the fulness of joy (2 John 12).

2. *Fellowship Expressed.* Meanwhile the spirit of the man is shown in his prayer that peace might be with Gaius, and the breadth of his interest and sympathy is shown by the salutation he sends from the friends and to the friends. Not only so, but there is a beautiful, personal, individual touch as he asks Gaius to salute the friends "by name."

Thus we see in marked contrast the three characters in that little community: the man who was proud, the man who was humble, and the man who was loving. Be it ours to avoid the sinfulness of the first and to follow the sincerity of the other two.

IV

REVIEW

It seems necessary to review quite briefly the teaching of these three portions of Holy Scripture. The doctrines were evidently important then, and they are no less important now. Circumstances change, but principles abide, and, although the conditions of life are very different today from those of the Apostle's time, the essential features are identical, and make these Epistles as vital as ever. What, then, are the essential truths found here, and what do they say to us today? They speak to us of six great needs. Although the general teaching will appear in outline form only, each aspect and element can be supported by passages in the Epistles. It will, perhaps, be best for each reader and student to find these for himself, and thus see how the Apostle's teaching is vital for our present experience.

I. A TRUE EXPRESSION OF LIFE

1. *Towards God*—Obedience.
2. *Towards Christians*—Love.
3. *Towards ourselves*—Assurance.

This is the threefold relationship of the believer, which must be shown in practical reality in daily life. When we are right with God, with our fellows and with ourselves, everything of necessity is right.

II. A TRUE VIEW OF SIN

1. *In relation to God*—Darkness.
2. *In relation to Christians*—Hate.
3. *In relation to ourselves*—Worldliness.

Here we see what evil really is in its threefold aspect. Towards God sin means darkness, including error of intellect and unrighteousness of life. As such it is marked by the spirit of antichrist. In relation to our Christian brethren sin of necessity shows itself in intense animosity, for there is absolutely no standing-ground between the love we ought to show and the hatred we ought not. In regard to ourselves, the atmosphere of worldliness is one of the deadliest forms of sin, against which we must ever be on our guard.

III. A TRUE CONCEPTION OF CHRIST

1. *As the Truth*—received.
2. *As the Life*—realized.
3. *As the Son*—confessed.

The Apostle all through lays the greatest stress on the Person and Work of our Lord as one of the essential, in many ways the most essential, features of true Christian living. As the Truth we accept and follow his teaching. As the Life we receive and reproduce his grace. As the Son we believe and profess the reality and blessedness of his redemption.

IV. A TRUE ATTITUDE OF SOUL

1. *Faith expressed in Christ.*
2. *Love expressed towards God and man.*
3. *Righteousness exemplified in daily conduct.*

Nothing can be required beyond these three elements, which sum up the whole of life. Our trust is fixed on Christ in all the glory of his Divine Person and redemptive work. Our love is centered on God, and on those for whom Christ died. Our righteousness is at once the proof of our new life and the expression of our genuine devotion to God.

V. A TRUE ENJOYMENT OF BLESSING

1. *Sonship*—past and present.
2. *Fellowship*—present.
3. *Heirship*—future.

These are the three elements of privilege which come to the believer in Christ. He experiences sonship, and rejoices to know that God is his Father. He exults in fellowship with the Father and the Son and his fellow-Christians. And he looks forward with hope, expectation, and anticipation to that future when he will see Christ and be like him.

VI. A TRUE GUARANTEE OF GRACE

1. *The Father's presence and witness.*
2. *The Son's Person and work.*
3. *The Spirit's power and witness.*

In this threefold way the Apostle shows the sure foundation and strong assurance of all those who have come to Christ. The witness of God concerning his Son; the witness of the Son concerning himself; and the witness of the Spirit concerning the Father and the Son are seen to blend, and also culminate in the believer's own witness in his heart that he is the blessed and joyous possessor of eternal life.

Thus the Apostle sums up his teaching. He had written the Gospel for the purpose of leading men to faith in Christ (John 20:31). He wrote the Epistles in order that the men who thus believed might have the blessed assurance in their souls concerning Christ and his redemption (1 John 5:13). He will still show men what they are to expect in and from. Christ in the future, when, through the Apocalypse, he will declare the glory of Christ's grace and government in relation to the whole universe. And so, concerning the past, the present, and the future, "Christ is all."

Testament prophets did not understand their own words, but were constantly endeavoring to discover the meaning (1 Pet. 1:11; 2 Pet. 1:19).

As to the *authorship*, there does not seem to be any valid reason for departing from the tradition of the Church in regard to the Apostle John. The substance and claim of the book also point in this direction.

The *date* is now usually regarded as that of the time of the Emperor Domitian, near the close of the first century.

The *title* is The Revelation of Jesus Christ, meaning the revelation which was received by Christ from God for us and given through angels by John. It is a "revelation" of his glory in relation to the world, the unveiling of the future in and through him. It is thus a book which emphasizes him and calls attention to him in all the glory of his Divine Person and universal sway.

Its *character* is that of a book of visions. "I saw" occurs over forty times. It is symbolical, a book which "signifies" (1:1), a communication by means of "signs."

IV

THE REVELATION

I

INTRODUCTION

There is, perhaps, no book in the New Testament as to which there are greater differences of opinion. Yet, as attention is so frequently, and at present so specially, concentrated on it, it seems necessary to endeavor to discover its meaning and purpose, especially because of what is its unique feature among New Testament books, the promise of a blessing on the reader and hearer of "the words of this prophecy" (1:3). But in view of these serious and often fundamental differences and notable difficulties, it has been thought best to provide material for study rather than to give my own conclusions, which would not be convincing to all readers.

The New Testament, as a record of divine revelation, is concerned with the past, the present, and the future. It includes a consideration of the Person of Christ in the Gospels, of the Church of Christ in the Acts and Epistles, and of the Rule of Christ in the Apocalypse. Thus, to use a well-known simile, we have respectively the foundation, the structure, and the completely furnished house. Or, to put it otherwise, the New Testament makes its appeal to Faith, to Love, and to Hope.

There would thus be a distinct incompleteness without this book of the Revelation, which corresponds to the prophecies of the Old Testament. Some, however, are deterred from studying it by reason of its difficulties; but, while these are real, they should not hinder us from giving the book the best attention possible. A blessing is assured to those who read, hear, and understand its message (1:3), and we know that even Old

II

ANALYSIS

It is important to gain an idea of the actual contents before proceeding to the interpretation of the book. It will be helpful to compare analyses by several writers.

1. Many, perhaps most writers, think that 1:19 provides a key to the book in its three divisions, with introduction (1:1–9) and conclusion (22:5–21):

(1) Things Seen (1:10–20).
(2) Things that Are (2–3).
(3) Things that Shall Be (4:1 to 22:5).

2. A clear and useful outline, and valuable as at any rate provisional, is by Rev. W. Graham Scroggie:

(1) 1:1–8. Introduction.
(2) 1:9 to 3:22. Vision of Grace.
(3) 4:1 to 19:10. Vision of Government.
(4) 19:11 to 22:5. Vision of Glory.
(5) 22:5–21. Conclusion.

3. Another by a well-known writer, Walter Scott, is as follows:

(1) 1:1–8. Introduction.
(2) 1:9–20. Things Seen.
(3) 2–3. Things that Are.
(4) 4:1 to 11:18; 11:19 to 20:3. The Period of the Great Tribulation (the second section being coterminous with but an elaboration of the first).
(5) 20:4–15. The Period of the Millennium.
(6) 21:1 to 22:5. The Post-millennial Period.

4. A writer of another school, Rev. E. H. Horne, divides it by concentrating attention on the repeated phrase, "it is done," and the opening of Heaven, giving three main parts:

(1) 4:1 to 16:17. The Present Age.
(2) 19:11 to 20:6. The Millennial Age.

(3) 21–22. The Eternal Age.

5. One comes from a thoughtful and able scholar on these subjects, the late Dr. Bullinger ("The Day of the Lord"):

(1) 1. Introduction.

(2) 2–3. God's People on Earth.

(3) 4:1 to 20:15. Fourteen Visions in Seven Pairs. Alternating between Heaven and Earth.

(4) 21:1 to 22:5. God's People on the New Earth.

(5) 22:6–21. Conclusion.

6. A very able and helpful discussion of the contents and plan, together with a full and clear analysis, is given in Dr. Swete's Commentary. He holds that the Apocalypse has two great divisions (1:9 to 11:14; 12:1 to 22:5), and his outline of the book in its "briefest form" is as follows:

Prologue and Greeting (1:1–8)

Part I. Vision of Christ in the midst of the Churches (1:9 to 3:22). Vision of Christ in Heaven (4:1 to 5:14). Preparations for the End (6:1 to 11:19).

Part II. Vision of the Mother of Christ and her enemies (12:1 to 13:18). Preparations for the End (14:1 to 20:15). Vision of the Bride of Christ, arrayed for her husband (21:1 to 22:5). Epilogue and benediction (22:6–21).

7. An American student of prophecy, the Rev. W. J. Erdman, D. D., has given an analysis which is deserving of notice because of its great clearness and fulness:

1. The Seven Churches

(1) 1:1–8. The Prologue.

(2) 1:9–20. The Son of Man.

(3) 2:1 to 3:22. The Seven Churches.

2. The Seven Seals

(1) 4:1 to 5:14. Introduction. The Throne, the Lamb, and the Book.

(2) 6:1–17. Progression. The Six Seals.

(3) 7:1–17. Episode. The Sealed and the Saved.

(4) 8:1. Consummation. The Seventh Seal.

3. The Seven Trumpets

(1) 8:2–5. Introduction. The Angel and Incense.

(2) 8:6 to 9:21. Progression. The Six Trumpets.

(3) 10:1 to 11:14. Episode. The Angel, the Little Book, the Two Witnesses.

(4) 11:15–19. Consummation. The Seventh Trumpet.

4. The Seven Personages

(1) 12:1 to 13:1a. Introduction. The Two Signs in Heaven.

(2) 13:1b–18. Progression. The Great Tribulation.

(3) 14:1–13. Episode. The First Fruits and the Three Angels.

(4) 14:14–20. Consummation. The Harvest and the Vintage.

5. The Seven Vials

(1) 15:1–8. Introduction. The Overcomers and the Seven Angels.

(2) 16:1–12. Progression. The Six Vials.

(3) 16:13–16. Episode. The Gathering of the Kings.

(4) 16:17–21. Consummation. The Seventh Vial.

6. The Seven Dooms

(1) 17:1–18. Introduction. The Babylon and the Beast.

(2) 18:1–24. Progression. The Doom of Babylon.

(3) 19:1–10. Episode. The Four Hallels.

(4) 19:11 to 20:15. Consummation. The Six Final Dooms.

7. The Seven New Things

(1) 21:1–8. Introduction.

(2) 21:9 to 22:5. The New Jerusalem.

(3) 22:6–21. The Epilogue.

Dr. Erdman says this analysis is an attempt to group the contents of the book according to what seem to be the lines of its structure. Also that the so-called three episodes are in each instance both retrospective and prospective.

But while these outlines will help toward a mastery of the actual contents, the analysis will depend very largely on the interpretation which is given to the book.

III

METHODS OF INTERPRETATION

The main lines of explanation must now be given:

1. Preterist

This regards the entire book as fulfilled in the past, within the time of the Roman Empire and in the life of the Apostle John, with special reference to A. D. 70. This is the view taken in two books: "The Parousia," by Dr. Russell, an English Congregational minister; and "The Christ Has Come," by E. Hampden Cook.

The question arises whether this view is really possible. It was not known in the early Church. It must be confessed that it is often (though not in the two writers named above) associated with rationalism and antisupernaturalism. And it seems to indicate the despair of any interpretation made according to the analogy of the Old Testament with its detailed prophecies, both fulfilled and unfulfilled.

2. *Idealist*

This understands the book as one of great principles, symbolically stated, with special reference to the persecution of the Church. It is thus a record of conflict and victory. A general view of the book on this interpretation would be:

(1) Introduction (1).
(2) The Church in History (2–3).
(3) Victory Anticipated (4–5).
(4) Great Judgments (6–16).
(5) Victory Accomplished (17–19).
(6) The Church Perfected (20:1 to 22:5).
(7) Conclusion (22:6–21).

This is the view associated with three books by Dr. Milligan, the volume in Schaff's Commentary on Revelation, the Baird Lectures on Revelation, and the volume in the Expositor's Bible; and with Bishop Boyd Carpenter in Cassell's Commentary.

The newest book taking this view is "Studies in the Book of Revelation," by Dr. S. A. Hunter, of the Western Theological Seminary, Pittsburgh. It is called "A Bible School Manual" and includes introduction, analysis, copious footnotes, extracts from many modern writers, and other materials. It gives an able presentation of the symbolical view, together with acute criticisms of other methods of interpretation. It is the best work available for the thorough study of this view of the Apocalypse.

A recent writer who may perhaps be included in this school, though he has distinctive features of his own, is Provost Erskine Hill, in Apocalyptic Problems. Up to the present time the treatment of only the first half of the Revelation has appeared, though its general line may be easily understood. To Mr. Erskine Hill the book is timeless and records the view of the angels about the various spiritual movements of all time. He does not identify this or that part with any historical period, past or present, nor does he allow a future specific application. The message of the book is said to be that "it reveals the power of self-sacrifice to solve the mystery of pain, and the power of the Living Christ to give his followers protection from all evil, and victory over all temptation" (p. 4). He thus faces the important question of the symbolism and its difficulties: "Imagine a learned scientist trying to explain the mysteries of wireless telegraphy to some untutored aboriginal tribe. The teacher would be confronted with the double difficulty of the crudity of his hearers' minds, and the extremely limited nature of their vocabulary" (p. 14). He is afraid of materializing Christ's sayings about the Advent, and he interprets the eagles of Matthew 24 as spiritual insight (p. 49f). The "sealed book" of chapter 5 is taken "to represent the problem of the existence of suffering in the world and the toleration of the sin which lies behind so much of it" (p. 91). But perhaps the most striking argument is his dealing with the "Coming of the Son of Man." In regard to the assertion of Christ in Matthew 10:23: "Ye shall not have gone over the cities of Israel till the Son of man be come," Mr. Hill thinks it refers to our Lord's first coming: "His Coming as Son of Man to the world of men was still an event of the future" (p. 56). "It was in his Mystical Body and on the Day of Pentecost that his first Coming as the Son of Man to the world took place" (p. 59). It is interesting that "coming" in the papyri is almost a technical term.

Now there is undoubted truth in this idealist view, but it may be seriously questioned whether by itself it is specific enough. Also, the relation of the book to the Old Testament and the connection and analogy with prophecies there would seem to demand something more definite. As the book is prophetic, it should be regarded and interpreted as such.

3. *Historicist*

This is the interpretation which regards the book from chapters 6–19 as a continuous revelation of the centuries of the Christian Church, and it is thought that the fulfilment has now extended to the sixth vial (16). According to this view the Euphrates (16:12) symbolizes the Turkish power, the Reformation is referred to in chapter 10, and the papacy in chapters 17–18. Many great, honored, and scholarly names are associated with this view, including those of E. B. Elliott and Grattan Guinness.

The serious objections raised to this interpretation include the following:

(1) Is it likely that a knowledge of history would be required before an ordinary Christian could understand this book?

(2) Is it possible to interpret a passage like 6:12–17 of anything, however terrible, that has already taken place? The great day of the wrath of the Lamb, it is urged, cannot be predicated of any event in the course of Christian history.

(3) If past wars are carefully recorded in the book, how is it that the war of 1914–1918, the greatest in history, finds no place in it?

(4) Notwithstanding the remarkable agreement on many points, there are also great differences between writers of this school, and these seem to many to show the impossibility of identifying the references with historical events. Thus in interpreting the second trumpet (8:8, 9), the following various interpretations have been given:

The fiery mountain means Satan; Genseric; a great heresy; Vespasian; the Prelacy; Rome.

The sea means the nations; the Church with its baptismal waters; the Sea of Galilee; pure doctrine.

The destruction of the fishes means the slaughter of Christians; the Jews; the Vandals; monks.

To the same effect are some recent words of the Rev. W. Graham Scroggie, who has pointed out how "the most distinguished exponents of this school hopelessly differ among themselves." He gave these instances:

Elliott interprets the sixth seal of Constantine, but Faber sees in it the French Revolution.

Bengel sees in the star fallen from heaven (10) a good angel, but Elliott regards it as Mohammed.

Mede takes the locusts of chapter 9, which torment men for five months, to mean one hundred and fifty years of the dominion of the Saracens; but

Vitringa says they mean the Goths and the Jesuits.

Mr. Scroggie reasonably adds: "So long as there is such variance as that among those whose general view is the same, dogmatism should be avoided."

The newest book based on this line of interpretation is "The Revelation of Jesus Christ," by H. C. Williams, in which the writer regards the Apocalypse as giving a threefold view of the future, each part ending with our Lord's coming. After the preliminary division in chapter 1, the book is divided thus:

(1) 2–3, regarded as descriptive of the whole period of the Church's history, culminating with the promise of Christ's coming (3:11, 20).

(2) 4–11, again culminating in the full realization of victory through the coming of Christ (11:15–17).

(3) 12–19, with a third reference to the coming of Christ (19:11–16).

The last two chapters are descriptive of the heavenly life of eternity, following the advent of Christ.

The general treatment is that of the Historicist School, though the writer has interpretations of his own which differ from those generally adopted by this prophetic school. He, too, makes much of the papacy as representing the antichrist, but he is possibly too apt to see the allusions to his own denomination in certain parts of the book, thereby confusing between primary interpretation and spiritual application.

4. Futurist

This, in general, means that, while chapters 2–3 refer to the present age, everything after 4:1 is still future, and will probably take only about seven years to fulfil, a time corresponding to the seventieth week of Daniel. On this view the Church will have gone from the earth, 1 Thessalonians 4 being fulfilled between chapters 3 and 4. The material from chapter 4 to chapter 19 is regarded as giving a series of pictures rather than a chronological sequence. One writer, Walter Scott, thinks that 4:1 to 11:18 is parallel with 11:19 to 20:3, the second emphasizing details of the first. Great names are also associated with this interpretation, including those of Seiss, B. W. Newton, J. N. Darby, Sir Robert Anderson, and many more.

The view is objected to by adherents of the other schools, especially the Historical, on several grounds, e. g.:

(1) Is it likely that the whole course of Christian history would be disregarded?

(2) How can the word "shortly" be interpreted on this view?

In view of all these differences of position, the student must face the question for himself, and, meanwhile, some of the matters calling for consideration may be mentioned.

IV

SOME PROBLEMS

As a help to the interpretation, the following questions call for careful consideration:

1. Does 1:10 refer to the "Lord's Day" (Sunday, the first day of the week) or to "the day of the Lord" (the future)? Many, perhaps most, favor the former, but, on the other hand, it is urged:

(1) 1:9ff refers to John being "in the spirit," and this, with other references, seems to indicate a vision of the future (4:2; 17:3; 21:10; cf. Ezek. 11:1; 37:1; 40:2).

(2) The title, "Lord's. Day," for Sunday is not found so early as this date.

(3) The origin of the term, Lord's Day, is pagan, not Christian. In pagan Rome the first day of the week was called Dominica (the Lord's), to which was to be added Sol, the sun; or in Hebrew, Baal, Lord.

The important point which turns on this interpretation is that in the latter view the whole book, including chapters 1–3, would be future, and it is urged that this is borne out by the references to the book as prophetic (1:3; 22:19; cf. 11:6; 19:10; 22:7, 10, 18).

2. Does 1:19 really indicate a division of the book? Many writers of different schools urge this and say that it is unthinkable that there should not be something of and for the past and present in the book, even though it be only chapters 1–3.

But Alford and others render the words thus: "What thou sawest and what they are" (i. e., signify). This is urged in the light of 1:20, where "are" certainly means signify.

One proof alleged in favor of this interpretation and at the same time in support of the view that the messages to the seven churches refer to the same period as that covered by the remainder of the book is that the visions from chapter 4 onward throw light on the spiritual history of the period from without, as the messages themselves throw light on the spiritual history of the churches from within. It is urged that there is a connection between the sevenfold series of visions and the seven churches, and the following conspectus is given:

The Ephesus Church (2:1–7). In the midst seven stars in right hand; threat to remove lampstand out of its place.

The Ephesus Period (4:1 to 7:3). In the midst seven-sealed book in right hand; seven lamps, eyes, spirits; mountains and islands "moved" (same word as above) out of their places.

The Smyrna Church (2:8–11). Tribulation; faithful unto death; second death; hurt.

The Smyrna Period (7:9 to 11:14). The great tribulation; two witnesses slain; death; slay; hurt.

The Pergamos Church (2:12–17). Hold fast my name; Satan's throne; the hidden manna; the doctrine of Balaam.

The Pergamos Period (11:15–19). Fear thy name; the kingdoms of this world become Christ's.

The Thyatira Church (2:18–29). The woman Jezebel; the morning star; the rod of iron; depths of Satan; keep works; faith and patience; false prophetess; her children killed.

The Thyatira Period (12–13). Woman clothed with sun; the twelve stars; the rod of iron; Satan; keep commandment; patience and faith; false prophet; God's children killed.

The Sardis Church (3:1–6). A few with undefiled garments; "they shall walk with me in white"; name confessed before the Father.

The Sardis Period (14). 144,000 not defiled; they follow the Lamb; without fault before the throne of God.

The Philadelphia Church (3:7–13). Worship before thee; a pillar in the temple; the name of the city of God—new Jerusalem; the trying of them that dwell on the earth; the hour; I will keep thee out of the hour.

The Philadelphia Period. (15–18). Worship before thee; the temple; the great city Babylon; they that dwell on the earth; one hour; come out, my people.

The Laodicea Church (3:14–22). White raiment; supper; faithful and true; amen; spue out of mouth; sit in my throne; stand at door.

The Laodicea Period. (19–20). Fine linen; marriage supper; faithful and true; the word of God; out of his mouth a sword; set on throne; the Judge.

There is certainly a close comparison at many points, but whether it is close enough to prove inter-relation will be a matter of opinion. Yet the view seems suggestive enough to provoke further study.

3. What is the interpretation of the messages to the seven churches (2–3)? They must have had a primary meaning for the churches addressed. See Ramsay's "Seven Churches of Asia."

Some consider that the seven sections represent seven periods of church history to the present day. But there is great difference of opinion as to the divisions of the periods, and a good deal of arbitrariness is seen in the attempt to make them harmonize with the progress of the history. If they are to be regarded as explanatory of Church history, it is more natural to think of them as emphasizing principles which are necessary all through the age. Thus, the loss of the first love and the consequent need of repentance in the first church are certainly true of much Christianity today.

Others say that the spirit of the message is so unlike that of the Church teaching of the Epistles to the Ephesians and Colossians that it is impossible to think of these messages as applicable to a New Testament church. On this view, the whole book being future, the churches refer to some communities of believers, Jewish probably, which will be on the earth after the Church, the body of Christ, has been taken away.

4. Are the seals, trumpets, and vials continuous (twenty-one), or parallel (three sevens)? One thing of interest, and perhaps of importance, is that the six seals correspond very closely to the Olivet discourses of Matthew 24:4–11:

False Christs, Matthew 24:5. First seal, Revelation 6:1, 2.
War, Matthew 24:6, 7. Second seal, Revelation 6:3, 4.
Famine, Matthew 24:7. Third seal, Revelation 6:5, 6.
Pestilence, Matthew 24:7. Fourth seal, Revelation 6:7, 8.
Afflictions, Matthew 24:9. Fifth seal, Revelation 6:9–11.
Earthquakes, Matthew 24:7. Sixth seal, Revelation 6:12.
Milligan elaborates this parallel with great force and suggests that the Apocalypse is John's version of the Olivet discourses. If this is true, the seals, trumpets, and vials are coterminous and represent different aspects of the same judgment. This is the general view favored by Mr. James H. McConkey in his "The Book of Revelation," who also regards the seals as covering the entire period, the trumpet and the vials being coterminous and parallel.

Dr. Gray refers to the Biblical law of recurrence, by which an outline is first given and then details follow. He illustrates this from Isaiah 1, which he thinks covers the whole of Isaiah's work, and then the same is given in detail as in chapters 2–4. And so, on this view, the seals (4–7), trumpets (8–14), and vials (15–18) are a parallel, the sixth seal being coterminous with the seventh trumpet (11:17, 18). Then the seventh seal goes back and starts a new series of judgments in the seven trumpets and the seven vials, chapter 20 being concerned with the final judgment. Hence the rest of the Apocalypse comes under the seventh seal (8:7; 18:24). Mr. Graham Scroggie prefers to interpret these sections, not by a recurrence or doubling back, but by the principle of inclusion, the seven trumpets being included in the seventh seal, and the seven vials in the seventh trumpet.

V

SOME GENERAL SUGGESTIONS

The following points will also perhaps help in the study of this book.

1. The Apocalypse cannot be properly understood without a knowledge of Old Testament prophecy, especially Daniel 2. The vision of Christ in Revelation 1 is strikingly like that of Daniel 10, as the following comparison will show:

Daniel 10:5, 6, 8–14	Revelation 1:13–17
Behold, one—a man.	A Son of man.
Clothed in linen.	Clothed with a garment to the foot.
Loins girded with fine gold of Uphaz.	Girt about the paps with a golden girdle.
His body was like the beryl.	His head and hair like wool and snow.
His face as the appearance of lightning.	
His eyes as lamps of fire.	His eyes as a flame of fire.
His feet like polished brass.	His feet like fine brass.
His voice like voice of a multitude.	His voice as the sound of many waters.

There remained no strength in me: for my comeliness was turned in me into corruption, * * * then was I in a deep sleep on my face, and my face touched the ground.	And when I saw him I fell at his feet as one dead.
And behold a hand touched me, which set me upon my knees and the palms of my hands.	He laid his right hand upon me.
Fear not, Daniel.	Fear not.
I am come to make thee understand what shall befall thy people in the latter days.	Write the things which thou hast seen * * * the seven stars are * * *
Shut up the words and seal the book to the time of the end (12:4).	Blessed is he that readeth, and they that hear * * * and keep those things that are written, for the time is at hand (1:3).

It is impossible to question the close parallels here, and if so, it is more than probable that the time, place, and people of both books are the same. "Thy people" would be Israel; "the latter days" bring us to the period of the Revelation, "the day of the Lord." The difference between the two accounts is that Daniel was told to shut up the words and seal the book *to the time of the end,* whereas John is told: "Blessed is he that readeth, and they that hear the words of the prophecy, and keep those things that are written therein, *for the time is at hand.*"

2. It is urged by some that all the symbols are Jewish, and not one, even the white stone, is Gentile, and that it is an essentially Jewish book. If this is so, the interpretation is certainly made easier by the limitation to Jewish life.

3. The recurrence of the sevens is particularly noteworthy, as illustrated in Erdman's outline given above.

4. Careful distinction must be made between the symbolical and the literal elements. While the book is full of Oriental symbolism and imagery, yet the literal interpretation should be given primary place whenever possible. And even the symbols, like figures of speech, express realities.

5. Much depends upon whether the book refers to the Church or to the Kingdom. But even if it is impossible to determine this, it is important to remember that Church and Kingdom are not identical. The Lord's Prayer alone shows this, for it would be manifestly impossible to substitute Church and say: Thy Church come. The usage in the Gospels (Kingdom), in Acts (Kingdom and Church), in the Epistles (Church), and in Revelation (Kingdom) points in the same direction. While the spiritual principles of the Kingdom obtain now, the Kingdom in full reality is not yet revealed, nor will be till the Lord comes. A kingdom is impossible without a king. The Church is an instrument for bringing in the Kingdom, but the "Kingdom of God" is far wider than the Church and means God's rule over the whole universe.

6. The idea of a double fulfilment of prophecy is worthy of attention. We see something of this in a comparison of Acts 2 with Joel 2, where it is evident that the Day of Pentecost was not a complete fulfilment of Joel's words. There must still be some further realization to give the prophecy its full import. Then, too, the realization of Malachi 4:5, 6, in John the Baptist does not exhaust the meaning, for the words clearly indicate some further and future fulfilment.

Dr. Scofield, on Matthew 24:4–11, suggests that these words are at once characteristic of the whole of the age and also of the last week of Daniel's vision, which, on this view, is regarded as still future.

Some writers endeavor to blend the Historical and Futurist views by means of a primary and secondary fulfilment, one in the present, and the other in the future, but this is difficult and perhaps impossible. At any rate, leading scholars of both schools maintain that the two positions are incompatible.

7. But whatever may be the true interpretation of the book as a whole, there are two points on which it is possible for all to agree and in this agreement to obtain much spiritual profit from the study.

The first of these is suggested by the title, The Revelation of Jesus Christ. It is a book which unveils, not conceals, the Lord. It is full of him, and the thoughtful student will not fail to see that he is the subject and substance of every part. The following outline, adapted from one by the Rev. W. Graham Scroggie, will show how full the book is of Christ:

I. The Manifestations of Christ.
    1. Personal.
        (1) His Deity.
        (2) His humanity.
        (3) The God-man.
    2. Official.
    3. Dispensational.
II. The Messages of Christ.
    1. The passages.
    2. The teaching.
    3. The standpoint.
III. The Relations of Christ.
    1. His relation to Heaven.
        (1) To the Father.
        (2) To the Spirit.
        (3) To unfallen angels.
    2. His relation to earth.
        (1) To the wicked.
        (2) To the righteous.
    3. His relation to hell.
        (1) To the devil.
        (2) To demons.
IV. The Work of Christ.
    1. In the church (chastening).
    2. In Israel (restoring).

3. In the world (judging).

V. The Victories of Christ.

   1. The fruit of His cross.

   2. The establishment of His Kingdom.

   3. The overthrow of His enemies.

The second of these points is the remarkable and close connection (by contrast) between the first three or four chapters of Genesis, and the last three or four chapters of the Apocalypse. This comparison has often been shown, and the following, taken from "The Apocalypse of Jesus Christ," by W. W. Mead, is eminently worthy of study and meditation. *Cf.* Companion Bible, Appendix 3.

Genesis 1–4 speaks of:	Revelation 19–22 speaks of:
1. The First Creation.	1. The New Creation.
2. The First Sabbath.	2. The holy Rest in the New Creation.
3. The First Adam—the Head of the Old Humanity.	3. The Second Adam—the Head of the New Humanity.
4. Eve—the wife of the First Adam, sinning condemned, sorrowing.	4. The Second Eve—the Bride of Christ, holy, exalted, glorious, "in exceeding joy."
5. The Garden of Eden.	5. The Paradise of God.
6. The Fall of Man.	6. Man's full Redemption and Restoration.
7. Sin.	7. Perfect Holiness.
8. Communion broken.	8. Communion restored, perfect, eternal.
9. Death.	9. Eternal Life.
10. The Promise.	10. Its complete fulfillment.
11. Loss of Eden.	11. Restoration to the greater bliss of Paradise.
12. Exclusion from the Tree of Life.	12. Access to and "authority over the Tree of Life."
13. Earth Cursed.	13. Earth's full deliverance from the Curse.
14. Satan in the Garden, tempting and bruising.	14. Satan bruised, and in the Lake of Fire.
15. The Seed of the Serpent (Cain and his line), dominant, persecuting, building cities, gaining the world.	15. The Serpent's Seed—the Antichrist, the False Prophet, and the False Bride, overcome, dispossessed of the Kingdom and cast into the Lake of Fire.
16. The Seed of the Woman (Abel and Seth), persecuted, killed, and of no reputation.	16. The Seed of the Woman—Christ and His Bride, risen, victorious, triumphant, in the City of God, possessing "the Kingdom and the power and the glory" "unto the ages of the ages."

And so in spite of the difficulties, it remains true that a blessing is promised to the reader and student of this book (1:3), and those who have given most attention to it know by experience that the promise is abundantly fulfilled.

Note: After having noted the various points that seem to call for attention, I may perhaps be allowed to add that of all the books referred to, I would strongly recommend two as, in my judgment, the most illuminating and satisfying: (1) "The Book of Revelation," by Scroggie (The Book Stall, 113 Fulton St., New York City, $1.60), and (2) "The Book of Revelation," by McConkey (Silver Publishing Company, Bessemer Building, Pittsburgh, Pa.). They should be read in this order.

BIBLIOGRAPHY

The Life

While books on the Gospel usually take the Apostle's life into consideration, the only book which I have been able to find dealing specifically with this subject is "John Whom Jesus Loved," by Culross.

The Gospel

Commentaries (including Greek)

The Gospel According to St. John. Bishop Westcott. 2 vols.

Meyer's Commentary on the New Testament: St. John. 2 vols.

Commentary on St. John's Gospel. Godet. 3 vols.

Commentary on St. John's Gospel. Tholuck.

Commentaries (English)

St. John's Gospel, with Introduction and Notes. George Reith. 2 vols.

The Gospel of John. Erdman.

The Analyzed New Testament: The Gospel According to John. G. Campbell Morgan.

The Gospel of John. Marcus Dods (The Expositor's Bible).

The Gospel of John. Whitelaw.

St. John. McClymont (The New Century Bible).

Expository Thoughts on St. John. Bishop Ryle. 2 vols.
The Pulpit Commentary. 2 vols.
Exposition of the Gospel of St. John. Govett. 2 vols.

Expository Studies

The Divinity of Christ in the Gospel of John. A. T. Robertson.
Studies in the Gospel by John. White.
Bible Readings in the Gospel of John. Henry Thorne.
Exposition of the Gospel of John. W. Kelly.
The Central Teaching of Jesus Christ. Bernard.
Addresses on St. John. Various authors.
Expositions of Holy Scripture: St. John. Alexander Maclaren. 3 vols.
Our Lord's Signs in St. John's Gospel. Hutchinson.
Christ in the Bible: John. A. B. Simpson.
The People's Bible: John. Joseph Parker.
The Holiest of All. Maclaren.
The Inner Witness of the Fourth Gospel. Keister.
The Seven Signs. Brockington.
The Life Indeed. Holdsworth.
Quiet Talks on John's Gospel. S. D. Gordon.
The Christ From Without and Within. Clark.
The Eight Signs of St. John's Gospel. Madeley.

Doctrinal Studies

The Origin of the Prologue to St. John's Gospel. Rendel Harris.
St. John's Gospel. Oosterzee.
The Johannine Theology. Stevens (Gospel and Epistles).

The Epistles

Commentaries

Commentary on St. John's Epistles. Ebrard.
The Pulpit Commentary: Peter, John, Jude.
The Epistles of John. Westcott.
The International Critical Commentary: The Johannine Epistles. Brooke.
The First Epistle of John. Haupt.

Expository Studies

First Epistle of John. Levi Palmer.
The First Epistle of John. Candlish. 2 vols.
Exposition of the First Epistle of St. John. Stock.
Nine Lectures on the First Epistle of John. J. N. D.
Love's Keen Flame. McIntyre.
Eternal Life: Expositions on John's Epistles. Gibbon.
First Epistle of St. John. Watson.
The First Epistle of John. Cameron.
The Tests of Life. Law.
Fellowship in the Life Eternal. Findlay.
An Exposition on the First Epistle of St. John. Morgan.
Exposition on the Epistles of John. Kelly.
The Life of Divine Fellowship. Lithgow.

The Revelation

An effort has been made to distinguish these works, but the characterizations are of necessity only partial, because the books often possess other features than those indicated.

Apocalyptic Problems. Erskine Hill (Symbolical).
Daniel and the Revelation. Tanner (Historicist).
The Apocalypse of St. John. H. B. Swete (Grammatical).
The Apocalypse Expounded. Govett (Futurist and Expository).
The Book of Revelation. Clarence Larkin (Futurist).
Exposition of the Revelation. Walter Scott (Futurist).
Thoughts on the Apocalypse. Newton (Futurist).
The Revelation. Gaebelein (Futurist).
Studies in the Book of Revelation. S. A. Hunter (Symbolical).
The Revelation of St. John. Milligan (Practical).
The First Century Message. Morgan (Practical).
The Apocalypse, or the Day of the Lord. Bullinger (Futurist).
Revelation. Kelly (Futurist).
Notes on the Revelation. Snell (Futurist).
Light on the Last Days. Blanchard (Practical).
Studies in the Revelation of Jesus Christ. White (Expository).
Simple Studies in the Revelation. Pettingill (Futurist).
The Book of Revelation. McConkey (Futurist).
The Seven Churches in Asia. Mackennal (Practical).
The Apocalypse of Jesus Christ. Mead (Futurist, Practical).
Christ in the Bible: Revelation. A. B. Simpson (Practical).
Lectures on the Revelation of St. John. Vaughan (2 vols) (Practical).
The Book of the Revelation. Lecture Notes. Scroggie (Outline of Study).
The Revelation of St. John the Divine. Gowen (Practical).
The Last Prophecy. Elliott (Historicist).
The Patmos Letters. J. L. Campbell (Practical).
Lectures on the Apocalypse. Seiss (3 vols) (Futurist, Practical).
Studies in the Apocalypse. Charles (Critical).
The Revelation of John. Case (Critical, Modernist).
Studies in the Book of Revelation. Moorehead (Futurist).
Lectures on the Revelation. Ironsides (Futurist, Practical).
The Apocalypse of John. Beckwith (Symbolical).
The Book of Revelation. Milligan (Symbolical, Practical).
The Apocalypse of St. John, I to III. Hort (Grammatical).
Revelation, in Ellicott's Commentary. Boyd Carpenter (Symbolical).
The Book of the Revelation. C. Anderson Scott (Practical).

ABOUT CROSSREACH PUBLICATIONS

Thank you for choosing <u>CrossReach Publications</u>.

Hope. Inspiration. Trust.

These three words sum up the philosophy of why CrossReach Publications exist. To creating inspiration for the present thus inspiring hope for the future, through trusted authors from previous generations.

We are *non-denominational* and *non-sectarian.* We appreciate and respect what every part of the body brings to the table and believe everyone has the right to study and come to their own conclusions. We aim to help facilitate that end.

We aspire to excellence. If we have not met your standards please contact us and let us know. We want you to feel satisfied with your product. Something for everyone. We publish quality books both in presentation and content from a wide variety of authors who span various doctrinal positions and traditions, on a wide variety of Christian topics that will teach, encourage, challenge, inspire and equip.

We're a family-based home-business. A husband and wife team raising 8 kids. If you have any questions or comments about our publications email us at:

<u>CrossReach@outlook.com</u>

Don't forget you can follow us on <u>Facebook</u> and <u>Twitter</u>, (links are on the copyright page above) to keep up to date on our newest titles and deals.

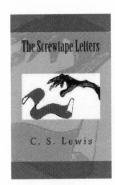

The Screwtape Letters
C. S. Lewis
$7.99
www.amazon.com/dp/1535260181

I have no intention of explaining how the correspondence which I now offer to the public fell into my hands.

There are two equal and opposite errors into which our race can fall about the devils. One is to disbelieve in their existence. The other is to believe, and to feel an excessive and unhealthy interest in them. They themselves are equally pleased by both errors and hail a materialist or a magician with the same delight. The sort of script which is used in this book can be very easily obtained by anyone who has once learned the knack; but ill-disposed or excitable people who might make a bad use of it shall not learn it from me.

Readers are advised to remember that the devil is a liar. Not everything that Screwtape says should be assumed to be true even from his own angle. I have made no attempt to identify any of the human beings mentioned in the letters; but I think it very unlikely that the portraits, say, of Fr. Spike or the patient's mother, are wholly just. There is wishful thinking in Hell as well as on Earth.

A Grief Observed
C. S. Lewis
$6.99
www.amazon.com/dp/1534898409

No one ever told me that grief felt so like fear. I am not afraid, but the sensation is like being afraid. The same fluttering in the stomach, the same restlessness, the yawning. I keep on swallowing. At other times it feels like being mildly drunk, or concussed. There is a sort of invisible blanket between the world and me. I find it hard to take in what anyone says. Or perhaps, hard to want to take it in. It is so uninteresting. Yet I want the others to be about me. I dread the moments when the house is empty. If only they would talk to one another and not to me.

How to Be Filled with the Holy Spirit
A. W. Tozer
$9.99
www.amazon.com/dp/1517462282

Before we deal with the question of how to be filled with the Holy Spirit, there are some matters which first have to be settled. As believers you have to get them out of the way, and right here is where the difficulty arises. I have been afraid that my listeners might have gotten the idea somewhere that I had a how-to-be-filled-with-the-Spirit-in-five-easy-lessons doctrine, which I could give you. If you can have any such vague ideas as that, I can only stand before you and say, "I am sorry"; because it isn't true; I can't give you such a course. There are some things, I say, that you have to get out of the way, settled.

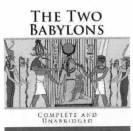

The Two Babylons
Alexander Hislop
$8.99
www.amazon.com/dp/1523282959

Fully Illustrated High Res. Images. Complete and Unabridged.

Expanded Seventh Edition. This is the first and only seventh edition available in a modern digital edition. Nothing is left out! New material not found in the first six editions!!! Available in eBook and paperback edition exclusively from CrossReach Publications.

"In his work on "The Two Babylons" Dr. Hislop has proven conclusively that all the idolatrous systems of the nations had their origin in what was founded by that mighty Rebel, the beginning of whose kingdom was Babel (Gen. 10:10)."—A. W. Pink, The Antichrist (1923)

The Person and Work of the Holy Spirit
R. A. Torey
$5.75
www.amazon.com/dp/1533030308

BEFORE one can correctly understand the work of the Holy Spirit, he must first of all know the Spirit Himself. A frequent source of error and fanaticism about the work of the Holy Spirit is the attempt to study and understand His work without first of all coming to know Him as a Person.

It is of the highest importance from the standpoint of worship that we decide whether the Holy Spirit is a Divine Person, worthy to receive our adoration, our faith, our love, and our entire surrender to Himself, or whether it is simply an influence emanating from God or a power or an illumination that God imparts to us. If the Holy Spirit is a person, and a Divine Person, and we do not know Him as such, then we are robbing a Divine Being of the worship and the faith and the love and the surrender to Himself which are His due.

The Problem of Pain
C. S. Lewis
$6.99
www.amazon.com/dp/1535052120

When Mr. Ashley Sampson suggested to me the writing of this book, I asked leave to be allowed to write it anonymously, since, if I were to say what I really thought about pain, I should be forced to make statements of such apparent fortitude that they would become ridiculous if anyone knew who made them. Anonymity was rejected as inconsistent with the series; but Mr. Sampson pointed out that I could write a preface explaining that I did not live up to my own principles! This exhilarating programme I am now carrying out. Let me confess at once, in the words of good Walter Hilton, that throughout this book "I feel myself so far from true feeling of that I speak, that I can naught else but cry mercy and desire after it as I may". Yet for that very reason there is one criticism which cannot be brought against me. No one can say "He jests at scars who never felt a wound", for I have never for one moment been in a state of mind to which even the imagination of serious pain was less than intolerable. If any man is safe from the danger of under-estimating this adversary, I am that man. I must add, too, that the only purpose of the book is to solve the intellectual problem raised by suffering; for the far higher task of teaching fortitude and patience I was never fool enough to suppose myself qualified, nor have I anything to offer my readers except my conviction that when pain is to be borne, a little courage helps more than much knowledge, a little human sympathy more than much courage, and the least tincture of the love of God more than all.

Out of the Silent Planet
C. S. Lewis
$7.92
www.amazon.com/dp/1536869929

The last drops of the thundershower had hardly ceased falling when the Pedestrian stuffed his map into his pocket, settled his pack more comfortably on his tired shoulders, and stepped out from the shelter of a large chestnut-tree into the middle of the road. A violent yellow sunset was pouring through a rift in the clouds to westward, but straight ahead over the hills the sky was the colour of dark slate. Every tree and blade of grass was dripping, and the road shone like a river. The Pedestrian wasted no time on the landscape but set out at once with the determined stride of a good walker who has lately realized that he will have to walk farther than he intended. That, indeed, was his situation. If he had chosen to look back, which he did not, he could have seen the spire of Much Nadderby, and, seeing it, might have uttered a malediction on the inhospitable little hotel which, though obviously empty, had refused him a bed. The place had changed hands since he last went for a walking-tour in these parts. The kindly old landlord on whom he had reckoned had been replaced by someone whom the barmaid referred to as 'the lady,' and the lady was apparently a British innkeeper of that orthodox school who regard guests as a nuisance. His only chance now was Sterk, on the far side of the hills, and a good six miles away. The map marked an inn at Sterk. The Pedestrian was too experienced to build any very sanguine hopes on this, but there seemed nothing else within range.

Claiming Our Rights
E. W. Kenyon
$7.99
www.amazon.com/dp/1522757481

There is no excuse for the spiritual weakness and poverty of the Family of God when the wealth of Grace and Love of our great Father with His power and wisdom are all at our disposal. We are not coming to the Father as a tramp coming to the door begging for food; we come as sons not only claiming our legal rights but claiming the natural rights of a child that is begotten in love. No one can hinder us or question our right of approach to our Father.

Satan has Legal Rights over the sinner that God cannot dispute or challenge. He can sell them as slaves; he owns them, body, soul and spirit. But the moment we are born again... receive Eternal Life, the nature of God,—his legal dominion ends.

Christ is the Legal Head of the New Creation, or Family of God, and all the Authority that was given Him, He has given us: (Matthew 28:18), "All authority in heaven," the seat of authority, and "on earth," the place of execution of authority. He is "head over all things," the highest authority in the Universe, for the benefit of the Church which is His body.

Home Geography for the Primary Grades
C. C. Long
$7.95
www.amazon.com/dp/1518780660

A popular homeschooling resource for many generations now. Geography may be divided into the geography of the home and the geography of the world at large. A knowledge of the home must be obtained by direct observation; of the rest of the world, through the imagination assisted by information. Ideas acquired by direct observation form a basis for imagining those things which are distant and unknown. The first work, then, in geographical instruction, is to study that small part of the earth's surface lying just at our doors. All around are illustrations of lake and river, upland and lowland, slope and valley. These forms must be actually observed by the pupil, mental pictures obtained, in order that he may be enabled to build up in his mind other mental pictures of similar unseen forms. The hill that he climbs each day may, by an appeal to his imagination, represent to him the lofty Andes or the Alps. From the meadow, or the bit of level land near the door, may be developed a notion of plain and prairie. The little stream that flows past the schoolhouse door, or even one formed by the sudden shower, may speak to him of the Mississippi, the Amazon, or the Rhine. Similarly, the idea of sea or ocean may be deduced from that of pond or lake. Thus, after the pupil has acquired elementary ideas by actual perception, the imagination can use them in constructing, on a larger scale, mental pictures of similar objects outside the bounds of his own experience and observation.

In His Steps
Charles M. Sheldon
$3.99
www.amazon.com/dp/1535086262

The sermon story, In His Steps, or "What Would Jesus Do?" was first written in the winter of 1896, and read by the author, a chapter at a time, to his Sunday evening congregation in the Central Congregational Church, Topeka, Kansas. It was then printed as a serial in The Advance (Chicago), and its reception by the readers of that paper was such that the publishers of The Advance made arrangements for its appearance in book form. It was their desire, in which the author heartily joined, that the story might reach as many readers as possible, hence succeeding editions of paper-covered volumes at a price within the reach of nearly all readers.

The story has been warmly and thoughtfully welcomed by Endeavor societies, temperance organizations, and Y. M. C. A. 's. It is the earnest prayer of the author that the book may go its way with a great blessing to the churches for the quickening of Christian discipleship, and the hastening of the Master's kingdom on earth.

Charles M. Sheldon.
Topeka, Kansas,
November, 1897.

Made in the USA
Las Vegas, NV
23 April 2023

71012499R00065